What It Takes

Books by Charles D. Ellis

The Partnership: The Making of Goldman Sachs

Winning the Loser's Game

Investment Policy

Joe Wilson and the Creation of Xerox

Capital: The Story of Long-Term Excellence

The Elements of Investing (with Burton Malkiel)

Wall Street People, Vol. I and Vol. II

The Second Crash

Institutional Investing

The Repurchase of Common Stock (with Allan Young)

The Investor's Anthology

Classics I and II

What It Takes

Seven Secrets of Success from the World's Greatest Professional Firms

Charles D. Ellis

WILEY

John Wiley & Sons, Inc.

For David F. Swensen, PhD, who invented the world's first financial derivative, reinvented endowment investing, shared his expertise widely as a teacher and adviser and wrote the best book on professional investing, chose making a life of service and values over making a fortune, brought more wealth to Yale University than any major donor, sets an example of excellence for all in his profession, and has more friends and admirers than he'll ever know.

Contents

Foreword

It is easy to admire the virtues of the five professional services firms featured in this book, but we also learn how very difficult it is to sustain excellence at the highest level from generation to generation. This should not be surprising. None of the ten largest corporations in the U.S. economy in 1900 still ranked in the top ten 50 years later, and, indeed, only three actually survived as companies. To maintain leadership in the face of competition, great firms must continually improve the nature and quality of their products and services and their own internal organizations.

Many readers of this volume will know at least some of Charley Ellis's many contributions to research and education in finance and business history. In this new and instructive book, Charley Ellis offers us some of the wisdom of his experience observing "what it takes" to be best-in-class as a professional services firm. Greenwich Associates, the firm Charley founded in 1972 and led for nearly three decades, provided research-based consulting to most of the world's strongest organizations in the financial services industry. The insights in this book thus rest on both keen observation and deep experience.

Charley develops his ideas within a clear conceptual framework, organized around seven essential attributes of a successful professional services firm. But the power of this book, as we have come to expect from Charley, resides in the compelling narratives he relates about the firms chosen as exemplars of excellence: McKinsey, Goldman Sachs, Capital Group, the Mayo Clinic, and Cravath, Swaine & Moore. Charley is a master storyteller, and his stories of people, their decisions, and their interactions communicate his conceptual arguments far more powerfully than any abstract discussion could. As always, Charley entertains us as he enlightens us.

As one who had the pleasure of working with Charley during his service as a Fellow of the Yale Corporation and Chair of our Investments Committee, I know firsthand that he practices the doctrines he preaches. He actively encourages every organization he touches to live by the principles he illustrates in this book.

What It Takes offers a roadmap for the kinds of organizational improvements that Charley has helped bring to many enterprises during his career. He shows us vividly how innovation and commitment to excellence can drive success, and how easy it is to fall behind. Whatever type of organization we serve, there is much to learn from this book.

—Richard C. Levin
President, Yale University
New Haven, Connecticut

Introduction

What It Takes is the story of what sets the *great* professional firms—the best firms, the acknowledged leaders in their industries—apart from all the rest. It is a blueprint for creating, building, and sustaining great organizations of all kinds.

For the 50 years that I have acted as a behind-the-scenes adviser on both strategy and tactics to several hundred firms in the Americas, Asia, and Europe, the questions that this book seeks to answer have been the burning ones for me: Which are the best firms? And what makes them the best? What principles and what concrete actions bring them to the top? How do they overcome external challenges from competitors and changes in the times, and the even more difficult internal challenges that either success or setbacks can create? How do they recover when they stumble?

All the firms included here are large and have been around for many years. To be sure, many smaller companies may mature into great firms. But for the purposes of this study, organizations have to be large enough that they are not dependent on a few individuals, and must have long enough histories that they are not creatures of one era, a few specific products, or a few major clients.

To identify the firms to include, I asked almost every firm leader I met three questions: At which firm in your industry would you most like to spend your career? Which firm would the most discerning clients like to use to handle their toughest challenges? And which firm's success is most durable, even as its leaders turn over or its environment changes?

Remarkably, there was a clear consensus in each of five fields. The outstanding leaders are McKinsey in consulting, Cravath, Swaine & Moore in law, Capital Group in investment management, the Mayo Clinic in health care, and Goldman Sachs in investment banking.

Yes, Goldman Sachs. While it has taken a well-deserved pounding since 2008 on a number of fronts, it was for decades the undisputed leader in its field. And it is working hard to regain that reputation and a dedication to the principles that brought it to preeminence in the first place. That intriguing struggle is covered in Chapter 10.

Once the firms were identified, I conducted over 300 formal interviews with their leaders during the past decade to determine what they believe are the secrets of their success. The results are revealed in these pages.

At the outset, I expected to find major differences from one field to another. But surprisingly, the essential lessons these firms teach are few and nearly identical. Olympic athletes supply a good simile. While they see themselves as obviously separate—"he's a pole-vaulter; she's a swimmer; he's a downhill skier, and I run the 440"—the gold medalists are essentially the same: superb athletes with unusual heart and lung capacity, and in great physical condition. They are highly disciplined, voracious competitors willing to spend unconscionable hours mastering every technique of their event.

So it is with the great firms and the superior people who create and maintain them. This book details how the great firms set themselves apart by the way in which they execute the following "simple" keys to success:

Mission—an overarching sense of purpose that motivates exceptional people to make personal sacrifices and dedicate their careers to the firm's work. (Chapter 1)

Culture—a set of values focused on using teamwork and self-discipline to repeatedly achieve superior results. The culture translates the firm's mission into specific, often idiosyncratic practices. Colleagues become a tribe. (Chapter 2)

Recruiting—bringing in the most capable, motivated new people. "Obvious!" you say? Wait till you see what work, costs, and sacrifices this entails. (Chapter 3)

Developing people—helping new colleagues get up the learning curve as fast as possible and maximizing their professional and personal development throughout their careers. (Chapter 4)

Client focus—tying clients to the firm by consistently meeting or exceeding what the most demanding clients expect when working on their most difficult issues. (Chapter 5)

Innovation—repeatedly finding new ways to serve clients. This can even include reinventing the whole organization to achieve game-changing advantages over competitors. (Chapters 6 and 7)

Leadership—steering the ship by bringing the other six factors together. (Chapter 8)

This study includes many stories of success. But along with the success stories comes the reality that for the top-ranking organizations there is only one new way to go—down. Even harder than becoming the best is staying the best. External challenges are tough—changing markets, competitors, clients, technologies, and regulation. But the internal challenges are often more difficult—growing lumberingly big or complex, the cockiness that success can breed, politics, weaker second-generation leaders, and finding the balance between profit-seeking and professional values. Professional firms are living organisms; none is assured of enduring success. They must always adapt. So a certain paranoia is needed to lead a great firm. And, as we see in Chapter 9, it also helps to have a little luck.

All the organizations celebrated in this book have faced adversity, sometimes of their own making. Chapter 10 examines how several of these firms have handled—and mishandled—recent mishaps and are struggling to right themselves.

Finally, Chapter 11 is the sad and instructive tale of a leader that stumbled and never made it back. Fifty years ago, Arthur Andersen & Co. was considered the finest professional firm in the world, period. It was the best major auditor and the leader in using computers. But then its leaders, standards, and organizational structure changed, and near-term profitability became paramount. Andersen's commitment to professional excellence got degraded in a long series of initially reversible stages until its essential culture had been destroyed from within.

Anyone familiar with how Mike Bloomberg has reconfigured New York City's mayor's office or how Lou Gerstner revitalized IBM or Rick Levin has been leading Yale University or General David Petraeus led the coalition forces in Iraq will appreciate how the lessons of *What It Takes* are applicable to the leadership teams at the top of all sorts of organizations. The elements of excellence are exemplified every day by diverse corporations in many fields, including Apple, Google, IBM, GE, ExxonMobil, Tupperware, John Deere, Caterpillar, Singapore Airlines, Duane Reade drug stores, Wegmans grocery stores, W. L. Gore, and Four Seasons Hotels, and at institutions as varied as the Hospital for Special Surgery, Memorial Sloan-Kettering, and the Navy SEALs. At the top of every organization, it's always all about people. The great firms are not dependent on any one remarkable leader or on a favorable environment. They sustain excellence over several generations of leaders who, knowing how many formerly leading firms have faded or fallen, are wisely on high alert for the unknown unknowns and their own misperceptions.

One of the most valuable qualities of a great firm is a superior capacity to see itself objectively and to learn and change on multiple levels and thus to continuously improve. Most organizations resist this; that is why organizational learning is so rare. What separates the great firms from their good competitors is not so much learning about external factors as internal learning—how individuals can be more effective at communicating and working with other members of their organization. As the network of effective members grows and as the effectiveness of each member of the network increases, small differences compound and the productivity of the network rises geometrically. This capacity to learn depends in turn on a clear mission, effective recruiting, developing people skillfully, innovations that serve clients, and multilevel leadership—a compelling virtuous circle of the lessons in *What It Takes.*

I

ACHIEVING
EXCELLENCE

Chapter 1

Mission

An Inspiring Long-Term Purpose

"**N**o, Herb. *No!*" exclaimed a rasping, nearly cracking voice from the back of the large room in Florida where 500 McKinsey & Co. partners were gathered for the firm's 1996 global leaders conference. They had been listening to Herbert Henzler, the architect of McKinsey's great success in Germany.

Henzler's talk—backed up as usual with slides on a giant screen—focused on a series of key words representing the bold actions he felt were needed to ensure McKinsey's future. Each word was a screen-dominator: INNOVATE. IMPROVE. MODERNIZE. REFORM. The last one-word slide had been followed by a four-word slide: REFORM OUR BUSINESS SYSTEM.

"Herb! *No!* There's something wrong with your slide!" The elderly, hunched man was now almost jogging up the middle aisle between row after row of chairs that filled the meeting room. "We are *not* a business. We are a *professional* firm! We have a professional system, but never a . . . a . . . *business* system!"

The agitated interrupter was McKinsey's former managing partner, Marvin Bower. Despite his 93 years, Bower exuded such assured authority that the room went silent. Henzler's face flushed as he froze at the speaker's podium. Attention centered on Bower. He had devoted his long career to making McKinsey a *professional* firm—never "just a business"—and on this vital distinction he felt he had to be right at all times. As he had done again and again over his 60 years of service, Bower reminded the group: "If there is the shadow of a doubt on something being good for business but not truly professional, *do not do it!*"

Having made his declaration, Bower returned to his seat near the rear of the room. Ken Ohmae, McKinsey's storied leader in Japan, was the conference's next speaker—and the next to be stopped cold in his tracks by Marvin Bower. Ohmae began by lamenting the hierarchical rigidity of Japan's *zaibatsu* corporate complexes and their consequent resistance to all consultants, including McKinsey. As usual, Ohmae had a bold, creative solution: At least some of the people in the inner core of Japan's largest corporate organizations would have to be replaced by open-minded new executives who would be interested in outside ideas and new ways of thinking. The solution, he said, was clear: McKinsey should get into executive search. Implied in Ohmae's strategy, of course, was that McKinsey would have preferential access to consulting assignments through those new executives McKinsey would place through its executive search: *We helped you get your job, so now why don't you help us get some consulting work with your company?*

Back on his feet, Bower was calling out as he again hurried to the front so he could be seen and heard by everyone: "Ken! Ken! We do *not* do headhunting. It would not be *professional* to go around pinching the best people from our clients. That would be a clear-cut conflict of interest." Once again the elderly man stopped any discussion of McKinsey's being a business. Bower was living another chapter in his lifelong commitment to McKinsey's being a truly professional firm in which every professional had an individual obligation to dissent.

True to that core value, Bower was leading by dissent, and as so often before, he prevailed. "Marvin took a central role at Florida, lambasting the 'innovators' when any of their ideas conflicted with the firm's priority drive for professionalism and so must be opposed," recalled Charles Shaw, a longtime senior partner. "He carried the day. Looking back to that day years later, I'm convinced that his argument—both emotionally and intellectually—made a valuable contribution to our long-term success as a professional firm. It clarified *for* McKinsey what *was* McKinsey."

■ ■ ■

Every great firm has a clear, long-term purpose—an inspiring, engaging mission. This North Star provides the firm's professionals with extra confidence in the meaning, value, and significance of their work and justifies the intensity of their engagement beyond "making a living" to making a purpose-driven life. In an old story, a pilgrim came to the construction site for what would become Chartres Cathedral and asked the stonecutters what they were doing. One tersely said, "Squaring this stone." Another proudly said, "Squaring this stone to build a strong wall for a major building." And the third, with joy in his heart, said with a wide smile, "Building a great cathedral to honor the glory of God!" With which stonecutter would you want to work?

Most young men and women coming out of the leading graduate schools—each with wide-ranging freedom of choice—will take the upper-middle pathway of a good job with a good firm, knowing they will earn more than enough to enjoy their time on earth. But a few of the best will choose a more demanding path. Wanting their careers to be more than just a series of high-paying jobs, they will seek employers with a truly compelling mission. For the most capable few who want to make a significant difference, good is not nearly good enough. And these purpose-driven people are as indispensable to each great organization's achieving its mission as being part of a great firm is essential to them. Only mission-driven organizations can consistently attract, inspire, and engage exceptional professionals in the continuously demanding work of producing superb service for the most interesting clients. And only mission-driven organizations can attract and keep important clients dealing with important challenges. That's why only organizations with a compelling mission can achieve and sustain excellence.

■ ■ ■

Marvin Bower's seminal contribution to McKinsey was understanding and articulating the value to the firm and its people of living for and with a higher purpose or mission: being not just a business but a *profession* and all that that implied. As a young man Bower had graduated from Brown University and gone on to Harvard Law School because he wanted to join Cleveland's leading law firm, the firm that eventually became Jones Day. But he failed to make the top 5 percent in his class and the *Harvard Law Review*, so he was rejected. Determined as always, Bower decided to return to Harvard, this time to the business school, and try again. He made the top 5 percent at Harvard Business School and was a student editor of the *Harvard Business Review*. This time the Jones Day firm admitted him.

Determined to understand what had made that firm great, Bower did what he would so often do during his later years at McKinsey: He made a list of the key factors. Client interests were always put first and clearly ahead of the firm's; confidences were always maintained; no assignment was taken unless it was really necessary and could not be handled by the client company's in-house counsel; partners always felt both the freedom and the responsibility to disagree with clients if that was in the client's interest; and partners consistently took time to coach associates on ways their work could be improved and on how they could keep their fees relatively low by being more creative than other firms in solving problems.

As a young lawyer serving as secretary to numerous bondholder committees organized to work out defaulted bond issues, Bower saw a pattern. The CEOs of the failed companies had needed information for sound decisions, but their employees, deferring to hierarchy, hadn't dared tell the insulated CEO what was really going on. Bower estimated that the managers could have saved 10 of the 11 companies if only frontline knowledge had been taken to the CEO. He became convinced that top management of corporations needed the same quality of independent, expert professional advice on *business* problems as his law firm was giving on *legal* matters. He began discussing with his wife, Helen, the great opportunities—and the risks—of switching from law to business consulting.

Early in 1933, Bower was working for a bondholders committee during a corporate reorganization in Chicago. Also on the committee was James O. McKinsey, the son of an Ozarks farmer, who had
started a relatively small accounting and management engineering
firm. McKinsey, impressed by a paper Bower had written on clothing manufacturing, asked about his career plans and offered to interview him. Bower was reluctant at first because his wife feared moving
near "Chicago gangsters." But when Jones Day cut all staff salaries by
25 percent, Bower decided to interview with "Mac" McKinsey. As
McKinsey explained his firm, Bower sensed that aside from its work
in accounting it was becoming just the kind of professional firm he
was interested in—working on business and management problems the
same way law firms worked on legal problems.

Bower joined McKinsey in late 1933 as one of the world's first
"career consultants." This was a change from the norm of experienced
industrial executives becoming consultants for stints of a few years
and then either "returning to industry" or retiring. Bower went into
McKinsey determined to do as much as he could to help it develop
into the kind of firm he envisioned.

James O. McKinsey's success in consulting peaked at Marshall
Field & Co., the big Chicago retailer, where he directed a major
study in 1935. He charged what was then considered a substantial fee:
$50 a day. At Marshall Field, McKinsey's shocking report—delivered
orally after just four months—recommended selling the 24 Fieldcrest
mills in the South, as well as the Chicago Merchandise Mart, the
nation's largest dry goods business, and the wholesale division, which
had been the traditional core of Marshall Field's business but was a
long-term money loser.

Having reported losses for five straight years, directors of Marshall
Field urged McKinsey to become chairman and CEO and implement
his comprehensive overhaul. Recognizing that advising was not doing,
McKinsey, who had an incorrigibly high need for achievement—his
work was his life—and a desire for real wealth, decided to take this
challenge, test theory with practice, and try to prove that he could
implement his concepts.

The work at Marshall Field—cutting off whole divisions, closing departments, firing hundreds of old-timers, and restructuring

every part of the business—was exhausting and produced a dozen threats on Mac McKinsey's life. He saved Marshall Field but ruined his health: he caught a cold that became pneumonia before penicillin was available and died suddenly at age 48 in 1937. As Bower lamented, "My personal loss was that the man I admired most—my hero—was gone. My career loss was that I had had less than two years to learn from my mentor."

Although his firm had specialists in functional areas, McKinsey always preferred to take the generalist point of view required of top management. His holistic diagnostic approach centered on major policies and the strategies needed to implement them. Basic to McKinsey's concept of management consulting was not just figuring out how to produce more efficiently, but deciding whether to be in a particular business at all. "Mac McKinsey's greatest contribution to consulting, as well as to business," Bower believed, "was his concept of the integrated nature of managing a business and the process of management as [organizational] components interacting. Mac's second contribution to consulting was his demonstration of independence by thought and deed and his willingness to tell the client the truth just as he saw it. From Mac, I learned basic concepts and ways of managing. Most important is the concept that making major improvements in a business can best be achieved when tackled as a whole. Mac also thought managing should be kept as simple as possible."

With the foundation laid by Mac McKinsey, Marvin Bower became the architect and chief builder of what would become the world's largest and most admired firm of top-management consultants. Monthly Saturday training sessions with everyone coming provided Bower with the pulpit from which he would preach the policies and unifying practices he traced back to Mac McKinsey, particularly devotion to the "professional approach." The firm moved deliberately away from overtly selling its professional services; Mac McKinsey had believed that if clients were well served, McKinsey's services would sell themselves. (Others would argue that, while not calling it "sales," once it gets started the firm is accomplished at persuading clients to enlarge or extend engagements and is exceptionally successful at developing regularly repeating clients.) This belief in the importance of serving clients well led naturally to the view that each client is a client of the whole firm, not just of an individual consultant, and so must have full access to all the firm's resources. Mac McKinsey made another enduring impact on the firm through his conviction that a professional firm should invest in its reputation by having its offices well located and attractively furnished.

An effective mission has to resonate both within the firm and outside. Bower insisted on the term *management consulting* to get away from such alternatives as *efficiency experts* or *management engineering*, which he found unprofessional. He insisted that consulting should be recognized as a profession and as a career. Training would be rigorous and continuous. Since major prospective corporate clients operated nationally, Bower saw that the firm must also be nationwide, with offices in major cities, and that those offices must all be identifiably part of a "one-firm firm:" Policies and procedures would be the same in all offices. A series of consulting guides—leaving room for judgment where unusual circumstances warranted some variation—were carefully prepared on such topics as manufacturing, organization, and management information and control.

Descriptive terms and phrases matter in defining a firm's mission. When others proposed a marketing brochure for the firm, Bower's first impulse was to condemn the idea as unprofessional. However, he changed to hearty agreement when he saw that creating the brochure—with himself leading the process—could be an effective device for getting internal agreement on values even before any external distribution. The result was a 42-page hardcover booklet titled *Supplementing Successful Management*. Bower made sure it explicitly committed McKinsey to becoming a truly professional firm.

Advocating the professional approach at every opportunity, Bower led the firm from 1950 to 1967, finally stepping down at age 64. During this period McKinsey decided to concentrate on consulting and get entirely away from accounting and actuarial services—and from executive recruiting, which had brought conflicts of interest, little professional satisfaction, and inadequate compensation. (In his proposal at the Florida conference, Ken Ohmae had touched an old nerve.) Bower gave talks, wrote memos, and frequently admonished his associates until two colleagues took him aside and said that while they agreed with him on McKinsey's mission, he was hurting his own cause with so much repetition. Bower accepted their advice on method and promptly began what he called "persuasion through pointing up success," watching for opportunities to commend others for taking the professional approach and leading from behind rather than from the front. But it was still Marvin Bower persisting with the same message.

As the unrelenting advocate of the professional approach—and making it stick and flourish—Bower put McKinsey on a different pathway. Booz Allen Hamilton, then its major competitor, helped unintentionally by proudly emphasizing that it was a *business*. Bower's commitment to professionalism eventually—he would have preferred the word *inevitably*—led to McKinsey's having a substantially stronger business. Today's partners believe this is a direct consequence of subordinating the firm's business to the higher disciplines of the profession, which, of course, put clients' interests first.

As Bower once explained,

> By applying the professional approach broadly, rigorously, and consistently, we have developed a "secret" strength in attracting, serving and maintaining relations with clients. This strength also serves firm interests in other ways and distinguishes McKinsey from most consulting firms. Yet there is really nothing secret about this strength. All we have done is to instill in our consultants the standards of the older professions, which are well known and to which most management consultants now subscribe. Our strength comes from a deeper understanding of the great values of the professional approach to clients *and* to the firm—and from a broader, more rigorous, and more consistent application of that approach so that it comes naturally in our thoughts and actions.

The quest for professionalism in a field where that had not been the norm led to two allied goals: Help clients make substantial, lasting, positive improvements in their performance; and build a great firm that can attract, develop, excite, and retain exceptional people. The persistence established the enduring value of an inspiring mission that has given a compelling answer to the question every potential client and every potential consultant will ask and must answer: Why McKinsey?

Without the determination to define and ensure the firm's commitment to being always a professional firm, McKinsey would never have become the world's finest firm in consulting. It couldn't have served clients so well or provided such great working and learning experiences for the many consultants who have so enjoyed their years at McKinsey. Similar clarity of mission and overarching purpose is the essential foundation of superb organizations in every field.

■ ■ ■

For insiders, a firm's mission is the big idea about why we are here and why we care so much and work so hard. Sometimes the mission emerges as a way of reconciling conflicting influences. At Capital Group Companies, a world-leading investment group that now manages well over a trillion dollars for millions of investors, the mission is a balance of three seemingly conflicting goals. The conflict was beginning to surface in the early sixties. In 1961, and again in 1963, the firm's reluctant leader-in-waiting, Jon Lovelace, got seriously ill and was away from Capital for many weeks. Recovering from adversity can be a good time for extended reflection and personal decision. During his second convalescence, several of Capital's mutual fund directors visited Lovelace to say that his future role was on their minds. His father, the firm's founder, Jonathan Bell Lovelace, was 67 and still had not stated any plans to step down. Young Lovelace resolved to overcome his diffidence and take up leadership, provided the other key people would join him in a novel three-way commitment to the organization's purpose or mission.

Two camps had been developing within Capital concerning the organization's primary purpose. Some in the firm emphasized service to *investors*; others emphasized returns to Capital's *owners*—akin to the professionalism versus business debate that so aroused Bower at McKinsey. At Capital, instead of choosing between "investors first" and "owners first"—in those days the conventional choice was "owners first"—Lovelace proposed that Capital would aim as fully and continuously as possible to balance achievement for *three* groups: investors, owners, and the firm's professionals, always focusing first on the investors. The proposal carried special weight because Jon Lovelace, through share purchases, had made himself a significant owner of the then only marginally profitable firm.

Jon met with his father and other principals in 1963 to gain agreement on this corporate objective. Shortly afterward, his father announced the selection of his son as his expected successor. The unusual three-way balance came to be seen in and beyond the firm as a seminal contribution to Capital's long-term success both by preempting a potentially divisive internal debate and by providing a meaningful organizational purpose or mission: always doing what's really right for investors. Over the long term, the interests of all three groups come together, because if investors do well, so will Capital's associates and owners.

Capital Group is unusual in its industry. While most mutual fund groups focus on "asset gathering" (sales), Capital focuses on *investing*—achieving superior risk-adjusted long-term investment returns for clients. The most important policy questions at Capital *always* center on serving the long-term interests of long-term investors. With its own kind of benevolent paternalism and self-discipline, Capital puts investors' interests first most strikingly in the unusual way it introduces new mutual funds. The strongest test of a professional firm's principles comes when it deliberately does *not* do something that is being done by competitors and would be highly profitable. The mutual fund industry norm is to "sell what's selling" by introducing new funds of a particular type whenever investor interest indicates an opportunity for more sales. Capital goes the other way with, eventually, favorable long-term results for its investors. At Capital, unlike most fund families, no new mutual fund will be launched unless the firm's investment professionals say, "Over the long run, investing in this fund *now* will prove to be a good idea for investors." For example, Capital was the clear leader in emerging-markets investing for institutional investors in the eighties when the emerging markets enjoyed a multiyear run-up. By the early nineties, retail investor interest was high. Many other fund families, often with far less experience or capability, were offering mutual funds that specialized in emerging markets. Brokers pleaded with Capital to offer an emerging-markets fund to individual investors, knowing it could be a big seller. But Capital refused. It wouldn't offer such a fund because it would sell *too well* to retail investors who wouldn't understand the real risks of investing in less developed countries, especially the risk of sudden major changes in valuation that would inevitably result in investor disappointment.

Then in 1999, *after* the average emerging-markets mutual fund had lost half its value since 1993 and retail demand was consequently low, Capital was ready to roll out a retail fund that would invest in emerging markets. With financial crises in Southeast Asia and Russia and the collapse of the Long-Term Capital Management hedge fund having substantially reduced investors' expectations, and with most competitors' emerging-market mutual funds experiencing net redemptions, Capital launched New World Fund. It would invest, near the market bottom, in a carefully composed portfolio of emerging-market sovereign debt and the shares of international companies headquartered in developed countries but doing substantial business in emerging markets—*not* companies headquartered in emerging-market countries where regulation and accounting practices might be questionable and corruption rife. Starting when it did, the fund has performed well. Similarly, Capital introduced the American High-Income Municipal Bond fund in 1994—at the very bottom of the municipal bond market. Riding the recovery in fixed income, that fund later ranked in the top 3 percent of its fund category.

Over and over again, Capital's mission of serving the real interests of long-term investors provides the True North for all sorts of operational decisions as well as the galvanizing purpose of the organization's investment professionals.

■ ■ ■

Powerful missions are often easy to summarize but never easy to achieve. At Mayo Clinic, True North is even clearer than at Capital Group. Mayo has no shareholders and no profit-seeking professionals. It is controlled by a foundation and staffed by salaried employees. Even as medical science has advanced rapidly, Mayo's mission continues to be defined by one simple, clear, and compelling statement: The needs of the patient come first. All the rest, complex and costly as health care can so often be, is implementation. Of numerous examples, here's one: When some patients complained that they were not sleeping well, a few interns stayed up all night to see if they could discover causes. In that single night, they learned why patients were not sleeping well: There were lots of noises. Phones rang, doors slammed, metal clipboards snapped back into place, and x-ray machines were noisy when wheeled down the hall. Among the many solutions: Phones were connected to lights so no ringing was needed, soft pads were put on clipboards, and the time at which x-rays were taken was changed. As a result, patients could rest more peacefully and this accelerated their recovery.

The founding Mayo brothers—William J. Mayo and Charles H. Mayo, widely known as Dr. Will and Dr. Charlie—were inspired by their father, Dr. William Worrall Mayo. As Dr. Charlie once said, "If we excel at anything, it is in our capacity for translating idealism into action." Dr. Will specified three factors as crucial to the long-term success of Mayo Clinic: continuing pursuit of the ideal of service, not profit; continuing primary concern for the care and well-being of each individual patient; and continuing interest by every staff member in the professional progress of every other staff member. More recently, three additional implicit factors have been made explicit: willingness to change in response to changing needs, striving for excellence in everything undertaken, and conducting all activities with absolute integrity. The primary focus at Mayo Clinic is always on the original core commitment: The needs of the patient come first.

"It has to do with a value system," said Robert Waller, the clinic's CEO from 1988 to 1998. "Mayo was very fortunate to have founders who were just uncanny in setting down a set of values that have served us so well for so many years. We're taking the best care of patients we can. And I think we've always tried to stay focused on a common mission: meeting the needs of our patients. We try very hard to send home a happy patient."

Contemporary health care in a large organization that centers on patient care and also emphasizes medical education and research is clearly a complex undertaking. Because each patient is unique, health-care services are unusually personal, but are delivered when the "customer" or patient is most dependent, anxious, and vulnerable, wearing an anonymous hospital gown and often feeling depersonalized. This reality is why Mayo Clinic's service-centered culture is so treasured by patients. They experience the clinic's many deliberate expressions of care at times when they most need to know they can trust and rely on the care. "Mayo Clinic is an idea," explained one Mayo physician. "It's the concept that the patient is the center of what we do. And we've built everything else around the patient with this idea in mind."

■ ■ ■

Great missions are long-term in perspective and known to insiders and clients as a commitment to be trusted. In the late 1970s, Goldman Sachs's co-chairman, John Whitehead, was becoming increasingly concerned that the firm's great successes might unintentionally weaken its strong commitment to its chosen mission. For 40 years, the firm had worked to rebuild after the 1929 market crash and the dramatic failure of its investment flagship, Goldman Sachs Trading Corporation. During the sixties and seventies, Goldman Sachs had made itself Wall Street's most profitable firm. At least as important to Whitehead, it was on its way to becoming Wall Street's best firm because it was admired for being the firm corporate executives could trust. (Decades later, Whitehead's concerns would be dramatized by the heavy blows to Goldman Sachs's reputation following the financial collapse of 2008.)

Even with unusually low turnover, the firm's steady growth meant that 8 to 9 percent of its people were new each year—so over three years, one out of four of its people would be new. Thinking through the implications, Whitehead worried that the firm could lose some of its treasured qualities. He needed an answer to a gnawing question: "How could we get the message to all those individuals who were new to Goldman Sachs in such a way that they would understand our core values, come to believe in them, and make the firm's values *their* values in everything they did every day?"

Whitehead collected what he thought were the unwritten principles of Goldman Sachs, thought about them for a few weeks, and then spent a Sunday afternoon writing them out longhand. The list began with 10 major statements, but his partner, George Doty, a devout Catholic, said that that seemed sacrilegious—too close to the Ten Commandments. So the list was expanded, eventually to 14. With a few changes by other partners, "Our Business Principles" was set in type and copies sent to all employees and their families at their homes, carefully addressed to John Smith & *Family*. "I was simply putting down on paper the things that we had really lived for as long as I could remember," said Whitehead. The first three numbered maxims were these:

1. Our clients' interests always come first. Our experience shows that if we serve our clients well, our own success will follow.
2. Our assets are people, capital, and reputation. If any of these is ever lost, the last is the most difficult to regain.
3. We take great pride in the professional quality of our work. We have an uncompromising determination to achieve excellence in everything we undertake. Though we may be involved in a wide variety and heavy volume of activity, we would, if it came to a choice, rather be best than biggest.

These principles rang true to the people of Goldman and, during its great growth years, they defined the firm's mission in a way that resonated with clients and set the firm apart. "My commitment to the traditional corporate mission at Goldman Sachs was certainly not religious," said partner Gene Fife. "It's because it's a very smart way to do very good business."

Never willing to be seen as a one-trick pony, Whitehead put out another set of guidelines or tactics for business development—and these *were* 10 commandments:

1. Don't waste your time going after business we don't really want.
2. The boss usually decides—not the assistant treasurer. Do you know the boss?
3. It's just as easy to get a first-rate piece of business as a second-rate one.
4. You never learn anything when you're talking.
5. The client's objective is more important than yours.
6. The respect of one person is worth more than acquaintance with 100.
7. When there's business to be done, get it!
8. Important people like to deal with other important people. Are you one?
9. There's nothing worse than an unhappy client.
10. If you get the business, it's up to you to see that it's well handled.

The firm's precepts didn't stop with the written ones. Nothing was ever done for prestige, and prestigious clients were often charged the most. Every banker was always expected to succeed on two top-priority standards: Serve the client *and* make money. If you must cut fees to win or keep business, do *not* cut fees. Making money—always and no exceptions—has been the principal principle of Goldman Sachs. But there has been an important change away from the traditional two-step of making money through service to clients to an aggressively direct focus on making money.

While some professional firms still try to manage and control their employees with top-down rules, a rules-based management cannot keep up with the speed of change in most professions and the need to address a wide variety of specific situations where values-based decisions are suddenly called for. Hard decisions come up for action much too quickly for gathering all the facts or for leisurely deliberation, and difficult decisions about doing the right thing are always in the gray zone of uncertainty. But action must be swift—so values must be unambiguous. With a principles-based management, responsibility for decisions can be pushed down to the men and women on the firing line. Since they should know their firm's culture and values and they must know the detailed realities of their specific business, they can be held accountable for knowing and doing the right things in the right way.

■ ■ ■

In contrast to Goldman Sachs's Business Principles, some enormously powerful mission statements are brief. Cravath, Swaine & Moore strives to be the most effective law firm on the most difficult cases involving U.S. law. The statement is succinct, but the execution it inspires can require herculean commitments.

The greatest commitment that Cravath or any law firm ever made began on January 17, 1969, the final Friday of Lyndon Johnson's presidency, when Attorney General Ramsey Clark filed suit charging IBM with monopolizing the general-purpose computer market. According to the filing, IBM had committed that offense by bundling together hardware, software, and support services; by introducing new computers at unfairly low prices; by announcing new models far in advance when it knew it was unlikely to be able to deliver the models on the announced schedule; and by giving educational institutions unreasonably large discriminatory price discounts. The Justice Department asked that IBM be broken up into "several discrete, separate, independent, and competitively balanced entities." Thus began the case that would drag on for no less than 13 years and attract numerous other litigants along the way.

"When IBM, one of America's most admired companies, turned to Cravath, we were awfully proud of the firm being asked to undertake the assignment and were determined to demonstrate the capacity to handle it," recalled Samuel Butler, who later became presiding partner. "IBM was at the time an unbelievable undertaking for Cravath. Afterwards, the firm knew if we could do IBM, we could do *anything*." The history of the IBM case would illustrate Cravath's commitment to its chosen mission.

Cravath had done relatively little recent work for IBM, the most important company in one of the most important industries in America. But a key link was senior partner Bruce Bromley, who had defended IBM in another antitrust suit back in 1952. Bromley reached over several other partners to select 38-year-old Thomas D. Barr to lead the Cravath legal team—committing virtually all its litigators—and take overall responsibility for what would become and remain the firm's largest client. Bromley, then in his eighties, read the trial transcript every day and made strong comments. Recalls partner John R. Hupper, "When push came to shove, we all pitched in."

Barr's strategy for IBM was massive, costly, complicated—and eventually successful. The case led to 2,500 depositions, 60 million pages of documents, 726 trial days, 856 witnesses for the defense, 12,280 exhibits, and 104,000 pages of transcripts. Over its 13 years, the case cost the Justice Department at least $15 million. IBM paid Cravath fees of $50 million, plus over $25 million of costs.

In early October 1972, the *New York Times* reported that IBM and the Department of Justice would meet in Washington "in a major attempt to work out a settlement of an antitrust suit filed against the giant computer maker almost four years ago." Just one week previously, tough, aggressive T. Vincent Learson, IBM's chairman and CEO, had made a surprise announcement that he would step down

at 60, after only 18 months in office, in favor of the more concilia-
tory Frank T. Cary. Later that month, Cravath's Barr met with the
Department of Justice in an unsuccessful attempt to work out a resolution and a consent decree.

Barr then requested postponement of the trial until after the 1972
presidential election, contending that "pressure from the press and the
election might lead the Justice Department to present nonnegotiable
demands and an ultimatum which would force us to defend our good
name." During the 90-minute hearing, exchanges between Barr and
Raymond M. Carlson, the government's lead attorney, became so acri-
monious that Judge David N. Edelstein urged both men "not to get
too personally involved." This instruction from the bench would soon
prove ironic.

Edelstein, chief federal judge for the Southern District of New
York, denied Cravath's request for postponement in the first of a long
series of decisions unusually hostile to IBM—and Cravath. Judge
Edelstein became an active and partisan participant in the long trial
proceedings, regularly helping the government lawyers and making life
difficult for Cravath lawyers, particularly Barr. Combative exchanges
and maneuvers by Barr and Edelstein provided an increasingly conten-
tious sideshow to the trial.

Barr presented evidence that IBM's share of data processing was
considerably less than the Justice Department's six-year-old estimates.
He argued that while IBM had grown substantially, the industry had
grown even faster, and that the business was not just equipment but
complex systems requiring total engagement by supplier and customer
working as partners to solve complex customer problems. The appropriate definition of the relevant market was critical. IBM had installed
over 70 percent of the 84,000 computer systems in the United States
and over 50 percent of the 58,000 in other countries. The government argued for a narrow definition of the market, contending that the
industry included only eight companies selling computer systems. IBM
argued that the industry included thousands of diverse competitors.

In January 1974, Cravath opened a "temporary" office near
IBM's Armonk, New York, headquarters. Over the next 10 years,
it would become the center of a firm within the firm. Casual dress
and $10,000 hazardous-duty bonuses were in; Cravath's traditional

18-month training rotations for associates were out. So were free evenings and weekends. While associates on the IBM case were nominally free to move elsewhere after two-year stints, many believed asking to do so would wreck their partnership prospects. "Most of us never had the guts to ask for a transfer," said one associate involved in the litigation. One associate, Joseph Sahid, billed 24 hours in a single day, only to be topped by another, Ronald S. Rolfe, who worked on a plane to California and, thanks to the three-hour time difference, billed 27 hours in a single day! (Both later became partners.) In contrast to Cravath's thorough, tightly disciplined, persistent pressing forward, the government lawyers were almost never prepared and often had to ask for delays.

For IBM, Cravath created a massive system of document retrieval—the first that worked on anything like such a scale—so documents could quickly be assembled by key words. Page after page of document after document were put on punch cards by keyboard operators typing out every word. And, to be certain of accuracy, every card was typed twice. This belt-and-suspenders duplicated work was done for the unheard-of volume of *one million* documents.

The IBM team, with just 20 percent of the firm's lawyers, was providing 35 percent of the firm's billings. Even with 30 to 40 lawyers in White Plains, Barr needed more help as he built up Cravath's litigation practice for the IBM cases. George Gillespie, a career specialist in the trusts and estates practice, was declared an expert on investing and therefore on the way capital markets really work. He helped figure out one of the main constraints on the several peripheral equipment makers that were suing IBM: They couldn't raise the capital needed to finance accelerated expansion. Gillespie also identified two expert witnesses: Arjay Miller, president of Ford, and Warren Buffett of Berkshire Hathaway. "Warren," said Gillespie, "was absolutely spectacular as a witness and key to IBM's case. He blew the government away!" Miller, like Barr, got a taste of Edelstein's hostility, recalling: "At no time in my life have I felt so abused and demeaned as I did at the hands of Judge Edelstein."

Cravath's aggressiveness and tenacity came to the fore in dispatching numerous "peripheral" suits by other companies. During discovery in the Control Data case, Barr created a decisive strategic advantage by a tactic perfectly suited to one of Cravath's unusual self-disciplines. The firm had produced an enormous volume of IBM documents and demanded as much from Control Data. Cravath being Cravath, before delivering IBM's documents its lawyers took the substantial time to read every one to be *sure* they knew all their contents. In contrast, counsel for Control Data relied on paralegals to review more than two dozen boxes of papers. This was a fatal blunder. Cravath lawyers found hard evidence of Control Data's plans to join a conspiracy to allocate markets and fix prices. Barr promptly filed a counterclaim that could have bankrupted Control Data and that did compel its lawyers to take him to lunch and plead: "Let's settle."

Government lawyers were excited by the idea that they could take advantage of the homework being done for the lawsuits by the private corporations, particularly Control Data's computerized database of the facts in the extensive documents IBM had provided. When Control Data informed the Justice Department on a Sunday evening of its settlement with IBM, the government's lead lawyer quickly moved to acquire the vital database. It was already too late. As part of the settlement, Cravath partners George Turner and John Hunt not only had negotiated the destruction of the database, they had spent that weekend supervising the shredding. Once again, Cravath had created a decisive strategic advantage for its client.

The other major ancillary lawsuits against IBM were also overcome. For the suit brought by Greyhound Corp., Barr's team was so small that for a time he had to concentrate entirely on this one case. His first action was to seek and win a transfer from Chicago to Phoenix, which meant that, like the Cravath team, Greyhound's Chicago lawyers were also out-of-towners. After two intensive months of brilliant cross-examination and well before IBM's own case was even presented, Barr moved for a directed verdict in favor of IBM. Barr won.

Telex was next. The long-working Cravath associate Joseph Sahid, suspicious that the personnel files provided by Telex were too thin, insisted on going to Telex's offices in Oklahoma. There, in the office of a former IBMer, he found a folder marked "IBM Confidential," containing corporate information improperly removed from IBM. With the aid of other Cravath lawyers, he filled a grocery cart with incriminating evidence. Even so, Judge Sherman Christiansen found IBM guilty of violating the Sherman Antitrust Act and fined IBM a record $259 million in damages. This put Barr, a former U.S. Marine, and his team on war footing. Telex's victory was reversed on appeal and IBM was awarded $18.5 million in damages. Telex appealed to the Supreme Court, but then agreed to settle.

For the suit brought by California Computer Products, Barr stepped back; he was needed in New York for the federal case. A leading Los Angeles firm was retained and supervised by David Boies, 34 and a third-year Cravath partner, who was summoned back from Bombay where he had been trying a case against the Indian government. Boies flew 11 hours to Tokyo and then took a 12-hour flight to JFK, arriving on a Sunday morning. In another illustration of Cravath intensity, he immediately received a huge pile of CalComp papers to study before meeting with Barr on Monday. Boies moved his family to California and organized over a dozen Cravath lawyers there in a pattern of 8:00 A.M. to 2:00 A.M. workdays. Every day throughout the trial, the day's transcript was obtained at about 10:00 P.M. by a team of Cravath lawyers, who took it apart and reorganized the contents into proposed findings of fact to support the series of propositions Cravath sought to prove for IBM. Each was cross-referenced to specific pages in the original transcript. If any proposition needed more documentation, Boies was quickly told so he could pursue it in court the next day.

CalComp's lawyers were stunned by the enormous effort expended on a simple motion to dismiss. The transcript Boies worked from had more than a thousand cross-references. "I had never encountered anything like that in my life," recalled CalComp's lead attorney, Max Blecher.

> The sheer manpower that took—the *cost*—I just felt overwhelmed. I've often wondered how they could operate if the client imposed any cost control at all. Everything showed this attitude. They buried us with paper. They produced reams of paper in futile endeavors. They made requests for admissions of fact that were ridiculous. We stacked up the paper—it was five or six feet tall!*

---

*Some thoughtful observers believe Cravath's forcefulness and virtually unlimited spending distorted the judicial process.

In court, Boies performed remarkably effectively. Memorably, he had CalComp's CEO read the text of his own recent speech, saying, "I really don't characterize IBM as competition" and "Our real competitor isn't IBM." Boies concluded by making an oral motion for a directed verdict at the close of the plaintiff's case. In just two hours, Cravath's motion was granted.

On June 1, 1981, Cravath rested its case in the main suit brought by the government. Barr had stated in court a willingness to negotiate with Ronald Reagan's new head of antitrust, Stanford University professor William Baxter, who held a conservative view on antitrust enforcement. In mid-July Baxter called Barr and explained that he felt insufficiently conversant with the IBM case to enter into negotiations, but was open to resolving either specific matters or the whole case before October 1. Barr proposed a series of weekly informational meetings. Baxter agreed. The Justice Department lawyers indignantly argued that they could and should provide any requisite "education" themselves; but Professor Baxter wanted to hear both sides, so eight all-day Saturday briefings were scheduled. In briefing after briefing, Cravath overwhelmed the Antitrust Division lawyers on facts, concepts, and every aspect of thoroughness.

On January 6, 1982, the Saturday briefings were stopped and the government lawyers agreed that the longest-ever antitrust suit should be dismissed as without merit. Two days later, IBM gave a celebratory party for all its lawyers at an expensive Manhattan discotheque called Regine's. "We lost only one of the twenty-one cases," recalled Evan R. Chesler, who in 2007 became Cravath's presiding partner, "and that loss was reversed on appeal." IBM had not been a regular Cravath client before the case, but ever since, IBM has averaged nearly 10 percent of Cravath's annual billings. "After the Department of Justice dropped the charges, we found that clients were lining up for our services. And they haven't stopped."

For Boies, as for other partners working on the IBM case, this was one of the formative experiences of a lifetime. "It was not only the biggest antitrust case going but the biggest trial," he said, "and we were into the guts of one of the most exciting companies in the most exciting industry. It's too simple to say if it hadn't been for this case there would have been another one. Without IBM, we'd be different lawyers and we'd be different people." But one thing would never be different: the mission of Cravath—to be the most effective law firm on the most difficult cases.

■ ■ ■

Every great firm has differentiated itself from other strong firms in its profession by committing itself to a challenging and inspiring purpose with compelling value for its professionals *and* its clients. The long-term mission needs to be translated into everyday practice, providing the unusually capable and ambitious people with the guidance and discipline necessary to ensure constancy. Aligning culture with mission is a central responsibility of leader-managers at all levels.

Chapter 2

Culture

How We Do Things around Here

All strong organizations, from global religions and major nations to street-corner gangs, develop norms of behavior, beliefs, and values that comprise their cultures. Culture translates mission into daily operating practice and bonds group members together. For an organization to rise to greatness, and particularly to sustain excellence, its internal culture must be complementary to its mission or purpose.

A vibrant culture is expressed in consistent standards of behavior and in decisions made every day by many different people in many different situations. Just as character eventually dominates physical strength in people, culture will eventually prevail in organizations. What appears soft in the short run is strong in the long run; what appears hard often proves brittle and transient. Group members reproduce their firm's values and expected behavior almost instinctively, and teach others. New people, to be accepted, must demonstrate that they are committed to the values and the expected behavior. In time, as the firm's cultural norms become part of them, they become recognized as "culture carriers."

Sustained commitment to excellence—particularly in ethics— attracts, keeps, and motivates exceptionally talented people who care intensely about achieving professional excellence at a level other professionals admire. Robust ethics and consistent care for clients are central to the cultural values of every great professional firm. They express themselves in policies and practices, in language and symbols, and in commitments of individuals to each other. For those who belong in the leading firms, the conventional "sacrifices" of long, intense hours and limited recreation are not really sacrifices at all. The true sacrifice would be to spend their careers in a less-than-best firm. As Aristotle said, "We are what we repeatedly do. Excellence, then, is not an act, but a habit."

The people at great firms work harder than their competitors— both longer, more demanding days and more days and nights each week. While producing more, they also insist on producing at the highest quality. They take pride and find great meaning in what they and their firm can achieve for clients. Leaders need to send consistent messages about what does or does not fit the cultural ideal. It takes time and memorable events to accumulate the experience through which individuals learn to understand, value, and eventually "own" an organization's culture. Strong cultures are exceedingly difficult to replicate. They can only develop over time through robust leadership and repeated successes. That's why if a superior professional firm begins to lose its competitive edge, some of the best prospective clients will go elsewhere, and then some of the most promising young professionals will, too. If such slippage is not promptly reversed, it will accelerate, as we will see it fatally did at Arthur Andersen & Co.

Each firm's culture is *sui generis*, but all great firms are remarkably similar in their demanding core values: intensity of commitment, persistent drive for improvement, unusually high quality standards, personal modesty, devotion to teamwork, long-term focus on serving clients well, ruthless objectivity, absolute integrity, and an unrelenting determination to excel. Of course, all this is a lot to ask. That's why only those who know that these daunting commitments are right for them can be sure that being part of a great firm is what they really want—and need.

■ ■ ■

Every exemplary firm's culture has many sources, particularly various leaders' initiatives, failures, and successes, and the competitive environment. The Mayo Clinic's culture of professionalism, consensus, egalitarianism, and idealism is the confluence of the personal values of the doctors Mayo with the conservatism and traditional thoughtfulness toward others of Upper Midwest Lutheranism. Add to these "Minnesota nice"—the plain qualities of service, thrift, modesty, and respect for individuals characteristic of the region's Scandinavian, Swiss, and German farmers. Blend in the confident devotion to service of the Sisters of St. Francis, who have been involved in the clinic's main hospital since its founding. Combine all this with the values of medicine as a calling and you have the necessary ingredients of a great culture.

The doctors Mayo—father and two sons—were the leaders in developing the culture in the late nineteenth century. As Dr. Will Mayo explained,

> Every man has some inspiration for good in his life. With my brother and me, it came from our father. He taught us that any man who has physical strength, intellectual capacity, or unusual opportunity holds such endowments in trust to do with them for others in proportion to his gifts. We want the money we receive to go back to the people from whom it came and we think we can best give it back to them through medical education.

At Mayo Clinic, the culture is so strong and so important to so many people at all levels that anyone joining must quickly learn to accept its dominance. As old hands will advise, "Mayo does not change for you." Widely held pride in the institution is balanced by rigorous self-criticism. Mayo people are hard on themselves and always on guard for possible shortcomings. People who are not comfortable with the Mayo culture usually leave within a few years. Those who stay for five years usually stay for life.

The Mayo adventure began in 1845 when, with no farewells to family or friends, 26-year-old William Worrall Mayo decided to leave Manchester, England, and try America. He had studied Latin, Greek, and chemistry and got his first job in New York City as a chemist at Bellevue Hospital. After leaving Bellevue for one year of study at Indiana Medical College, Mayo got his degree and in 1854 went west to St. Paul, then a town of only 4,000 inhabitants where citizens still worried, with good reason, about attacks by Indians. Moving on to Rochester, Mayo, known as "the little doctor" because he was only five-foot-four, made a living by combining medicine, farming, and local political office, including several years as a state senator. Keen on becoming a surgeon, he went back to New York City for several months in 1869 to study surgery and gynecology.

Medicine was far from today's sophistication. In those days, for good reason, most sick people went home; only poor people went to hospitals. The stethoscope was novel, and the clinical thermometer had not yet been invented. Microscopes were first used in 1870, and even 20 years later most physicians had never seen one. Few diseases could be specified. Causes were largely unknown. Surgery was for emergencies only. But medicine and surgery, in which the Mayos would specialize, were going through several simultaneous revolutions. Anesthesia was new, untried, and little used, but would later give surgeons enough time to complete the complex procedures that could save lives.

Returning to Rochester, Mayo built a sizable practice with his wife's active help. As boys, both Will and Charlie worked as prescription clerks in the drugstore below the Little Doctor's office. Later they went on rounds with their father, learned to use his microscope, and began learning a doctor's basic skills. Still later, they advanced to preparing sutures for surgeries. The boys learned the principles and ethics of physicians: The life of a doctor must be one of service; he must respond to every call whether or not he would ever get paid.

On a hot August day in 1883, a powerful tornado destroyed much of Rochester, killed several people, and hurt dozens. When found in the rubble, the seriously wounded were taken to hotels and offices for emergency care. Forty were taken to the convent of the Sisters of St. Francis where the Mayos and other doctors worked through the night. When nursing was needed longer than the volunteers could continue working, the 24 Sisters of St. Francis took on that responsibility even though their calling was teaching, not nursing.

Based on this dramatic experience, Mother Alfred Moes had an idea: Build a hospital in Rochester. She went to Dr. Mayo, but he said, "No. Rochester is too small and a hospital would cost too much."

"How much?" asked Mother Alfred.

"Forty thousand dollars!"

She quickly countered, "Just promise me to take charge of it and we will set the building before you at once"—even if his cost estimate of $40,000 was accurate.

Over five years of spartan living while giving sewing, knitting, and piano lessons, the sisters saved $25,000 and bought land for another $2,200. They presented the $25,000 to the Little Doctor, who said $25,000 would pay not only for a hospital but for "the best that money could buy," and went East to study hospital design. Two years later, the first patients were admitted to the new 27-bed hospital. From its beginning, the hospital admitted both paying and charity patients of any race or creed. Those "everyman" values were not everyone's: Religious prejudice against Catholics was surging in the upper Midwest, and many local doctors refused to use the sisters' new hospital. Mortality rates at the hospital were rising—apparently because local doctors were sending only their riskiest patients to Saint Marys Hospital—so the sisters decided to require a Mayo examination before admission. About the same time, the Mayo brothers decided to use only Saint Marys and told their patients to pay the hospital first and their fees second. The result: The Mayo brothers had an unintended monopoly on the best hospital in a wide area.

The Mayo Clinic was soon prospering with standard fees and large volume. The brothers were doing and learning from 4,000 operations a year. Volume drove them up the experience curve, and the Mayos were unusual in their continuing commitment to learning: reading about advances in medicine for one full hour each day and, at different times, spending at least a month each year visiting leading practitioners to learn new ideas and techniques. They also presented papers regularly on their advances in surgery.

The brothers' values became the core of the Mayo Clinic culture. Their father had taught that no man had a right to great wealth while others were in poverty, so they achieved balance by not charging patients who couldn't afford their services—but they clearly expected others to pay. After all, a doctor needed good equipment to keep up with modern medicine. In 1895, the x-ray was discovered by Wilhelm Röntgen, a German physicist, and five years later the Mayos had an x-ray machine in their office. The commitment to having the most advanced equipment available continues to be central to Mayo Clinic's culture and its compact with physicians.

The brothers had one joint bank account and put all they earned into it, with each taking out what he needed until year-end, when they divided whatever was left. Over the years, about half their income was spent; the other half was accumulated with the intention that someday it would be recycled to the community from which it had come. In the late 1890s, to guard the Mayo Clinic from the disruption that might come with any partner's death, the Mayos worked out a contract that limited the partners to participation in the income of the clinic. On retirement or death, a partner would get one year's income but would have no ownership interest in the assets or property of the clinic. After two years of grumbling by some of their partners, Dr. Will's view that "whatever was good for the practice and its patients should therefore be done" led to a quiet confrontation: Either all would sign or the partnership would be broken up. The other partners signed.

Patient volume tripled between 1908 and 1912, and the Mayo brothers realized that their increasingly strong group practice should continue after they had retired. At the peak of their practice, they moved to perpetuate Mayo Clinic beyond their own years. They had given away their accumulated savings to institutionalize the clinic but still owned the properties and the capital of the partnership. They wanted to turn this into a permanent endowment for Mayo Clinic. On advice of lawyers, they incorporated the Mayo Properties Association in October 1919 as a charity without capital stock to be overseen by nine trustees. The properties were valued at $5 million and the contributed securities added another $5 million—a total of $10 million (about $140 million in today's dollars). The "voluntary association of physicians" would be governed by a self-perpetuating board of "able men of future generations."

The next step, in 1923, replaced the personal partnership with a voluntary association, and all former partners, including the Mayo brothers, went on fixed salaries. Finally, the Properties Association leased its buildings and equipment to Mayo Clinic at an annual rent equal to the clinic's net income, which would then be invested in medical research and education. Administration was vested in a board of governors and supervision of all professional activities became the responsibility of an executive committee of five appointed by the governors from a list of 15 nominated by the professional staff. At Dr. Will's initiative, the various tasks of administration would be overseen by standing committees with rotating membership appointed from the professional staff.

In 1983, the Mayo Medical School, initially part of the University of Minnesota, opened as an independent degree-granting institution. It is best known for its residency training program. With over 1,000 residents and fellows, it also has a strong PhD program and continuing education programs covering virtually every allied health discipline. The launch of Mayo Medical School accelerated basic science, and the infusion of large numbers of young doctors energized Mayo Clinic.

Mayo Clinic today continues to express three main themes: The interests of the patient come first; care is best achieved by pooling talent across many specialties; and clinical care is delivered with time-concentrated efficiency via "single destination" medicine. Mayo Clinic's great distinction is in execution—caring for each individual patient—and the essence of distinctive execution is recruiting outstanding people who will dedicate their careers to achieving the organization's mission by acting on its core values. "Everyone is centered on our sense of purpose, our mission," explained neurologist Charles M. Harper. "With *very* few exceptions, everyone at Mayo walks the walk every day. Those who leave often come back to say, 'I didn't realize how good Mayo Clinic really is until I left.'"

Each great firm's culture takes abstract concepts down to specific actions and connects specific tasks to the organization's inspiring mission. When Discovery was recently filming a TV documentary on Mayo Clinic, a woman with a strong German accent was shown one evening cleaning a hospital room. Asked on camera why she was cleaning so carefully, she captured the clinic's values and culture in the powerful simplicity of her reply: "I'm saving patients' lives."

■ ■ ■

Most major law firms passed a tipping point in their transition from profession to business in the 1980s. Federal district judge Harold Baer, Jr., wrote, "In some firms we find that profits have replaced *pro bono*; production has undercut professionalism; and compensation has overtaken collegiality." A challenge for law-firm leadership came with the switch from deciding whether ever to terminate a partner to how to have the least bloodshed. Partners were "encouraged" to practice elsewhere or were "retired" before turning gray.

But Cravath remained Cravath, different from other law firms because of the partners' unusually strong commitment to the firm as an institution. "Cravath is the Elysian Fields," declared partner Jeffrey A. Smith. "The air here is different and everybody contributes to that air. We have great cohesiveness because we all know we're lucky to be here." For partners, a big reward is simply knowing that they have become proficient at doing the quality and quantity of work expected of a Cravath partner. For those with a need to excel, it is a privilege to be working with other smart, fully engaged professionals. Partner Katherine Forrest noted, "On vacation, we're all always on call. One-third of any vacation day will be spent 'at the office.'" Partners cheerfully say, "You've gotta love it to work this hard."

Loyalty to Cravath is not just an expectation, it's a cultural requirement: Don't *ever* hurt the firm. The bonding created by the everyday gatherings of partners at the lunch table and by intense teaming during 12- or 18-month training rotations nurtures the relationships that connect partner to partner and partner to partnership. The lead litigator rotates from case to case so whoever leads in one case will support in another; that way, everyone sees how good the firm's other lawyers are. Cravath is both an institution and a tribe: an institution that stands for values the current partners are responsible for protecting and perpetuating and a tribe bonded by deeply shared beliefs, behavior, and experiences. Those who have engaged together in particularly intense and difficult experiences will talk for years about those shared adventures. Shakespeare's "We few, we band of brothers" is frequently cited by partners. As partner Julie North put it, "You can only understand the collegiality of Cravath by being here yourself." The collegial environment is bolstered by moderate size, working with long-term clients, explicit interchangeability among partners in serving any client, calendar-based rotation of associates assigned to partners for training, avoiding lateral hires, and "lockstep" compensation (everyone who made partner in the same year is paid equally).

Still, close friendships outside the firm are not the norm among Cravath partners, at least in part for lack of time. "We are colleagues, not social pals," said Allen Parker, the deputy presiding partner. Not all partners like all partners, but all know how to put aside personal feelings and work rationally together on key issues with passion and calm, doing all they can for the client and for the firm. Partner Jack Hupper explained, "Being able and *knowing* you are able to call on other partners and associates for help—even at nine at night—certain you will get a swift and affirmative response, is a galvanizing strength."

The Cravath partners' dining room may be considered the best and most exclusive club in the legal profession, but partners are quick to say that it is just a conference room. The food is just a selection from the cafeteria. The waitstaff knows what each partner likes to drink—no alcohol—and brings it automatically. Partners go there because it's so convenient. They typically stay only 15 minutes, usually using those few minutes to talk about clients or the law. The first arrival at the long table sits in the middle and everyone coming in later sits at the next open seat or fills in seats left by partners who have finished. There are no cliques and no saved seats. No work is done at lunch, but partners are always asking each other "What are you working on now?" or getting caught up with familiar faces or getting to know new partners. Awhile ago the partners moved to a bigger room with a bigger table, but it didn't work well because they couldn't converse easily across that table, so they went back to the old table.

Tom Barr epitomized the Cravath work ethic, the dominant force in the firm's culture. Incorrigibly gung-ho, with a Marine Corps recruiting poster affixed to the inside of his coat closet, Barr built the firm's IBM team with symbolic acts like scheduling tennis with colleagues at 6:00 A.M. (Despite early grumbling, almost everybody eventually said they loved it). Barr said,

There is no conceivable substitute for hard work. You can't intuit the facts. If there's one rule of thumb, it is that the side that works the hardest wins. . . . I don't know any good lawyer who doesn't work his ass off. Until you've done everything you can do to win, you're not free to stop. There isn't any other way to do it. If you don't want this, you shouldn't be a litigator.

According to North, "Tom Barr's forceful personality shaped us. We speak in his voice today. Building teams; keeping together; finding a way; always moving up."

At many major law firms, a non-lawyer business manager may come around and say, "Your hours are short. Get 'em back up there—pronto!" Not at Cravath. As partner Bill Whelan said, "We're not very good at policing the hours booked and don't really want to be because it could hurt other areas of our compact that we value." Cravath expects partners to motivate themselves, but there are limits. For the new young partner who might be thinking *I've sacrificed in the past, but now I'm a partner*, Cravath has a message: You're never "in." The intensity of the work never stops. There's no starting gun and no finish line. Cravath partners typically bill 2,250 hours a year, versus 1,850 at Davis Polk and 2,000 at Sullivan & Cromwell. Cravath's work-intensive lifestyle is not one that partners at other firms would embrace, but Cravath partners thrive on it. "We believe partners should be there for clients seven days a week," said Evan Chesler.

One of the greatest challenges for the leaders of Cravath or any professional firm is adapting internal culture to external social changes. Over the decades the firm has faced conflicts between its espoused values and its customary practices. Choices had to be made, and making choices was sometimes difficult for the firm and for the individuals. Ed Benjamin became Cravath's first Jewish partner in 1964 despite the adamant opposition of a senior partner, Hoyt Moore, who declared: "No Jew is joining any firm where I'm a partner!" It was a defining statement that backfired: The partnership was promptly dissolved and a new partnership immediately formed—without Hoyt Moore. A year later, three more Jewish associates became Cravath partners. (Observers of the profession believe that some of Cravath,

Swaine & Moore's best competitors are firms formed in the fifties and sixties by Jews who had been attracted to the legal profession but had not been accepted as partners at the then leading New York City firms.)

Bayo Ogunlesi, a very able lawyer and one of Cravath's first African-American associates, eventually left to head up investment banking at Credit Suisse First Boston. "Losing Bayo was a serious loss, and we still have not rebuilt a community of African Americans," observed a partner. The firm has also struggled in efforts to develop a community of Asians. This is one of the limitations caused by Cravath's reluctance to recruit laterally from other law firms, combined with its inflexible "lockstep" compensation; other firms can use compensation as leverage to get partners to promote diversity. Similarly, Cravath can't get established in bankruptcy or derivatives or investment company law practice without lateral hires.

Another major change came with the increasing number of women going into law. Female partners are now in double digits and 70 women are midlevel Cravath lawyers. Typically women at Cravath defer having children until they have made partner, and some have live-at-home househusbands. Part-time partners are not okay with Cravath. A few years ago a group of female associates voiced various complaints, including that the female partners were not "accessible" to them. Sam Butler acknowledged that "Davis Polk has done much better on this than we have; we lose women to them, but not men. A big part of the reason is that we insist on the fairness of what Americans call equal treatment." Then he smiled and confessed, "We treat *all* associates badly."

Another test of a tribal culture is how it deals with a beloved and extraordinarily capable young leader who leaves. For Cravath, that leader was David Boies. He rose swiftly to prominence through his stellar role in the IBM antitrust case where his formidable talent, capacity for work, and grasp of economics made him a key contributor. But Boies, having left, became an apostate. "David is a great lawyer but was always on the outside boundaries and was the perfect one to stretch them," said Jeff Smith. "David loved the complexity of the issues at Cravath—and put up with the rest of it. Over the years, we and David became less and less enamored of each other. He became more interested in 'me' than in 'the firm.' He was our prodigal son. But when he left, we never missed a beat. His leaving has been to our mutual benefit."

The intensity of work at Cravath has long had a bracing effect on those who strive to excel. One of Cravath's exemplars, John J. McCloy, joined as an associate in 1925 and became a popular partner in 1929. (In one of a series of important roles in public service, he was the head of the German occupation after World War II.) McCloy's perseverance was dramatized in the Black Tom case, in which 10 years of unrelenting pursuit—involving a battery of Cravath lawyers, invisible inks, German saboteurs, check stubs in an abandoned suitcase, a labor leader in Ireland, two rejections by the Mixed Claims Commission, a change in U.S. laws, Russian secret agents, a small container of poison gas, negotiation with Hermann Göring and Rudolf Hess, and the lucky discovery of a vital handwritten note—eventually produced a $21 million settlement in favor of the firm's client, Bethlehem Steel. As McCloy reflected on his Cravath experience, he explained why it had meant so much to him: "The work habits I developed were of lasting value. . . . I knew I could accomplish any task and that I could be the type of person others depended on, rather than the type who had to depend on others."

■ ■ ■

Personal modesty, social reserve, and deliberate absence of arrogance are characteristic of great professional cultures. Capital Group "is clearly a culture of strong individuals in an industry notoriously afflicted with egotism," according to James F. Rothenberg, president of the Capital Research & Management unit. "Yet we accept and quietly seek anonymity as individuals in the work we do. We prize the reality that even among our professional peers, Capital, as an organization, is underappreciated and not fully recognized." Capital's culture has no place for stars and no interest in public recognition for individuals. Internally, the organization is remarkably flat. Everyone uses first names; all offices are modular; lots of people may be chairman of this unit or president of that, but nobody seems to care about titles, particularly the current title holder.

Everyone acts quite respectfully of everyone else; no one is put down and discussions are always appreciative of others' thoughts and feelings. (This is true to such an extent that some worry that Capital people may be too nice to each other.) Circumspection fits comfortably with the disciplined professional values that have long been a hallmark of Capital. "When I joined," recalled Robert L. Cody, "the firm was known to all of us in the industry for having consistently high standards in every area. The one word for Capital was and still is 'integrity'—both moral integrity and intellectual integrity. That commitment goes right back to Jonathan Bell Lovelace."

There have been few breaches of the organization's zero tolerance on matters of integrity over the past 80 years, but there have been breaches. Years ago, one trader let it be known to Wall Street firms that he wanted in on promising new issues for his personal account. Found out, he was promptly dismissed. In the seventies, the wife of an analyst who came from a Boston mutual fund organization was trading ahead of Capital's mutual funds in her personal account. Although it took some time to learn all the facts, the analyst was then obliged to leave immediately. Capital learned a painful lesson back in 1983, when a senior administrative officer was found siphoning money from a money market fund. The amount was large: approximately $2 million, but this was determined only after an extensive in-house investigation.* Some felt that while he hid as much as he could for as long as he could, the only reason he was caught was that somehow he wanted to get caught. Others felt that, as so often happens in white-collar crime, he came to believe he was too smart to get caught and so got careless. The SEC conducted a major investigation and imposed sanctions barring the man from the mutual fund industry, but decided not to press criminal charges. Nor did Capital. Determined to find out what had gone wrong and why, Capital realized that no large organization can assume that not one of its people would ever lie, steal, or cheat, so it designed a series of cross-checks into its systems. Ensuring integrity requires extra care in recruiting and training, and rigorous searching out of unexpected problems.

---

* Initially, the amount diverted was thought to be only $40,000. And it first appeared that all or most of the money was going to fund an overcommitted pledge to the Boy Scouts.

Ten years later, a similar test of culture arose at Goldman Sachs. Michael L. Smirlock had joined the firm after achieving academic distinction as a young professor at Wharton. Having just been named partner at 36, Smirlock was head of the $14 billion fixed-income investment management unit. In March 1993, he deliberately "reassigned" some $5 million of securities from one account to another, apparently to make investment performance look better. Smirlock's actions were discovered on a Friday, and that Saturday he was dismissed and reported to the regulatory authorities. "It's so hard to understand," commented partner Mike Armellino. "He was young, brilliant, articulate, and he didn't take any money doing it. But he sure ruined his career." In a fast-moving financial organization with lots of people making decisions that involve substantial amounts of money, temptations are many. So discipline must be known to be decisive.

Professional firms and individuals spend most of their lives working with uncertainties and complexities where answers are neither clear nor certain. By Warren Buffett's definition, unethical behavior is what you would not want your parents or children to read on the front page of your local newspaper. As Justice Potter Stewart said of pornography, "I can't define it, but I know it when I see it." For management, one great challenge, of course, is to anticipate ethical questions before they take shape and take appropriate remedial action ahead of need. Another is to flood the culture with positive affirmations of highly ethical behavior and standards. Then, as Ronald Reagan said, "Trust, but verify."

McKinsey's Marvin Bower once said sadly, "There may also be a belief that since we employ only people of good character, it is out of place to discuss ethics with them. The history of human experience and the current lowering of standards in the older professions show that any such belief is not well founded." Every large organization faces misbehavior. A Cravath partner, to facilitate his liaison with the vulnerable young wife of an associate, repeatedly sent the associate out of town. Associates found this despicable and protested. Fairly soon, the partner left to take a senior position in the federal government. For other reasons, he was not taken back into the firm when the government job ended.

Ethical questions and difficulties frequently cluster around change and newness: new people, new services, new markets. Vigilance is particularly important when the proportion of "new" versus "old" people is too large for the culture carriers to instill all the behavioral norms in all the new people. Special vigilance is also needed when the nature of the work is changing rapidly and those who favor traditional values can be called "out of touch" or "unrealistic." Times do change, but core professional ethics and values do not go into or out of fashion. Firms' values come in three guises: values on display in *signs* or posters, values supported by management's *statements*, and values driven by management's *actions*. A firm that celebrates its core values externally is often signaling its weaknesses, while celebrating core values *internally* is an important way to clarify what is or is not accepted.

With 15 to 20 percent of its staff new to the firm each year, persistent attention is needed to protect McKinsey's values from being "left for later." Values need to be refreshed—not too frequently, but regularly—to sustain those bonds and connections. So on one "Values Day" each year, the leaders in every McKinsey office talk specifically about values—often with an outside speaker to add interest—and then engage all members of the staff in case-based workshop discussions to relate the guiding principles to everyday operations.

Many important McKinsey values were derived from Bower's experience at the Jones Day law firm in Cleveland. Bower was unrelenting in his campaign to inculcate the values he believed clients most respected. McKinsey's commitment to stated values was clarified when a consultant who had been the firm's largest revenue producer one year was obliged to leave the firm because he had been hoarding clients in direct conflict with McKinsey's firm-first commitment to total collaboration. Donald Waite, a McKinsey director emeritus, remarked, "In annual and biannual individual evaluations, the 'soloist' will be among the first to learn that team play really counts at McKinsey."

Decisive action to ensure clarity about professional values is defining, particularly for those *not* involved in the particular situation. When the firm's fundamental values were violated, Bower swiftly sent a clear message to the organization. Chuck Ames, a longtime senior partner, remembered another instance involving a top performer:

> The best performing associate in the office was very smart and was working on a top management organization study. He had

recommended an organizational change [at the client corporation] and the creation of a new officer position—and then recommended himself for the position. The CEO called Marvin to tell him and Marvin asked the associate if this were true, and he said yes. So Marvin said, "You have thirty minutes to clear out. You're all done. If you need some help, I'll be glad to get the building services to help you get your things out, but you're *out.*" That was it. Losing that consultant was a real loss to the firm, but that didn't make any difference to Marvin. His position was that you live by our principles or you're out of here. When I told the consultant I was sorry to hear about this, he said, "No, Marvin did the right thing. I violated principles, I got caught, it's the right thing— throw me out."

"Values are everywhere at McKinsey—clients first, obligation to dissent and being *sure* everyone understands your point of view," recalled Leigh Bonney, a McKinsey consultant for eight years. Values are far superior to rules and regulations. "We must be wary of any 'religious' convictions," said Ian Davis, a former managing director. "Every organization has core values, so it's meaningless to say 'We are values driven.' The values of a Wall Street trading room or al-Qaeda or the Mafia *are* values—but they are not *our* values."

McKinsey learned from experience that its strong beliefs— obligation to dissent, no hierarchy, and up or out—are not universal values. For example, without adaptation none of these three ideas works comfortably in Japan. The Japanese *know* from their strong cultural traditions that hierarchy is as it should be; that dissent, particularly by the young, is wrong; that meritocracy is not always right; and that "up or out" conflicts with loyalty to employees and lifetime reciprocal responsibilities. Davis had to speak with the parents of many of the professional staff in Japan to try to show them why McKinsey's values were not evil. As he acknowledged, "Being a one-firm firm *is* sometimes tedious, and one set of values can get in the way of other values."

According to Jon Katzenbach, a former senior partner, "Values reinforcement must come primarily from within the culture and through the informal organization. The informal organization must strongly reinforce the values to make them real." McKinsey consultants

at all levels are encouraged to speak out on any perceived values deviation. "Speak up and speak out" stories are spread widely. A daily question is: Why would we suggest doing X if it's not best for this client?
"There is a tension, hopefully a dynamic and constructive tension but
all too often a destructive tension, between the disciplines and priorities of the *business* and the priorities and disciplines of the *profession*,"
said Davis. "Dealing successfully with that tension is where leadership
as opposed to management will be most telling." Former senior partner
Terry Williams observed: "Money versus professional values is a con-
stant struggle." D. Ronald Daniel, former head of McKinsey, agreed:
"Devotion to professionalism, if not pursued relentlessly, will inevitably
drift and fade toward commercialism."

■ ■ ■

That struggle is particularly fierce in Wall Street, where the money is
so substantial and visible. The traditional culture of Goldman Sachs
traces back to the values of the Sachs family, admired for modesty, philanthropy, and integrity. Integrity became the core value for Sidney
Weinberg, who headed the firm from 1930 to 1969. His successor, Gus Levy, accelerated Weinberg's drive for more and then even
more business, often testing the limits Weinberg had set on acceptable
behavior. Levy set the standards of personal commitment by coming in at 7:00 A.M. when competitors were starting no earlier than
nine-thirty or ten, *and* having at least one and often two client dinners
almost every night. He flew coach and expected everyone to answer
his own phone, work in rolled-up shirtsleeves, eat a quick lunch at the
trading desk in order to keep on working, and call everyone else by
first name (except "Mr. Weinberg").

The culture of Goldman Sachs became a unique blend of the
drive for making money and the characteristics of family. More than
any other Wall Street firm, Goldman Sachs celebrated teamwork and
team play. Expressions of being part of "our crowd" were simple: Go
to every employee's major life events—every wedding, every funeral,
and every bar mitzvah; always get there early and make sure you're
visibly social. More than at any other firm, the partners of Goldman
Sachs turned out, over and over again, for weddings, funerals, and other

family events. At the same time, internal competition for a partnership was so intense that it was important to have a mentor or "rabbi" who would coach, sponsor, and protect you.

Personal anonymity was expected: no press, no self-promotion, and no claiming credit. Public relations were handled by Ed Novotny, whose business card had no indication that he worked for Goldman Sachs and whose office was in a different building; his job was to keep the firm out of the papers. The word *I* was *never* used. *We* was the appropriate pronoun for any success—and some joked that most people in the firm didn't even dare talk about going to an *eye* doctor. Cost discipline was another principle. Fly coach; staff leanly. Quietly aggressive salesmanship was clearly a principle. So was working harder and for much longer hours than the people at any other firm. Open, extensive internal communications became another commitment. Part of this was "posting:" keeping everyone informed. For thousands of Goldman Sachs people around the world, the last 30 to 45 minutes before going to bed at night and the first 30 to 45 minutes in the early morning are devoted to receiving and replying to voice messages and e-mails.

Absolute loyalty and discretion were expected—absolutely. While strong feelings, including personal dislikes and deep angers, were evident to the partners *within* the partnership, an impenetrable cone of silence kept almost all internal tensions invisible to outsiders. No other major firm came even close. One remarkable demonstration of the we–the separation between insiders and outsiders—was the speed with which, for many years, long-serving partners who left the firm went from being insiders to being outsiders. While this may have strengthened internal bonding, it was an obvious missed opportunity for the organization and a personal loss for those who, after devoting the most important years of their careers to the firm, were virtually ignored. In recent years, Lloyd Blankfein, who became CEO in 2006, introduced many changes, engaging alumni in the work of the firm, often as highly paid consultants; organizing a website for alumni; and hosting enjoyable annual dinners for alumni on each continent, with in-depth presentations on the business.

The culture of Goldman Sachs was a blend of the values and expectations of three very different sources—the Sachs family, Sidney Weinberg, and Gus Levy—organized, codified, and promulgated by

John Whitehead in the 1970s as the firm was accelerating toward Wall Street leadership. The first three Business Principles are about the firm's mission (see Chapter 1). The others are about its culture:

4. We stress creativity and imagination in everything we do. While recognizing that the old way may still be the best way, we constantly strive to find a better solution to clients' problems. We pride ourselves on having pioneered many of the practices and techniques that have become standard in the industry.

5. We make an unusual effort to identify and recruit the very best person for every job. Although our activities are measured in billions of dollars, we select our people one by one. In a service business, we know that without the best people, we cannot be the best firm.

6. We offer our people the opportunity to move ahead more rapidly than is possible at most other places. We have yet to find the limits to the responsibility that our best people are able to assume. Advancement depends solely on ability, performance, and contribution to the firm's success, without regard to race, color, age, creed, sex, or national origin.

7. We stress teamwork in everything we do. While individual creativity is always encouraged, we have found that team effort often produces the best results. We have no room for those who put their personal interests ahead of the interests of the firm and its clients.

8. The dedication of our people to the firm and the intense effort they give their jobs are greater than one finds in most other organizations. We think that this is an important part of our success.

9. Our profits are a key to our success. They replenish our capital and attract and keep our best people. It is our practice to share our profits generously with all who helped create them. Profitability is crucial to our future.

10. We consider our size an asset that we try hard to preserve. We want to be big enough to undertake the largest project that any of our clients could contemplate, yet small enough to maintain the loyalty, the intimacy, and the esprit de corps that we all treasure and that contributes greatly to our success.

11. We constantly strive to anticipate the rapidly changing needs of our clients and to develop new services to meet those needs. We know that the world of finance will not stand still and that complacency can lead to extinction.

12. We regularly receive confidential information as part of our normal client relationships. To breach a confidence or to use confidential information improperly or carelessly would be unthinkable.

13. Our business is highly competitive and we aggressively seek to expand our client relationships. However, we must always be fair competitors and must never denigrate other firms.

14. Integrity and honesty are at the heart of our business. We expect our people to maintain high ethical standards in everything they do, both in their work for the firm and in their personal lives.

Whitehead knew that articulating these propositions was only a start. He and his co-leader, John Weinberg, lived by them. As tough commanders with combat experience and determination to excel, they knew they had to be absolute in requiring consistent adherence by everyone. Close monitoring on every dimension made it clear to everyone that the Two Johns would accept nothing less. Weinberg once fired a divisional head for having an affair with his secretary and not coming entirely clean with him when the story got into the press. "Assuring professional ethics are really lived by is a bit like being a zookeeper," commented partner Roy Smith. "You need lions and tigers to have a really good zoo, but you must also keep them under control—or reasonably so." Disciplined commitment across the firm made Goldman Sachs stronger and stronger, more and more widely respected and admired, and increasingly profitable—far more profitable than any other firm.

As with any strength, consistent success can produce a weakness. As the firm surged ahead, Whitehead had an increasingly grave concern that he decided to emphasize at an annual investment banking planning conference.

One thing worries me. It has done great harm to some of our competitors and could do serious harm to Goldman Sachs. What worries me is the early indication of a serious disease that can be quite destructive in a professional service firm. That disease has a name we don't like to use, but we must. It's arrogance. If *any* of you has any suggestions at *any* time on how we can prevent arrogance, you know I'd appreciate your help. Who would like to start this important discussion?

One hand went up. Whitehead turned toward the young banker. "And what can you suggest we do?"

"There's one really effective way to put an end to what you're worried about."

"And what would that be?"

"Hire mediocre people."

One form of arrogance is an individual or a whole firm deciding that it can set its own rules and standards of behavior. In recent years, as we shall see, Goldman Sachs leadership has been bluntly challenged by actions in specific transactions and by cultural changes that pulled the firm away from its first declared Business Principle: "Our clients' interests always come first." Since culture is the conversion of mission into daily behavior, a shift in either can and will affect the other. As always, the easiest direction of change is to shift down to a lower standard— usually in pursuit of short-term profits. That's why the great firms, to stay great, must devote so much time and talent to recruiting, training, and developing their people and to reinforcing high standards, and why leadership at all levels is so important to ensuring consistency in "how we do things around here."

Chapter 3

Recruiting

Getting the Right People

L ong before they ever face off in direct competition, the great
firms in every field separate themselves decisively from the many
good firms in their recruiting. They know their success tomorrow depends on recruiting and training the most capable young people
today. And they know that their toughest future competitors are—or
certainly should be—always striving to outdo them in recruiting.

Most firms confine themselves to middling futures by being "realistic" and making "reasonable" efforts in recruiting while aiming to
attract their "fair share" of the available talent. Young firms often make
crucial mistakes because, given their current obscurity, they feel they
have to compromise on the quality of the people they hire now, hoping they can somehow upgrade later. History shows that firms that
settle never get above the second tier. In the perpetual war for talent,
the best firms *never* settle. They always devote "unreasonable" efforts to

recruiting and have no interest in fair-sharing with competitors. They are determined to win an *unfair* share of the finest talent. They strive to out-recruit *all* their competitors *all* the time.

■ ■ ■

Every firm makes choices either by commission or omission. Only those that make recruiting a top priority can hope to advance in competitive standing. The hard work of intensive recruiting must always come first—for the firm and for the firm's leaders. That's why recruiting at Goldman Sachs is always led by one of the firm's most important partners and is that partner's number-one priority. "We can't be the best firm if we don't have the best people," is how John Whitehead summed it up. Partner Robert M. Conway recalled,

> John knew that recruiting was the most important thing we could ever do and that if we organized better and worked at it harder and with more skill, we could identify and attract better people more often. And if we did this consistently, we would build a better and better organization and could eventually become the best investment banking firm in America—and in the world. As John put it, and he really meant it, "If we ever stop doing recruiting very well, within just five years we will be on that slippery downslope, doomed to mediocrity."

When Conway was out recruiting at business schools, he always checked competitors' signup sheets to see who represented each of the other firms. "Every time, it was the same: Goldman Sachs always sent the more senior team."

Ford Motor Co. was for many years the firm's most prestigious client, so the answer to a young partner's question would have been a surprise at other firms. The partner was scheduled for interviews at Stanford Business School the next day but had just received an urgent call from Ford to go to Dearborn, Ford's headquarters. Alarmed, he plaintively asked the senior partner in charge of recruiting, "Which should I do?" The immediate reply confirmed Goldman Sachs's priority: "You go to Stanford. I'll cover you at Ford."

Among investment banking and securities firms, Goldman Sachs is today, and consistently has been for over 50 years, the most effective recruiter of the top business school graduates. All the negative press and the hostile congressional hearings after the Wall Street meltdown of 2008 have not changed that. If anything, reduced employment opportunities elsewhere on Wall Street have sharpened the competition to get into Goldman Sachs.

Selection is based on three equally weighted criteria: intelligence, as measured by grades and standardized test scores; leadership, demonstrated by having been repeatedly chosen by peers to lead sports teams and extracurricular organizations; and ambition to achieve, as determined during numerous interviews. Two dozen or more one-on-one interviews—some deliberately tough, some deliberately easy—give the candidate a cross-sectional view of Goldman Sachs and the ability to assess whether he or she would be satisfied with the long hours, travel, personal anonymity, and team discipline the firm's culture requires. Multiple interviews have long been the firm's tradition even though they are known to have a cost beyond money and time: Some people get lost to other firms, but Goldman Sachs isn't bothered. It doubts they would have had the right stuff.

Goldman Sachs does not look for top-quartile—or even top-decile—MBAs. Convinced that over the long run there is a decisive difference between the top 5 percent and the second 5 percent, the firm focuses on recruiting only those it believes are the very best young professionals, selecting carefully for such characteristics as leadership, drive, and appetite for hard work. Starting by hiring the 5 percent most qualified and capable, the firm then proceeds over the next few years to identify for advancement the 2 or 3 percent most effective team-playing contributors. The others can go to other firms.

Members of a firm can be especially effective at the institutions they themselves attended. At each college or graduate school where Goldman Sachs recruits, its team is made up of exceptional graduates from that particular school. They are on campus more frequently than competitors to chat with faculty about their courses and research and about the most promising students. They serve as guest speakers in classes and stay close to students who had worked at the firm after college before going back for an MBA or another advanced degree.

The best of these get invited back after earning their MBAs. In the eighties, recruiting was extended to include college seniors who would later go on to graduate schools. As the competition for talent intensified, recruiting was further extended in the nineties to college students looking for summer jobs between their junior and senior years. All these young Goldman Sachs "alumni" are expected to scout their classmates actively in search of superb candidates. The scuttlebutt network at colleges and graduate schools is always powerful. Students watch closely and talk about where the best seniors go. So do the faculty. Firms that have consistently been the best recruiters have strong momentum.

Recruiting the best extends into an unusual commitment to keeping the very best. Partner Michael Evans explained, "Where we differ most from other firms is in the attention we pay to retention. Goldman Sachs's standards of care for its professionals are simply the best in the industry. We hire the best and work hard year round to retain them through intensive training and mentoring." Recognizing the firm's unusual emphasis on teamwork and on fitting into a pattern of unrelenting work, Evans identified a potential problem: "The one possible negative of our approach is that the firm has less tolerance for nonconformist behavior."

Money motivates, of course, and for many years Goldman Sachs has paid more than other firms to people who develop rapidly and perform unusually well. But it also understands the strong attraction that the most talented and interesting people have for each other; how engaging it can be for unusually capable people to know they'll be on a steep learning curve; and how energizing it is to be striving to earn a position as part of a winning team. Being explicit about its high standards, hard work, long hours, and travel has turned out to be a powerful magnet for top people with ambition, particularly when they believe the competition to get ahead will always be fair.

■ ■ ■

In any firm, large numbers of interviews with each candidate are an important indicator of organizational commitment. Multiple interviews—often two dozen—teach the candidate more about the firm and its people and why it might be just right for him or her. The firm also gets more perspectives on the candidate, making it easier to find a potential weakness or a cultural misfit.

Capital Group learned from experience that it's helpful to have at least two associates interview any new candidate *twice* before asking lots of others to make time for a full series of interviews. Once that decision is made, Capital makes a major commitment to determining fit. Jim Rothenberg explained, "We think of hiring a lot like getting married. And if the marriage breaks up, we think that's really *our* fault."

Every year, Capital interviews two or three dozen MBAs at each major business school and then invites the most promising for two-day visits to headquarters in Los Angeles—and many more interviews. Interviews are exhaustive and exhausting as interviewers probe for such qualities as integrity, work ethic, humor, and perspective. "We look for a group of *C* words," said Karin Larson, who specialized in personnel: "common sense, curiosity, caution without being stubborn, creativity, and confidence without arrogance." Then begins the search for a match between the individual and the industry that he or she will research for investment potential. Such an alignment really matters, but it's something most people cannot easily find for themselves. An IBM engineer's résumé said he'd published some imaginative science fiction. This creative flair was central to his becoming a successful analyst of companies dependent on creativity—not high-tech companies but *retailers*.

Some Capital associates wonder about both the cost in productivity of having 20 people interview each serious candidate and the obvious risk that selection by consensus may eliminate the rare outlier who just might be an investment genius. But most feel it gives candidates a chance to see for themselves whether Capital is right for them. Self-selection is part of every effective recruiting process. Some candidates keep performing better as they do more interviews, but others get overconfident and coast. Some candidates find the process just too long and toss it in. In selecting people, as in making investments, said Larson, "if you ever feel you need to hurry to jump aboard, subsequent experience says *Stop!* Take all the time and care you need to make your very best decision. People will be with the organization for a long, long time, so it's easy to see why investing substantial time in making the really right decision at the beginning is always a rewarding investment."

Larson pointed to some specific reasons Capital recruiters take extra time. "You have to be cautious these days because many young people are attracted to investment management by the high compensation, not the nature of the work itself." Moreover,

> We know a high IQ is no guarantee that a person will be an effective securities analyst. Being too smart and always looking for just one more detail can really get in the way of good decision-making and superior understanding of what will really drive an investment. On the other hand, we strive to avoid the easy trap of locking someone out just because he's never owned a stock. Maybe he just never happened to get involved before; maybe he will be very good when he does get involved.

Capital seeks unusual diversity in national, cultural, and career backgrounds. The firm likes to mix people from four different sources: new MBAs; those with industry experience; professionals from other investment firms; and people from its own special in-house training program for college graduates, the Associates Program (TAP). The program began as an experiment and worked so well that it has become an important part of Capital's search for capable young people. During two years of training, each TAPer spends four months in each of six areas, such as administration, marketing, and investing. As a senior money manager explained, "Each position gives the TAPer enough time to go from *in*competent to competent and appreciate firsthand what it takes to do each job well. More than one in six eventually goes into investing." Among those most widely expected to provide organizational leadership in the future, easily half are TAPers.

■ ■ ■

At Mayo Clinic, recruiting is almost easy in some ways because the recruiting message is as clear to candidates as the Minnesota sky. Mayo knows what it is looking for. Its culture is strong and established, and its values are consistent and explicit. It uses its arduous recruiting process partly as a test. "We go through so many steps, we have so many people involved in screening and interviewing, even at entry-level jobs, that the people who survive the drawn-out process must really want to work here," said Matthew McElrath, former chair of human resources for Mayo Clinic Arizona. Mayo finds people who separate personal advancement from professional fulfillment as part of a strong team.

The clinic grooms and trains potential new physicians in its highly selective Mayo Medical School and its residency and fellowship programs. Both were created, in part, for the purpose of serving as long-term "interviews." In filling some 45 physician staff positions each year, Mayo Clinic has a great advantage in its ability to select the most like-minded prospects among the school's 50 graduating medical students and several hundred fellows, who represent 5 percent or less of the applicants to these highly selective programs. While studying at Mayo, the lone-cowboy type quickly realizes he is not going to be a good fit or professionally happy.

Mayo Clinic hires people for careers, not for jobs, and so talks explicitly about lifelong careers when recruiting. It is a "relational" employer that believes an investment in recruiting is an investment in success for both the clinic and the employee. "Many will focus on skills first, but I say go to values first," said McElrath. "Competency is irrelevant if we don't share common values."

Beyond one-on-one interviews, an unusual part of the hiring process can be a 90-minute "behavioral interview"—sometimes with three or four candidates together—conducted by several people from the hiring unit. Interviews cover a standard set of 8 to 10 topics, based on Mayo Clinic values and the skills needed for success in the particular position. Examples: "Describe a highly successful project" or "Tell me about a situation where you had to disagree with your boss to prevent a mistake being made." In describing their experiences, candidates inevitably show their styles of confrontation, and panelists can easily probe for details or feelings or reasoning. They'll also hear whether the candidate uses *I* or *we*. After this structured interview, often only one of the three or four is hired, and sometimes none.

■ ■ ■

Sometimes achieving organizational excellence requires a basic shift in recruiting philosophy. Almost 60 years ago, Marvin Bower impressed upon his McKinsey colleagues that the firm's real competition was not for clients or specific projects—much as it would vigorously compete for both—but for talented, committed people. If McKinsey won the competition for people, the clients and assignments would surely follow. As usual, Bower had a plan: Recruit MBAs. He believed McKinsey would do better with consulting based on analysis by bright young MBAs than with consulting based on the experience of mediocre managerial retreads. By implication, he planted doubts about firms with older, perhaps less imaginative and contemporary thinkers. The experienced executive often had had one bad experience: He might have lost out to another person for the top job. Also, his experience might give depth without breadth, which could show up as inflexibility or too little imagination in analyzing a client's situation.

MBAs who had much less experience were quicker studies and could be trained to a higher firm-wide standard. Initially, MBAs were so few relative to the whole firm that it took several years of steady recruiting before they were noticeably changing McKinsey. Bower stayed with it, reminding skeptical clients that most major discoveries are made by people under 35. Bringing young people to the firm made it easier to achieve internal harmony and get real teamwork. McKinsey's MBAs put increasing focus on the disciplines of objective analysis and problem-solving as a *firm*, not "Here's the way I used to do it—so now you should, too."

Discovering the usefulness of young MBAs brought another major advantage: As they were graduating from business schools, they were easy to find, and all were looking for jobs. In recruiting talented young people, McKinsey's main competition in the late sixties and seventies was Boston Consulting Group. BCG positioned itself as doing much more top-level strategy work and at the same time maintained that its consultants were living more balanced lives. BCG also offered large "exploding" bonuses, which would be withdrawn if not promptly accepted, to press the best MBAs—particularly those with large student loans to repay—into accepting its job offers quickly, before most had time to consider offers from other firms, particularly McKinsey.

McKinsey fought back with summer internships between first- and second-year MBA studies. Other consulting firms quickly followed. "Those were rocky days for McKinsey," former managing partner Ron Daniel recalled. "We always took the position of a championship team—that we have no competitors—and would point out that we hire more consultants each year than BCG employs in total." But privately the firm realized that it had to change to make itself the best recruiter by having some of its best people doing all recruiting and getting well rewarded for it. Daniel observed, "While the best we recruit today are not clearly smarter than the best recruits of years ago, the average is clearly higher." A main reason for the substantial strength of McKinsey's recruiting is that Daniel made it his personal priority for many years.

In the seventies and eighties, the McKinsey pipeline was filled primarily with top-quartile MBAs from Harvard, Wharton, Stanford, and Tuck, plus the top 5 percent from Virginia, MIT, Columbia, and Europe's INSEAD and occasional "walk-ins." In the early nineties, the firm grew so much that the top 25 percent was expanded to the top 35 percent. When Daniel recommended recruiting PhDs and law school graduates, he got much the same negative reaction Bower had gotten to hiring MBAs 20 years earlier. *You won't get the best people because they'll get, and accept, the jobs they have been training for. They won't know enough about business strategy, marketing, production, or finance— not even accounting. They won't have spent two years learning how to think through business problems—MBAs will have dealt with over one thousand cases—and won't know how to present their findings to senior business executives in the language of business.* Today the majority of new McKinsey consultants have advanced degrees other than or in addition to MBAs. About 600 consultants are MDs and several are MD/PhDs. McKinsey has more Rhodes Scholars than any other organization.

Today McKinsey's recruiting mission statement is clear: The firm strives to "attract, develop, excite, motivate, and retain exceptional people." Experience can matter, but analytical capability matters much more because anyone can learn but nobody can get smarter. Initial interviews are typically done on campus. Successful candidates then interview at the office of their choice to assess personality fit, since offices can differ slightly in tone or style. While each office makes its own hiring decisions, one partner oversees all McKinsey recruiting at a large source like Harvard Business School. For offices in Australia, Brazil, Canada, and other countries, McKinsey usually recruits the best one or two nationals from those countries who are graduating from larger schools like

Harvard or Wharton. An integral part of McKinsey interviewing has long been testing candidates with an unstructured problem to see how they think when facing a new, unknown situation. In the past, each partner used his own case, but more recently, said Rodney Zemmel, who oversaw the recruiting program in 2011, "We train to a norm to make the process systematic."

By the 1990s, the largest number of the most talented business graduates across Europe agreed: They wanted to go into consulting—at least for a few years—and the firm they most wanted to work for was McKinsey. In America, McKinsey was rated number one as a "dream company" to work for in *Fortune* magazine's survey of MBAs. By the end of the twentieth century, McKinsey was hiring one out of seven Harvard Business School graduates who ranked in the top third of their class. Today McKinsey's power in recruiting is hard to overstate. Even MBAs who don't want the job want the offer. The firm wins most of the time it competes with another consulting firm's offer. According to Zemmel, "When we compete with another firm, our offer is accepted eighty percent of the time. As you can imagine, that's almost always after the other firm has made an all-out effort to win each of those competitions."

Many great firms try to include as many candidates as possible in the first stage of the recruiting process—the "top of the funnel"— so nobody gets missed. McKinsey evaluates some 200,000 applicants per year worldwide, so the recruiting process must operate on a vast scale. At the same time, since the firm hires only one out of 100 applicants, the process designed to select that 1 percent has to be exacting. Administering this process, which is both highly personal to each applicant and global, depends on over 100 full-time professional administrators. Partners participate in recruiting with an average yearly commitment of four days, most of which are devoted to interviewing candidates. For the Americas, with roughly 500 partners involved, this equals eight consultant-years of the firm's most treasured resources or, in financial terms, about $30 million of forgone revenue.

Recruiting peaks for four months each year. During this period, "the firm is a recruiting *machine*," said Leigh Bonney. "It's all hands on deck. For Harvard Business School we designated two engagement managers full time for those four months." While other consulting firms delegate recruiting to HR or to those consultants with time available,

McKinsey's recruiting is done by the firm's best and busiest consultants. "Weak people recruit still weaker people, apparently to increase their own stature by lowering the firm average," warned partner Jürgen Kluge. "Very strong people are not afraid of competition and look hard for the very best people. McKinsey's recruiting must always be done by consultants who are clearly in our top third." Whoever leads recruiting at a major school may do so for two years, but because having evident client impact is essential to a consultant's standing in the firm, leaders will, as soon as possible, be back working with clients.

McKinsey, being McKinsey, keeps detailed records so the selection process can be evaluated rigorously by the results. The process is astonishingly effective—about 90 percent accurate in predicting who will be successful as a McKinsey consultant. Scores given during recruiting have proved far more accurate in predicting future performance than the person's work background or academic performance.

Halfway through the interviewing, the interviewers meet to assess the candidate and decide whether to continue and, if so, how. McKinsey's analysis of cost-effectiveness has led to the conclusion that the optimum number of interviews is eight. After that, the incremental accuracy of predictions of success in consulting does not justify the incremental cost. Discussion among experienced interviewers illuminates for the newer interviewers what McKinsey has learned to look for in order to protect the firm's culture and values. In "interview training days," new interviewers see videos, conduct mock interviews, and get coaching and critique. "We are, of course, concerned about false negatives," observed Rodney Zemmel. "If one interviewer has a false negative in one out of ten cases, two interviewers will have a double false negative in about one in 100 cases. This may sound good, but since we make offers to only one in 100, we want to do even better." McKinsey believes it could reduce recruiting costs by half if it dropped a third of the schools at which it interviews, but any one of those schools might be a pipeline to the one stellar person the recruiters wouldn't want to miss.

"Will X become a *partner*?" is the central question always asked in recruiting. Excellent problem solving is not enough to become a partner. "Successful consultants need three Qs; IQ, EQ, and RQ," offered director emeritus Peter Kraljic: "intellectual capability, emotional capability, and relationship capability—the ability to see things as others do from their perspective." Herbert Henzler, the former leader of McKinsey Germany, added,

> We look for "archetypal" people who are not mainstreamers but leaders and independent thinkers—lead dogs. Athletes know the importance of hard training. Victory and defeat are not very far separated. Only those with the appropriate habit of mind know that an unclimbed mountain can be climbed.

The reach of its recruiting has helped McKinsey increase diversity.* In North America, women now represent 40 percent of the firm's new consultants, though the proportion in Germany and elsewhere is lower. Diversifying the firm's gene pool is a strategic priority—by geography, by gender, by MBA versus other advanced degrees, and, more recently, by functional skills in such areas as risk management and information technology and by industry experience. (In the past, McKinsey consultants looked down on functional skills.) "We gladly interview all sorts of PhDs," said Zemmel, "even though we know we have more success with PhD *scientists* than with PhD poets." The emphasis on diversity now extends to diversity *within* the many Chinese consultants who are recruited each year. In China, most recent graduates are just not ready for the work of consultants. They have focused on excelling in classrooms and have not developed street smarts or the communication skills needed to work effectively within a team. Good communication within a team is vital when doing rigorous data analysis, creating ideas, or developing hypotheses, and later when working persuasively with clients on implementation.

■ ■ ■

Cravath partner Allen Finkelson asserted with the confidence for which the firm is well known: "The idea of working at the finest law

---

*As at most firms, diversity was not always a priority. When Marvin Bower first began recruiting MBAs, only men were even considered—there were no women in the business schools then—and interview evaluation forms had as the first factor on which to rate a candidate: "Regular facial features."

firm in the world is the real carrot." While Cravath partners respect and admire a few other law firms, they do not recognize any as equals. As presiding partner Evan Chesler put it,

> If we make an offer and the candidate has good judgment, he or she will surely accept. And if they don't accept, we'll then doubt their judgment. Cravath training is the best postgraduate educa- tion—education, not just training—a young lawyer will ever receive. In our recruiting, we sell education.

Cravath's recruiting focuses on the top graduates of the top law schools because performance in law school is an effective first approxi- mation of performance in legal work. The firm's recruiting success centers on its providing intensive education in the practice of law, its reputation for hiring the most capable and ambitious young lawyers, and the commitment of the partners to do the interviewing.

"Nobody coming into Cravath got only one offer, so everyone chose Cravath—an active choice for a firm of excellence," remarked tax partner Stephen Gordon. And George Gillespie explained, "Wachtell [Wachtell, Lipton, Rosen & Katz] is our strongest competi- tor. With their specialization in mergers and acquisitions, they're more profitable and they pay more than we can, so if associates want to spe- cialize in M&A, they'll go there. If they want a broader corporate prac- tice, they'll come to Cravath." Cravath partners don't run down other firms when recruiting, but partner Daniel Mosley did dryly observe: "Some firms position themselves as having a better lifestyle, but it's not clear that this is objective reality. When we work through the night with them, they're working through the night with us."

Since 2007 the starting salary at Cravath and other top-tier New York law firms has been $160,000. Most associates at the leading law firms come from the same top-10 law schools, which are about the same size as they were decades ago and collectively graduate about 2,500 new lawyers each year. So with Cravath's traditional focus on the top 10 percent, it has only about 250 to select from and, until recently, it wanted to hire nearly 100 associates: five times as many as it did 50 years ago. Competition for the fixed supply of new lawyers increased with the growth of the other major New York City firms, strong regional firms, and the New York offices of national law firms headquartered

elsewhere, as well as from the increased interest in lawyers by leading private equity and consulting firms. Another kind of competition
has come from lifestyle changes. Not all new lawyers or their spouses
want to live in New York City. Young lawyers are less accepting of
the long, hard hours accurately associated with the major New York
firms. Increasing interest in "balanced lives" among young lawyers—
particularly among women who want to balance their careers and
family commitments—can make it attractive to go to less demanding
regional firms or to in-house law departments of major corporations.

In theory, Cravath had some choices: Spread recruiting to more law
schools and try to pick off one or two stars from the lesser schools
or change its policy and bring in lateral hires *or* ease off on its high
standards *or* acquire another firm. Cravath won't relax standards and,
with rare exceptions, won't compromise on its policy of not hiring laterals because the partners don't like the impact on associates. Several
years ago, the recruiting partner expanded recruiting through the
Midwest to cover strong second-tier law schools like Notre Dame and
Michigan, hoping to find one or two outstanding people. It worked,
but was later dropped because it took too much time and effort. The
deans do not want Cravath to cherry-pick their best students, so
recruiters must treat all candidates equally. A graduate from a second-
tier law school told about his Cravath interview: Cravath's partner
greeted him at the cubicle door, saying, "To be perfectly honest with
you, the only person we might want is the editor of your law review,
and that's why I'm here, but you look like a nice guy and we're both
here, so why don't we have a friendly chat?" They talked awhile and
Cravath hired one person: the law review editor.

Cravath's recent strategic response to the recruiting problem of
substantially increased competition has been to change its economic
model. Instead of expanding the associates–partner pyramid to get
more leverage, the firm has reduced the number of associates taken
into the firm each year—from about 100 to about 50—and increased
its focus on bringing in even-more-exceptional associates to maximize
productivity. These outstanding associates will get even more attention
and training from partners, resulting, the firm hopes, in lower costs to
Cravath and stronger, longer-lasting bonds between the firm and associates so they will stay through their most productive associate years.

Cravath's eliteness is professional, certainly not social or ancestral. Stephen Gordon recalled that after growing up in modest circumstances in Syracuse, New York, and working in a bakery for $4.72 an hour during college,

> I'd read about Cravath in an article about the "price war" bidding for new associates pushing starting pay up to $26,000 in 1977. I thought that was very good money, so Cravath registered in the back of my mind. Coming out of Harvard Law School, we all had a moral certainty about the big New York law firms: awful sweatshops run by Brahmin partners who would never accept guys like me. But I decided to interview with one of the major firms so I'd know for the rest of my life what I'd turned down, and tried Cravath. My first interview was with a brash young Jewish partner. He and every one of the several other partners I met that day were smart, interesting, personable—and different. They all really liked doing the work they did. And they were each impressive in different ways. I knew it was supposed to be a bad place, but I really liked it.

One hiring partner who tried to meet all prospective associates at the end of their long day of interviews would ask everyone the same question: "During the interviews, did you find any surprises?" And 95 percent would answer, "Yes, I liked the people more than I'd expected."

■ ■ ■

With 20 to 30 percent higher pay than most law firms and less grinding hours, plus a more direct path to senior positions in corporate management, McKinsey has made increasingly successful forays into hiring law school graduates who are capable of rigorously analyzing business problems. The appeal of consulting in comparison to practicing law includes travel, opportunities for greater creativity, and work on more interesting, less structured, or predetermined problems. That's why McKinsey hires as many Harvard Law School graduates as most large law firms. "Management consulting is, for most people, an unknown," observed Peter Walker, a director in the New York office.

There are no clear specs. So when recruiting, we have an obligation to advise candidates that success as a consultant and a career in consulting are not destiny. It all depends on you. And whether someone has the right fit can only be learned by experience. So we say, "Try consulting. You'll learn a lot about the real nature of consulting and a lot about yourself—and about the fit."

McKinsey has established itself as an ideal first employer for MBAs not yet ready to choose a specific career. After Columbia Business School, with expectations of taking two or three years in consulting before settling on a real career, Donald C. Waite III was attracted to McKinsey because his interviewer assured him he would learn a lot. For Waite, that was a compelling attraction. "After thirty-six years at the firm, it still is," said Waite, who rose to be a director and head of the New York office. "Teamwork and learning are what working at McKinsey is all about."

In deciding on firms and careers, people choose not only the work they will do, but the values they will hold and the kind of people they will become. For many years, McKinsey and Goldman Sachs recruited mostly the same people. McKinsey might have hired 20 percent of the candidates Goldman Sachs would not hire, and vice versa, but for both firms most offers overlapped. However, just five years after hiring, the two groups of people would become very different. Investment bankers would say they wanted to go all out to make money awhile longer and then rebalance their lives later, but all too often they got so focused on maximizing dollars that they could only aim for "more"— and never rebalanced their lives. The overlap with Goldman Sachs in recruiting has declined considerably over the years—presumably because prospective traders are seldom prospective consultants. Making money is far less important or interesting for those who go into consulting, who often say things like, "We're making more than we need for the lives we want to lead anyway."

■ ■ ■

Systematic as the great firms' recruiting is, they remain open to unique opportunities and often blend selective senior recruiting with a strategy aimed primarily at current graduates. Few organizations are as negative about bringing in established outsiders as Cravath. No lateral hires—a policy laid down by Paul Cravath in the early twentieth century—assures those who commit to earning partnership that they will not have outsiders parachute in ahead of them. It also assures the firm that its partners will be "Cravath trained." Still, all good rules have a few deliberate exceptions. Over 100 years, only five partners have come in as laterals. In 1991, Jeffrey A. Smith was one. After Harvard College, he went to Penn Law School, liked Philadelphia, chose to live there, and made partner in a good firm. One day a headhunter called: "I'm so excited. I've got a search for a great firm that never uses search firms. They want to start an environmental practice. I know you'd never move, but I need your help: Who is very good in environmental law?"

"Which firm is looking?"

"Sorry, I can't tell you. I'm forbidden to reveal the name."

"Well, there's only one firm I'd ever consider."

"And it is . . . ?"

"Cravath."

"You guessed it."

Nine months later, having met virtually every partner at Cravath, Smith got the offer—with one unusual condition: He must come alone. No clients could be brought along. Six years later, he made partner at Cravath.

Capital Group interviews more than 50 experienced investment professionals each year even though fewer than 1 in 10 will eventually be invited to join. Capital will let able people at other firms know that if they ever want to talk, they should take the initiative. It likes to add experienced people during industry downturns because that's a win for everybody. Capital gets some very good people—they're leaving troubled firms so their former employers often feel relieved to have them safely and well placed—and they come to a place that really wants them. As a financially strong private firm, Capital can budget reserves for this sort of initiative: investing in people for the long term much as it invests long term for clients. Capital is explicitly committed to hiring ahead of need to accommodate future growth. During the bear market at the start of this century, while other firms were laying off people, Capital not only had zero layoffs, it hired several hundred new associates, including 16 senior professionals. Ten years later, for the first time, the organization laid off several hundred people. They were largely in information technology and investor services, which had been allowed to overexpand during an industry boom, but also included two dozen underperforming investment people. Tenure at Capital was no longer assured. It had to be earned.

■ ■ ■

Hiring ahead of need is chancy, of course. Even McKinsey can get caught in a mismatch of supply and demand when the market suddenly changes. For example, in 2001, aiming for 2,000 hires, McKinsey made 3,000 offers—and, with the dot-com bust, got 2,800 acceptances! Simultaneously, departures of young consultants slowed down for the same reason. Suddenly the firm was carrying an extra 1,000 people. Even though it obviously hurt their compensation for a while, the partners accepted the costs so McKinsey would be ready for growth when the economy recovered.

Over and over again, the great firms deliberately excel at recruiting stellar people at least in part because they are committed to an inspiring, overarching mission or purpose and the compelling values of a strong culture. Recruiting well is essential, and well begun *is* half done—but only half. Even the best recruiting is "one hand clapping." The other key to developing the strongest organization is the commitment to educating each recruit and developing everyone's ability and self-discipline to continue learning, because people change and the work of the great professions is always changing, too.

Chapter 4

Developing People

Training, Educating, and Organizing for Excellence

The right dimensions on which to measure the strength of any professional firm are the number of consistently first-rate professional people and how effectively they are organized. Having carefully recruited the best people, the great firms invest more time and energy than others in developing the skills of each individual—and they never stop. While the firms differ in some of the specific ways they manage their people, they all work in teams and foster a culture of teamwork. People are mentored, evaluated, and coached systematically on their teamwork effectiveness, and are bonded together by shared experiences in the past and the certainty of interdependence in the future.

In the early years of their careers at each of the great professional firms, beginners experience a powerful surge in learning. Typically called *training*, in the best programs it is at least equally *education*. Training is learning how to reproduce what predecessors have

developed as best practices; training suggests that the most an associate can learn is how to do what can be instructed—it implies that
the associate will often do less and can never do better. Education
is learning how to understand issues so thoroughly that appropriate
new resolutions—*new* best practices—will be developed. Learning to
reproduce what a leader can already do is always far less important
than learning how to be an effective leader.

■ ■ ■

"Cravath training," said Evan Chesler, "is the best postgraduate
education—education, not just training—you will ever receive." Cravath's
compact with new associates is explicit: Come here, get Cravath training,
and when you leave you'll be a better lawyer than you ever imagined.
Partners see this superb postgraduate education in law as a springboard
to a great legal career. That's the reason to join the firm as an associate, not with a specific ambition to become a partner. In fact, partners
believe that wanting partnership too much, having too much at stake
on that one decision, shows a lack of the judgment and balanced perspective required of a Cravath partner.

The firm devotes extraordinary, systematic effort to developing the skills of top law school graduates so it can select the best of the
best as Cravath partners. Partner Kris Heinzelman explained, "Cravath
trains associates in all aspects of corporate law—not just in one specific
specialty—so associates are flexible enough for anything and certainly are
not intimidated by anything new." Associates develop their skills through
several years of general legal experience before specializing and so should
"not be confined overlong to the work of one client or one partner."
The emphasis is on preparing them as future partners or senior associates to organize a team of lawyers, divide a complex matter into component parts that can each be addressed separately, and then recombine
those parts into the most effective resolution. Cravath trains each litigation
associate to be the best litigation generalist—not a *securities* litigator or an
antitrust litigator—believing that the best litigators will thrive on the challenges of handling a wide variety of cases. "We want litigators who will
be masterful across a wide range of cases, learning from each case how
to be better at *all* litigation," explained partner Julie North, though she

added: "We also accept that the 'next best' litigators will want to specialize so they can master one particular area." "The best training—and most of our training—is doing real work," said George Gillespie. "That's where we pass the Cravath 'secrets of the craft' along from partner to associate and from senior associate to junior associate." Partners agree that Cravath training is the most important strength—the firm's "secret sauce." Almost all partners are products of Cravath training, which fosters firm-wide professional bonding and diffusion of power across the partnership.

Basics matter. As Chesler emphasized,

> Our clear and explicit intention is zero defects. We may miss— but not often. Here's an example of training: When I send a letter, I look at the envelope to be sure it's correct. My assistant once asked me why and I explained that to the receiving party, details matter because they are perceived as signals. In an important matter for IBM—removing the stricture of the old antitrust consent decree—I wrote a letter to Judge Schwartz, who was presiding after we had achieved the removal of Judge Edelstein, explaining IBM's case for relief. A few days later I got a phone call from the judge saying: "I have your letter. I agree with your logic. I will end the constraints and will call the government's lawyers. Oh, one other thing," he said as he hung up, "I spell my name with a *t*." It did not matter one iota that Schwarz is a common spelling or that one of our partners uses that spelling or that our associate copied it exactly the way the Department of Justice had spelled it. The judge's name was incorrectly spelled in *our* letter. Basics matter. You can't soar like an eagle until you have learned *exactly* how to flap your wings. Cravath requires certain skills. We coach, but only the player on the field actually plays, so the player needs to develop the gyroscope that will *always* work for her or for him.

■ ■ ■

The Cravath firm's origins trace back to the early nineteenth century. By the 1860s, practicing lawyers were debating the value of the new law schools and what privileges, if any, their graduates should receive. The case for law schools advanced after Harvard organized a law faculty in 1870. By the closing years of the nineteenth century, as its workload tripled and became more complex, the still small firm saw the need to improve the quality of the staff. In 1896, for the first time, it hired a recent law school graduate as an associate. The firm was already one of the nation's oldest and, while never having grown beyond five partners, was described in 1898 as having "held equal rank to any of the great law firms of the City" for half a century.

The firm sometimes retained the services of a young outside lawyer named Paul Cravath, who had "an uncanny sense for the right solution of mixed business and legal problems and a capacity for bringing men to his views." In 1899, when the head of the firm heard that Cravath's partner was leaving private practice to teach law at Columbia, he invited Cravath, then 37, to join his firm as one of three senior partners. Cravath did, and the firm was soon styled as Guthrie, Cravath & Henderson.

Cravath brought with him the basic idea for a new kind of law firm. He was convinced that he knew how to build a great firm based in part on the ideas of Walter S. Carter, whose law office he had entered after graduating at the top of his class from Columbia Law School: Each year recruit one or two outstanding graduates from each leading law school, require them to work exclusively for the firm (an innovation), train them rigorously for several years, make the best performers partners, and oblige all others to leave, replacing them with the best new graduates.

Contrary to conventional stories, the Cravath System of training young lawyers, for which the firm is so widely admired, did not spring fully formed from the massive brow of Paul Cravath. It was developed over many years with experience and the thoughtfulness of others. But the core concept was Cravath's and, with his love of system, he was the principal architect. Moreover, his powerful personality was crucial to putting through several simultaneous changes to establish a radically new approach to training young lawyers and developing a firm of self-perpetuating excellence. Training associates to the highest standards has been the essential engine of excellence in the Cravath System for over 100 years. Paul Cravath's innovation proved so effective that all the other major law firms moved in the direction he had chosen.

New lawyers had traditionally been trained by having each partner train his own associates in his own way. To avoid inconsistent work habits or standards, Cravath introduced a firm-centered training program, inculcating the importance of teamwork, and insisted that all associates be trained within the firm. To be hired, they must have studied liberal arts in college and mastered the basic legal concepts of common law—best taught in the law schools at Yale, Columbia, or Harvard, where they must have excelled. In addition to brains, Paul Cravath also wanted personality and physical stamina. While they still typically come in from elite law schools, Cravath lawyers are almost never from affluent, socially prominent families. "We really don't care," said one partner. But the strong impression is that they do care—in reverse—really preferring always to make partners of those who, like themselves, made it on their own.

New Cravath lawyers are not thrown into deep water and told to swim; they are taken into shallow water and carefully taught strokes. Believing they will learn to be better lawyers sooner, Cravath rejects the conventional practice of assigning small matters to new associates without much supervision on the theory that a lawyer best learns how to handle cases by actually handling them. Under the Cravath System, a young lawyer watches his senior break a large problem down into its component parts, is given one of the small parts and exhaustively does whatever the part assigned to him requires. The neophyte learns to analyze each component of a complicated problem rigorously, a process impracticable in handling small, routine matters.

Over the years, training at Cravath has been made much more regular, predictable, and institutional. It is designed to enable associates to think and act like partners, who have to be inner-directed on strategy, policies, and techniques of law and have a mastery of the inherently creative process of handling challenging legal matters. Partners agree that it's not the long hours but the intensity of those hours that is so very hard. Can an associate take the stress? Can he or she take the sustained focus, the imperatives of meeting the schedule, the responsibility of decision, the pace, and the deadlines? Most of the learning comes from working on difficult issues of importance to major clients, which is why professionals say they "practice" law, "practice" medicine, and "practice" consulting: The best practitioners are always learning. Cravath partners believe associates have to learn for themselves so the learning is really *theirs*. Partners will help an associate by asking questions. For example, after a trial, a partner might ask, "Do you see why I did not object even though the note you passed said correctly that I could?" If the partner simply spells out his reasoning, he's only training, not educating the associate to think rigorously and independently. "Besides," observed Chesler with a smile, "we're all too busy to be giving a lot of instruction."

The results produced by the Cravath System have been described as "a crack cavalry regiment in which everybody would wheel into line and accomplish whatever was necessary even if it took all night long." Paul Cravath demanded results. "He expected perfection or as near to it as he could get and he seldom got quite as much as he expected," said one of his partners. "His first great object was to organize his firm and its staff so as to make it competent to do, as nearly perfectly as it could be done, any acceptable work which might be offered."

The firm's strategic commitment to its own way of training and educating associates is clarified by contrasting it to the "pool" system of managing associates used by most large law firms. Mergers, particularly unwelcome takeover bids, come up suddenly. Court proceedings get stopped, sometimes for weeks. Lawsuits often come as surprises. These sudden changes in demand are inherent in the practice of law and can be highly disruptive, particularly to the profitability of a law firm, because while the productive capacity of the firm can quickly be strained by the urgent demands of a surge in work volume, when volume drops off, the fixed costs of having a large group of associates and support staff continue right on. So the typical large law firm's economics depend on organizational flexibility, particularly in the way associates are assigned to specific matters. The pool system helps keep the supply side flexible.

In the pool system, work is broken up into bite-size pieces, which the partner who works with a particular client parcels out according to their difficulty to associates according to their abilities and experience. If work volume is up, the partner calls for more associates, saying, "I need one third-year and two first-years." Partners treat associates as fungible. If demand goes up a lot, the typical law firm hires more associates at whatever level of experience seems requisite. If demand drops off significantly, associates are let go.

Over time, while it does deal with a core economic and organizational problem, the pool process inevitably makes a firm less collegial and more impersonal.

Cravath rejects the pool system for several reasons. While it's clearly important to produce great work for clients in the short run, the firm believes it's even more important to develop great lawyers who will produce great work for clients in the long run. Persuaded that the best way to train young lawyers is to bond associates directly with a specific small team of partners and associates, Cravath will typically have two, three, or four partners work closely with an assigned group of associates over 12 or 18 months—12-month intervals in corporate law and 18-month intervals in litigation. Everyone on the team is motivated to produce the best results for the client *and* to help each lawyer develop. Associates get invaluable experience in understanding each client's total problem, the firm's specific strategy for dealing most effectively with the particular matter, and why the division of work into specific components makes sense, all of which increases each associate's future effectiveness.

Cravath partners believe associates will have learned in the 12 or 18 months of a rotation most of the transferable useful knowledge of that specialty they could learn if they stayed in it for the rest of their careers. So it's time to move on to a different team. The more diversity of substantial experience—the more different ways of thinking conceptually and tactically about how best to deal with complex new problems—the better an associate becomes as a many-faceted problem solver and the lower the risk of getting professionally "grooved" or caught in a rut.

"It's an amazing way to learn," said Julie North.

> The capabilities and confidence you learn through Cravath training will take you anywhere you most want to go. We really get to know each other personally and professionally and we all get practice in the skills of working as a team, which means so much at Cravath. We accept that we're sacrificing efficiency because we know we are gaining so much in effectiveness.

Each successful Cravath lawyer was, before coming to Cravath, a very successful *solo* performer—in school, college, and law school—and then, at Cravath, had to transform himself or herself into a *team* performer by joining and becoming a member of a team already in motion.

This major reorientation to teamwork can be destabilizing for the serial-achieving individualist. Highly talented individuals are naturally proud people. For those who were in the top 1 percent in school, the top 1 percent in college, the top 1 percent in law school—and *never* less than the top 10 percent in anything—to suddenly realize that at Cravath, for the first time in a lifetime, they are *not* in the top 1 percent—not even the top 10 percent or even the top 25 percent—can be deeply distressing. And it can be very hard for them to be in the *bottom* 50 percent at Cravath as, of course, half the associates must always be.

As associates grow in professional stature, those who evidence capacity for delegation get opportunities to expand the volume and raise the complexity of their own activities by giving younger associates the same kind of training they have enjoyed. Katherine Forrest paired with Evan Chesler for her first years and then with Tom Barr. "They showed me how to be the very best lawyer I could be. As an associate, you get to do all sorts of stuff you're not really ready to do. That's a great compliment and very challenging—and fulfilling. You feel like a star."

Partners say that Cravath is not so much a homogeneous one-firm firm as a close confederation of small practice units. In rotations, explained North, "you really go from one small law firm to another small law firm, working very closely with the partners in each unit, learning from them both different areas of law and also different ways of practicing law." This is important in litigation in a particular way: To be successful in court, a lawyer must be seen to be comfortable in his own skin. Each lawyer needs to find and develop his or her own "voice." So it's important to see the different ways of working and the different voices of different partners who are equally effective because they do what works best for them and their personalities. Cravath strives to teach litigation strategy and tactics better than any other firm—not just the *how*, but also the *why*. If a litigator thinks through all the alternatives far enough ahead, he can cause developments to evolve much more in the way he wants. Forrest explained, "We believe you need to know how the dominoes are set up and arranged and how one domino can cause another to fall down so you'll know exactly when to topple over that first domino and exactly where its falling will lead."

Courtroom trials on complex corporate matters are a vanishing phenomenon, partly because trials are so enormously expensive and partly because of alternatives such as mediation and dispute resolution. A corporate litigator can easily practice for 35 years and never go to trial. Yet Cravath needs to train litigators for trials, and the best way to do this is with trials. No law firm wants to lose a major case because its junior attorney didn't know how best to handle a case in court. To give young litigators experience, Cravath will charge lower rates to get trial experience for them.

At the end of each rotation, the partners in each working unit evaluate each associate's professional capabilities and achievements and how the associate can best improve. Summarizing these evaluations with the associate may take an hour, covering each matter worked on plus advice on how the associate will want to approach the next rotation. These end-of-rotation reviews are summations of the day-to-day feedback already given in the course of work. Feedback comes continuously in the way work is either accepted and used or marked up for change, so there should be no surprises in the end-of-rotation review. Critiques are also obtained from clients. The insights and suggestions fed back to the associate are passed on to the partners in the next rotation. The process of rotation helps ensure training consistency because no partner wants to hear a partner from the next rotation ask, "Why doesn't this associate know X or Y?"

Over the usual seven years as an associate, each young lawyer will have worked closely—sitting right beside them day after day for a full rotation—with as many as 12 to 15 partners. Those partners really get to know the associates, their capabilities, what moves them along, and how to calibrate the tone and content of anything they say. Rotations also prevent small loyalty groups or sub-tribes from forming. By pooling experiences and appraisals, the partners have a powerful process for determining which associates belong in the partnership. And each associate knows, too. If an associate is one of the 10 percent where the decision on partnership is not clear—maybe there was *one* screw-up or *one* personality conflict with a partner—the firm can defer judgment and decide after adding one more rotation.

One problem with rotations is that clients don't like change. Clients get attached to "their" associates and are not thrilled when they get rotated to other partners and other clients. In any change, everyone knows what he is losing and not what he is about to get, so Cravath has to explain the benefits. Chesler said, "We try to teach clients to understand the long-term benefits to them of our devotion to training that makes our partners and our senior associates so interchangeable and so capable of teaming up effectively to serve them unusually well."

Sustaining the firm's excellence, Cravath emphasizes, is particularly important for long-term clients. If a client is not willing to try doing things Cravath's way, the odds are low it will be a great long-term client. "We run our business with certain core principles," said Chesler. "It's not that we are completely inflexible, but *we* absorb the need for flexibility." For example, when a client complained that a rotation meant the incoming associate would need at least 90 days to learn enough about a case to be fully effective, Cravath decided two things: Go ahead with the rotation, but don't bill that associate's time for those first three months.

Over the past 10 years, another dimension has been added to Cravath training. Formal classes are now led by a group of partners on such topics as preparing witnesses, opening statements, and closing statements. Part of the motivation is the Bar Association's continuing education requirement, but Cravath decided that if courses would be required, it would be better if its own partners taught them. Clients' in-house attorneys are invited to join some of the sessions, which are, understandably, bowdlerized versions with some case details deleted. One partner teaches a basic patent law course so an associate won't freeze up if intellectual property law suddenly becomes important in a case. In deposition training, videos of partners taking actual depositions are used because associates find this a far better way to master skills than books or lectures on theory.

Paul Saunders gives a popular course on opening statements. He uses film clips, starting with Hollywood court martial movies and a video of the O.J. Simpson trial where the prosecutor's deliberately theatrical opening words to the jury were: "I have the hardest job in the world because I must convince you that a beloved American icon has done a profoundly dastardly deed." Saunders cuts in here: "No! No! *No!* He had *all* the facts on his side. He did *not* have 'the hardest job' at all. He had a powerful winning case. He had the *easiest* job—until he anchored the jury's thinking with that blundering statement about how tough he thought it was. If that conviction was lost anywhere, it was lost right then and there—at the opening!"

■ ■ ■

New doctors at the Mayo Clinic share at least one challenge with Cravath's new associates. In medical school, studying and learning are solo activities. In school, getting help on an exam from another student is cheating. Excelling alone is how a resident got into a great medical school and then won a great residency. Then suddenly everything changes. To be a great Mayo doctor, the new resident must understand that professionalism at the point of care means solving problems as part of a team, not alone. Residents also find they can no longer depend as before on memory. Now they depend on discovery—on figuring things out. Radiologist Stephen Swensen contended: "Nobody who is at Mayo Clinic could ever have been as good outside Mayo."

Each year, the typical Mayo Clinic employee participates in 17 different courses, some lasting a few hours and some, several days. Before nurses can go into the operating room, they must practice for 12 weeks in a simulation center not unlike the Link Trainers airline pilots use. With thousands of courses on offer, annual course registrations for all three Mayo campuses run over 940,000. Some courses are aimed at helping employees be more effective in their current positions while others are designed to help in career development. In addition, 3,500 employees receive tuition support for external career development courses. Mayo courses cover a wide range of subjects. Examples include effective use of interpreters, goal setting and personal and professional growth, workplace violence, mutual respect/sexual harassment, gaining trust and inspiring confidence to lead change, skills for handling challenging conversations, the manager's role in answering tough questions about salary, a manager's introduction to business law, and myths and facts about cancer-causing agents. The many courses have two objectives: enhance the performance capabilities of individuals in their current positions and enable them to take on larger responsibilities. The objective, said Dr. Michael Brennan, "is to prepare the workforce of the future with Mayo values."

History is important to Mayo training. Each year, a weeklong "Heritage Days" celebration for everyone at Mayo Clinic retells the story of the Mayo family and the early days of the clinic. Until recently, one training section had new nurses reading parts in a scene that tells about the early days of the clinic in which a Franciscan nurse, Sister Mary Joseph, who would serve for 47 years, recalled turning away and quivering with shame and indignation when a male patient's naked body was examined. After this upsetting experience, she protested. Getting no sympathy at all, she was told that prudery among nurses could lead to neglect in nursing; she must care for all patients, both men and women. This simple, instructional scene was performed thousands of times. Today a video is used.

Professionalism and teamwork as active commitments are best taught and learned by the informal curriculum of seeing what others do. "Culture development starts early," said internist Douglas L. Wood. "Most of our physicians come to Mayo for postgraduate training and they observe directly the meaning of Mayo values in various areas. We seek those who fit best." Physicians new to Mayo get special training in its values and professionalism: three weeks in their first year and two weeks in their second and third years. Communication skills are always emphasized. Stephen Swensen explained, "We have a hidden curriculum for new residents: What does it really mean to act consistently on 'the needs of the patient come first?' What do people do when nobody is watching? If the informal values do not match and reinforce the stated mission, they will dominate. When people come to Mayo Clinic and say, 'We want to copy your process,' we know it cannot be done." Patients often say things like: "Where do you get people like this who will always go the extra mile? If only I had people like this in my company, I could accomplish great things." What they do not recognize is that there's a *reason* people on the Mayo Clinic staff are as they are: years of deliberate training by management and a strong culture in harmony with both recruiting practice and the Mayo mission.

■ ■ ■

A few excellent firms believe that the best training is the least training. In sharp contrast to Cravath, Capital Group doesn't try to formally train its young investment professionals. It doesn't want to. Great long-term investment decisions are a unique combination of a creative understanding of how value develops, exhaustive information gathering, and thorough analysis of the relevant facts. Since each industry is unique, each new analyst creates his or her own training program, knowing that other analysts and portfolio counselors will gladly help with answers to questions. Successful investment research and decision making are always personal and often lonely tasks that differ too much from industry to industry for "common denominator" training. Conventional training might constrict creativity and originality. Investment analysts must learn for themselves. As Gordon Crawford, senior vice president of Capital Research, said: "There isn't much point to teaching how to do research. Each person should and will do it differently."

While Capital believes investment research really can't be taught, it believes that with time and diligent effort, the essential capabilities can be learned by exceptional people with the right motivation—the people Capital strives to recruit. Talent and motivation are both essential to achieving superior investment results in a fiercely competitive market dominated by many well-informed professionals at the world's leading investment institutions.

The primary management challenge at Capital is not managing investments or serving investors, as important as those two functions obviously are. Like all professional organizations, Capital's main challenge is finding and developing unusually talented professionals and designing its organizational structure around *them*, organizing them into effective teams that will achieve superior long-term results.

A new analyst typically studies individual companies and their industry for at least a year before making *any* investment recommendations. For the assigned industry, the analyst has to figure out what the important questions are and develop relevant answers by establishing deep relationships with executives at many companies and gaining a solid understanding of what drives or retards each company's long-term progress. This in-depth self-education usually continues for two or three *decades*—sometimes alone and sometimes in groups of analysts with shared interests—and will focus on making specific decisions to buy or sell based on complex, uncertain, and ever-changing information, always in competition with other professional investors. "It takes

10 full years for a capable industry analyst to reach his or her top performance," said Karin Larson. "But in most organizations, the analysts just won't have the opportunity to concentrate on one industry for anywhere near that long. That means our senior analysts have a very real competitive advantage versus analysts at other firms in analyzing companies and understanding investments."

Gordon Crawford, who covered media companies for more than 35 years, teaches beginner analysts that being nice is important because "life is short; everyone has too little time and so must make choices of where to spend that limited time. CEOs will, quite naturally, spend their time with those who are enjoyable to be with *and* have done their homework." Years ago, Howard Schow, then head of Capital Research, taught the organization what is now known as Schow's Law: "Hire only people who are very bright—and at least possible to like."

Investment management organizations need to make numerous risky decisions to buy or sell specific securities every day even though relevant information is always uncertain at the time of decision. So portfolio investing is a continuous process of great complexity. Success depends on simultaneous excellence in two remarkably different capabilities: individual intellectual creativity and collegial communication. "We treasure the major, innovative idea," said former chairman James Fullerton, "but even the best idea is only valuable to the extent it is *used*. If you like someone, you'll listen to his ideas. If you like each other a lot, you'll listen often and pay close attention. There is perhaps no business in which good communication of soft, emerging ideas is more important than the investment management business." In sharing information and ideas that might coalesce into great investment decisions, good listening is essential. And the keys to good listening are trust and confidence in each other. Of course, good communication depends on both the sender and the receiver because when he's *not* listening, the receiver is really in complete—negative—control of "communication."

Nobody grooms a successor at Capital. Because professionals have their own strengths and best ways to contribute, no one will want exactly the same job that was designed to suit someone else. Tailoring a job to each professional's evolving strengths leads to more productivity and greater individual satisfaction. Capital strives to enable associates to do their best not by controls but by removing impediments—even though, as Mike Shanahan, long one of Capital's strong leaders, conceded, "This is damned hard to execute successfully."

Associates at Capital are encouraged to focus on doing what they really like to do. Bill Hurt, chairman of Capital Strategy Research, explained, "People like to do what they do well. Very able people like to concentrate on what they do very well. And they don't much like to do what they do only fairly well. If, over time, you're not doing more and more of what you want to do, you'll wind up doing lots of things you don't want to do. And you only live once." Associates are cautioned that others may form an opinion of what they do best and then give them more and more of only that same type of work. Continuous change and personal growth are encouraged to help associates learn more about themselves and about things they don't know much about but that might actually be just right for them. Explained Shanahan, "We want each person to know they are being treated as a unique individual even when there are 100 others at least as good as they are. So the recurring key question is: Do you want to be as good as you possibly can be?"

The "do what you really like to do" approach is balanced by rigorous quantification of each person's actual investment results. Results are calculated daily using a four-year moving average, with yearly weights of 10, 20, 30, and 40 percent—from the furthest past year to the current year—against appropriate internal benchmarks. Results are the largest driver of compensation. "Objectivity is a god at Capital," said Hurt. "In Wall Street [securities firms], you want bright, articulate, motivated people, but you *need* people who will precipitate transactions because they are socially dominant and other people will act on their recommendations—whether good or bad. At Capital, we really don't want socially dominant people because that would get in the way of objectivity."

A typical Capital innovation came with the recognition that there could be an alternative to the traditional investment career progression from junior analyst to analyst followed by the usual switch to portfolio manager. Instead, Capital analysts are offered a comparable progression in responsibilities from junior analyst to analyst to senior analyst, with equal advances in compensation, ownership, and stature. Likewise, an associate could be both an analyst and a portfolio manager. Gordon Crawford was a full-time analyst for over 20 years and then, at his choice, became both an analyst and a portfolio manager. Crawford served on Capital Group Companies' board of directors for nearly 20 years—the last two as nonexecutive chairman—and then returned to full-time portfolio management. The impact on young analysts of seeing this kind of career progression is, of course, meaningful. So is the relentless measuring of investment results.

Striving for collaboration and cooperation does not keep Capital from hiring aggressive risk takers. The firm is filled with smart, rational professionals who are, by nature, highly competitive and never sentimental. "If such ambitious people were in a different cultural environment, their behavior would surely be very different," said Jim Rothenberg. "But to maximize results and collaboration, Capital structures its organization to channel competition outside—against the markets and competitors—not inside among our professionals." As Karin Larson sees it, "Managing a group of equity analysts is a lot like parenting teenagers. It's important not to hear everything and *not* to remember everything that's said."

To rationalize and harmonize all aspects of the working environment, organizational design is a top priority. At Capital, design comprises financial and nonfinancial compensation, professional challenges, and growth opportunities, with the emphasis always on effectiveness in communicating investment information and ideas. "It would be hard to find an environment where you are really so free to be all you are able to be—if you want it," said Parker Simes, formerly president of Capital's Japanese subsidiary. "It's fun and exhilarating. With virtually no politics or bureaucracy, we strive to be a true meritocracy."

Rigorous evaluation processes are typical of all the great firms. Capital's annual individual 360-degree review process (reflecting evaluations by co-workers at various levels) covers 10 criteria that have been identified over many years as the factors that make a difference in achieving superior long-term results. Everybody is encouraged to rate everybody he or she works with. Analysts evaluate each other, analysts rate portfolio managers and vice versa, so the process is truly balanced. Each analyst will be rated by 10 or more portfolio managers and each manager will be evaluated by at least as many analysts. Evaluations include numerical ratings on several standard factors and open-ended commentary on anything any reviewer thinks might be important, plus insights obtained through follow-up interviews.

The evaluations are compiled, with scores reported in quintiles, and shared with the associate in a session that usually takes an hour or more. "Associates want to know all they can learn about how well they are doing and how they can improve, even when they are already doing very, very well," said Larson. The review process is combined with annual self-appraisals and careful development of each associate's "franchise plan" of personal and career progress to help find the role that the associate can perform most effectively.

A significant characteristic is Capital's capacity to understand the extraordinary irregularity of investment results and give timely support to individuals during their particular periods of great stress. Investors who have been through a few ups and downs themselves appreciate what others are going through when their "downs" come along. As Crawford said, "It sure helps to have a good sense of humor because even a very good analyst will be wrong 40 percent of the time—and once in a while, very wrong." The secret to being truly tolerant during a colleague's difficult times is to be careful in recruiting so all those around the stumbler will want to give him time to get back on his horse and demonstrate the capabilities they know he has.

Teamwork and working in teams are central to Capital, as to all the great firms. As the organization grows, Capital restructures again and again into smaller teams so everyone will know each fellow worker well and everyone will see the impact of his or her own contributions. Having many right-sized working units is central to Capital's effectiveness in dealing with the inherent complexity of investing globally. Globalization of investing is creating the need for greater diversity. "To be a global investment organization, you have to be multicultural and multilingual," explained David Fisher. "Capital analysts and portfolio counselors were born in 38 different countries and speak 40 languages. If you walk down the hall, the order of people you'll meet are Canadian, Chilean, French, German, American, Brazilian, French again, Chinese, Argentinean, and Indian."

Open communication and teamwork are developed around shared interests. Analysts interested in telecoms or financials or emerging markets or other areas join together frequently. Sometimes they'll come together for a week of intensive company visits, sometimes for a week-end of discussions or a weekly global teleconference. Fortunately, communications technology has improved even more rapidly than the firm has grown. Conference calls link units from various parts of the world. Information on analysts' visits to companies is shared continuously via the Internet. Several daily Internet newsletters have wide internal circulation, and research "jamborees" bring large groups together to exchange information. A videoconferencing facility is used so often that the telephone company came up with an unusual usage-pricing arrangement: For a flat fee, it is left on all the time.

Great firms don't lose many professionals. "What's really different about Capital is reflected in what's got to be the lowest employee turnover in this business—by a ton," said Bob Kirby, a former senior portfolio manager. Only 2 percent of Capital professionals leave in a typical year. "Basically, people stay here because it's the best working environment in the business. You have just an awesome amount of freedom and flexibility to determine how you'll do your job—and then get measured on your results."

Unusually long careers enable Capital's analysts to develop detailed knowledge of companies, products, managers, and technologies, so they can understand the probable impact of current developments on long-term investment value. Long careers help professionals develop greater understanding of themselves and of each other so they communicate more effectively on complex investment decisions. The value of an organization's internal communications network rises with more and longer relationships. When an experienced professional leaves, any organization loses more than that one person; it also loses that person's network of relationships and understandings developed over years of experience with every other person in that network.

■ ■ ■

As at Capital, Mayo Clinic's success in managing people is shown by low voluntary turnover—among physicians, just over 2.5 percent per year on all three campuses. Among non-physician staff, turnover is only 5 percent in Minnesota. In Arizona and Florida, where turnover at peer organizations is over 30 percent, Mayo's is about 10 percent. People who have left have said just one week after leaving that they wished they were back at Mayo.

So that problem behavior can be addressed directly, Mayo's 360-degree reviews, including evaluations by patients as well as co-workers, are standard for allied health staff and, while voluntary, are increasingly used for physicians. The evaluations center on how the person does or does not exemplify a few core values. Among other things, checkpoints reflect whether the staff member:

- Fosters mutual respect and supports Mayo Clinic's commitment to diversity
- Fosters teamwork, personal responsibility, integrity, innovation, trust, and communication
- Adheres to high standards of personal and professional conduct
- Maintains and enhances professional and other skills
- Continuously improves processes and services that support patient care, education, and research

Assessments of physicians by peers and supervisors also consider three specific questions: (1) Does the physician always sign off with clarity at the end of his shift? (2) If a member of your family had X illness, would you want her or him to be treated by this doctor? (3) If you were setting up a private practice, would you want this doctor as your partner?

When a few physicians fell short on always showing respect to all—a corollary of hiring a more diverse workforce—regular surveys of staff satisfaction alerted department chairs that behavioral problems were not being dealt with. The surveys showed that 50 percent of staff did not feel comfortable speaking up to doctors if some procedure was not followed correctly. Management is coaching nurses and doctors how to relate better across races and nationalities to ensure that 100 percent *do* feel comfortable—and confident in the way they will be heard.

■ ■ ■

Training at Goldman Sachs depended for many years on improvisational one-on-one coaching in each unit while doing the work. The mentoring was not organized; it was up to each individual to find his own mentor or "rabbi." As a new associate in investment banking, Henry Paulson got a memorable lesson from partner Jim Gorter, longtime head of the powerful Chicago regional office and particularly effective in developing future leaders. Gorter returned Paulson's first important written work with "Good Memo!" written across the top—and every pronoun *I*—three or four per page—crossed out with a big *X*.

Gorter's advice on how to develop great client relationships was always the same: "It's not how quickly you start completing transactions, but how well you do your work. Do everything the right way—always. Don't chase near-term transactions. Go long term. Do it right and you'll get the really big business. Relationship banking is not a sprint, it's a marathon." Gorter taught Paulson a great lesson: "Secure people give all the credit they can to the other people on the team." The strength of this advice was amplified by comparison to partners who took credit, even more than they deserved, and seriously hurt their careers over the longer term.

Formal training at Goldman Sachs has gone through several stages. The first program was developed in the early 1970s by Richard Menschel and Roy Zuckerberg for a dozen trainees in security sales and scheduled at 5:30 to 7:30 on Wednesday and Friday nights. The time was rumored to have been chosen to conflict on Fridays with New York City's major social evening so salespeople would be obliged to show their commitment to the firm. As a further test, Friday sessions usually began as much as an hour late and invariably ran well past 7:30, often past 8:30 and sometimes past 9:00—too late for planning or accepting a social dinner invitation.

The featured event of each session was role-playing in front of the whole class with a "lucky" trainee trying to sell to either Menschel or Zuckerberg, who would play the role of a hypothetical customer who had all sorts of questions and was being difficult. Training continued for six months. Anyone who failed the final exam was recycled for another six months. The final exam was simple—and hard. Studying up on one of the firm's major research recommendations until he thought he knew it cold, the trainee would meet one-on-one with Menschel and make his presentation as rigorous and compelling as possible.

Usually Menschel asked question after probing question, but sometimes after just 10 minutes, he would surprise the trainee with, "You
make a really strong case. Buy me 10,000 shares." If the trainee said
"Thank you" and took out his order pad to write out the "buy" ticket,
he passed the exam. But if he said anything else, he failed, because saying anything else might somehow restart the process and lead to the
customer's reconsidering his decision. And this could lead to the customer deciding to wait and do more research. If so, the buy order
would be canceled. As the saying goes, the trainee salesman would have
"bought it back."

Several years ago Goldman Sachs, concerned about the need for
many more well-developed leader-managers as a result of the firm's
increasing complexity and global size, saw a need for a more systematic
approach to developing the effectiveness of its more than 1,000 managing directors. Most divisions had become as large as the whole firm
had been just 10 years before. Internet surveys and interviews sought
opinions within the firm on management and leadership development:
how much was going on, how effective it was, and whether the firm's
changing needs were being met. Consultants were interviewed about
the latest concepts in management development, and "best practitioners" in management education were visited to study what they did and
how well it worked. Early on, the firm recognized a major problem:
Its work ethic and reward system—and increasingly its culture—were
centered on being commercial. And "commercial" was increasingly
focused on near-term profit. So something as soft and abstract as a program of management training and development would be consistently
overshadowed by real transactions, particularly when the program was
new and unproven. Leadership for the new leadership program would be
crucial, so the head of GE's fabled Crotonville leadership-development
center was recruited. Although initially somewhat mystified by the
time and effort being invested in developing the program, he was soon
joining in 6:00 A.M. planning sessions—even before officially arriving
at the firm.

Pine Street, as the program was called, expanded its focus to
include what was identified as "leadership acceleration" for a group of
nearly 100 fast-rising managing directors. (Goldman Sachs University
would continue to focus on the skills training needs of vice presidents

and below.) The message given the selected managing directors was the same message Whitehead and John Weinberg had given each new partner 30 years ago: "Congratulations on your well-deserved promotion. We expect even more of you now. So take the pace up even higher and show us you can be a real leader."

Today all new employees participate in a weeklong introductory program that tells the history of the firm and introduces each of its main lines of business while emphasizing the core values of Goldman Sachs. Each division then conducts its own skills-centered training for several weeks or several months as needed. In one widely used case study, the direct superior of a trader in his eleventh year of steadily rising responsibilities and positive reviews learns that on his pre-employment statement, the trader had said he had never been arrested. But it's just been learned that he *had* been busted for possession of marijuana while in college. So now what should be done? The discussion is lively and usually concludes with consensus among the trainees that one mistake made a dozen years ago doesn't really matter. But it *does* matter. In the securities business, as the world has amply learned, there are too many temptations. If he could cut corners once, as he did on his job application, he can do it again. If, when challenged, he 'fesses up and shows genuine chagrin, a stern admonition will do. But if he bobs and weaves or prevaricates, he's out.

Pine Street quickly learned that to be embraced by the firm, courses had to be made specific to each division and that professors from great universities who didn't fully understand Goldman Sachs were not nearly as credible as the firm's senior leaders. Over 80 percent of Pine Street courses are taught by the firm's top line executives. Executive coaching was added, and when members of the management committee reached out for coaching themselves, it was quickly seen as not "remedial" but developmental. Each coaching relationship lasts several months, and to avoid organizational politics all coaches are external. Several dozen managing directors participate. Clients are invited to participate in some exercises. They enjoy the process and develop greater appreciation for Goldman Sachs as an organization. Even the most commercial people of Goldman Sachs recognize that having five hours one-on-one with an important client is a great way to develop a stronger business relationship.

Still, while participants' ratings rose steadily, measuring the profit return on Pine Street was elusive. When Paulson went to Treasury, support from the top fell away and the man from GE eventually retired. The firm's focus was increasingly clearly commercial. After the Wall Street meltdown, however, Lloyd Blankfein gave Pine Street increasing attention and recruited a new leader, George Parsons, to spur a turnaround, and over 6,200 managing directors, vice presidents, and partners were using Pine Street. But results were decidedly mixed. As Parsons acknowledged shortly after announcing his departure after just two years, "Leaders have to unlearn old ways of thinking and old skills and learn new ways of thinking and new skills. This is hard and doing this on the run is very hard." One managing director put it more directly:

> This is a cynical organization, and it's an organization that is so focused commercially that if it thinks that something is superfluous, it has no patience for it. If it doesn't see a direct correlation between what Pine Street does and making this place more commercially effective, the firm will forget about Pine Street in one nanosecond.

The commitment to both profits *and* clients is frequently and fervently articulated by the firm's top people. "It is not about you!" is a central message in every presentation to new Goldman Sachs employees. "Yes, you must enjoy the work to do it really well and be successful at the firm. But you cannot be successful here unless you understand that it's *not* about you; it's about meeting the needs of *clients*." Outsiders would be surprised by how strongly insiders preach the importance of "Our clients' interests always come first." But insiders have been surprised by how frequently outsiders—even former partners—have concluded that too many at Goldman Sachs no longer believe in nor practice what they preach. The Business Principles are still in frames on the walls and still appear in each year's annual report, but they may no longer be central to the firm's culture, norms, or priorities.

■ ■ ■

In almost every great organization, most learning develops while working with and for clients on specific challenges. Training at McKinsey, as at all the great firms, is largely done by doing the firm's work, so training is continuous for all consultants throughout their careers: gathering and analyzing data, organizing effective presentations and working in teams with clients to develop recommendations for change in such a way that clients will feel ownership of and commitment to the recommendations, and then working with clients on effective implementation. Only implemented recommendations count. This intensifies the challenge of managing each major engagement because the nitty-gritty of consulting on the details of effective implementation can be boring to bright, ambitious young consultants *and* can seem too costly for the clients.

A major part of consultant learning comes with the virtually continuous feedback given during each engagement. Another major part is the review within the team of each consultant's contribution at the end of each client engagement while memories are still fresh. In addition, at year-end, appraisals are accumulated into rigorous, firm-wide evaluations that determine younger consultants' compensation and advancement.

Quality control at McKinsey necessarily depends more on superior recruiting and on-the-job training than on direct supervision from headquarters, for several major reasons. Consulting work is a process and the firm works in many separate engagements—often in quite specialized and very different fields—all over the world. Moreover, McKinsey needs to be able to deploy teams with as many as 50 or 60 consultants. Communication between an expert specialist in one discipline and an expert specialist in another discipline on such a large team is always a challenge. Yet McKinsey's reputation and the effectiveness of its management both depend on senior consultants, principals, and directors making decisions every day on complex matters when far away from their home offices.

Each incoming associate is assigned to one partner who will be his or her mentor. The mentoring relationship is taken seriously by both mentor and mentee as an explicit responsibility. Explained Terry Williams, "McKinsey training has always been based primarily on apprentice consultants learning from experienced partners." Like Cravath, McKinsey recognizes the difference between training and education. "The apprentice model trains people to the standards the master already has, but does not go beyond the master," explained Ian Davis. "Education is different. Education develops the capacity to innovate. So McKinsey increasingly focuses on education. Besides, what can be copied within the firm can also be copied outside the firm—by competitors."

Picking up on a practice originated in the thirties by Mac McKinsey, the firm organized training after World War II so the work product would be consistent no matter who worked on a specific consulting engagement. During the school year, all consultants met every third or fourth Saturday for training and to pool their knowledge on a series of subjects. The group spent one whole school year working out a manual on cost reduction. Another manual was done on managing accounts payable, and another on managing receivables. "Then we did the same on personnel and then on manufacturing," said former senior partner Roger Morrison.

> We were training our consultants, and we were creating the knowledge capital of a true *profession*—plus strong bonding among the participants. Ironically, once we had done all that work to collect, combine, clarify, and codify our best thinking, we almost never went back to those manuals. We didn't have to because after doing the real work, we had the results and the process of getting those results in our heads and we had the benefits of disciplining ourselves and our thinking by working it all out together.

In the late fifties and early sixties, with MBAs coming to McKinsey in groups of 50 or 60 each year, the firm developed an intensive two-week Introductory Training Program (ITP) for groups of 25 at a time. A central purpose was to be sure young consultants would quickly learn to work together as teams, develop strong bonds with each other and to the firm, and get immersed in McKinsey's values and their operational validity. The consistency of orientation and values developed in ITP proved particularly important for the firm's international expansion as a one-firm firm.

All McKinsey consulting is done by teams, so effectiveness when working on teams is crucial to the success of every consultant. The firm depends upon aggressive thinking without aggressive behavior: Consultants are expected to be polite—with bold ideas. They are carefully combined into teams that bring together different perspectives and ways of thinking. Diversity is important: diversity in culture and experience, intellectual interests, and academic training; and differences in sex, age, race, and nationality. Teams are led by "engagement directors" who work with the client to define each engagement's purpose, scope, timing, and fees. The engagement director is responsible for the quality of the work, maintaining good relations with the client, protecting the firm and its reputation, managing costs, ensuring ethical behavior, and developing future principals and directors. "This is the most difficult role in the whole system," Michael Muth, a former senior partner, observed with a chuckle as he reflected on the "man-in-the-middle" realities.

Learning from the painful lessons of having to deal with the "good-enough" people taken on during World War II, McKinsey recognized that the only way to ensure it had the best people for consulting was to weed out all the others. In 1950, it gradually began to use the "up-or-out" policy then common among the leading law firms. Bower argued that up-or-out reinforced the firm's recruiting policy: McKinsey would hire only exceptional people, so if they did not excel in consulting they should leave and work for organizations that could better use their exceptional talents. If any consultants were treated as "workhorses" or second-class citizens, that would damage firm morale. Moreover, as Bower complained in his annual report to the partners back in 1952, the firm had been "slow to eliminate associates whose lack of capacity was well recognized."

Every firm with a rigorous up-or-out policy knows how hard it is to act on it consistently, and only the outstanding firms understand how important this discipline is to achieving firm-wide excellence. Today McKinsey's up-or-out policy requires separation unless a consultant demonstrates, at a prescribed pace, a superior fit with consulting. Each year McKinsey culls about 18 percent of associates, 11 percent of principals, and, since the up-or-out discipline never ends, 3 percent of directors. The firm understands that a reputation for constructive departures will strengthen recruiting, morale among the professionals who stay, and the firm's franchise—including future business.

McKinsey is objectively "hard" when making decisions about people but soft in implementation, repeatedly helping consultants find positions—often with clients—that are a better match to their particular skills and interests. For example, when the firm has decided a director should leave, it may allow two or three *years* for the actual departure. Many McKinsey people leave consulting for great careers as CEOs of major corporations. IBM's CEO Lou Gerstner, a McKinsey alumnus, quite sincerely asked Peter Walker, a director in the New York office, "Why are you still at McKinsey? You could be running something *big.*"

When McKinsey wanted to create a retirement policy that was equitable, would cause individuals no loss of face, and would work in all territories, senior partner Lowell Bryan led a retirement task force. Consultants in their late fifties generally were diminishing in effectiveness but understandably did not recognize this themselves. Those staying beyond 60 were all too often becoming a headache for the firm. In addition, the firm had accumulated far too many custom deals for retiring senior consultants. Some wanted an office and secretarial services. Some wanted a swimming pool. Some wanted to continue consulting.

Some leavers felt strongly that they had not been treated well in their leaving. As Ron Daniel put it, "It's not dog eat dog, it's *young* dog eat *old* dog!" Younger partners effectively drive older partners out of the firm, especially if they are not particularly well liked. One simple expedient is not making a particular effort to keep them fully informed, perhaps not telling them about an important meeting until it's too late to fit it into their busy schedules. For the good of the firm, a policy was set: Retire at 60 or sooner. The firm developed the Past Fifty-Five program, which may require a few consultants to leave a little too soon but protects the institution. Three months before turning 55, each consultant gets a "Happy Birthday" letter from the firm. Retirement between 55 and 60 is designed to match the consultant's probable decline in energy and effectiveness—partly due to the retirement of the client executives they've known best, partly due to fading energies, and partly due to increasing interest in activities outside work. The firm has tried to find a way of neutralizing incentives either to leave or stay by offering those who commit to retirement a golden handshake equal to 1.5 times their last three years' average compensation. The firm will pay another one-year bonus at age 60, basically to seal the retirement bargain and close the door. The policy was set so the firm could *make* consultants leave at 60; but leaving the choice of what year to leave before 60 meant each consultant could say, "I'm in control of this. It's *my* choice, *my* decision." Those few who really want to continue consulting can do so—if they perform. At the firm's top level, directors can stay until 65, subject to performance.

■ ■ ■

While compensation is important, the core of every great firm's success in managing people is the power of intrinsic motivation. Compensation is "hygienic." If it is unfair, it can be a major disincentive, but those who can do exceptional work often do what they do because they love it and feel it is central to who they are. At Mayo Clinic, all physicians are on salary. The salary system attracts physicians who appreciate how it fosters trust—trust among physicians and among patients who can be sure no physician has a financial incentive to perform procedures. Salaries align incentives with the interests of the patients and of the institution. The clinic's public trustees set salaries at the seventieth percentile of peers in the particular specialty or field in the open market. New physicians' salaries rise for five years until reaching the salary level for all experienced physicians. (In another sign of equality, physicians' offices are all "modular" in furnishings and the same size.) As recognition of the increased responsibilities involved, salaries are increased 5 to 10 percent for physicians becoming divisional or departmental chairs; all these medical executives continue to practice medicine, so there is a high level of trust of leaders. Chairs rotate about every eight years. To prevent any financial penalty for rotating out of a chair, the "chair's increment" continues until retirement. Since pensions are linked to total compensation, the incentive to take a chair, typically in a physician's late forties or early fifties, is significant. One benefit of all physicians being on salary is that, unlike many in private practice, Mayo physicians are expected to spend as much time with each patient, and order tests or engage other physicians, as they think best for the patient.

Physicians enjoy some important intangibles. Nobody has to worry about developing or running his own small business—which many doctors don't like doing—and each doctor is expected to be away learning or giving papers at professional conferences for 18 days each year. An indirect form of compensation is that everyone has the latest equipment to use. Mayo Clinic spends nearly $1 million annually on satellite time to facilitate three-way televised conferencing and nearly $100 million on equipment each year.*

Compensation at McKinsey and Cravath is also divorced from direct revenue production. McKinsey consultants who focus on analysis and presentations are not expected to look for billable mandates but for specific ways in which the firm can be helpful to each client. McKinsey stopped using revenue or profitability numbers in determining compensation over 20 years ago. Before that, it had taken another 20 years of step-by-step diminution to bring the use of revenues or profits as a base for compensation all the way down to zero because both advocates of change and opponents had strong beliefs and feelings. Decades ago McKinsey worked hard trying to determine how to value introducing clients versus doing the work and kept finding that dividing up the earnings brought consternation. While fairness and equity were McKinsey's mantras, different people contributed differently and valued contributions—theirs and others'—differently. Being and being seen to be equitable is hard when revenues or profits are involved because, for example, it can be harder to earn 10 million euros consulting for well-managed Daimler-Benz than to earn 40 million from a government-sponsored insurance organization with lots of self-generated difficulties to work on. And the division of a consultant's time between client work and non-client work needs to be recognized. So does the mix of clients: Did the consultant serve only two major clients or was he spread out across 10 smaller and less risky engagements?

Consultants at all levels are graded on a scale of 1 to 3 in three specific areas: non-client work, internal reputation, and "people impact." Non-client work includes recruiting and publications. Intellectual leadership can spread value-added advances through many consultants to many, many clients. That distributed value will eventually contribute

---

*The value of medical equipment can depreciate rapidly. An MRI unit bought for $1.6 million was sold five years later as "junk" for $50,000.

to increasing revenues and profits since financial gains derive from the firm's increased abilities to do great work with clients.

Internal reputation consists of several factors: Has the consultant had a big client impact, particularly an unexpected impact, that helped get the client to take action? Is the consultant, particularly a senior consultant, recognized externally as a leader by key people at client organizations? Does the consultant command respect internally? This is particularly important for young consultants because it leads to their being sought after to be on consulting teams.

People impact measures how well other consultants like working with you or how likely they are to seek you out as a coach. For example, do you, as a team leader, make last-minute changes in responsibilities? Do you, as a senior consultant, really help others on the team develop their skills and effectiveness? Or do you cause insecurity or even destroy the effectiveness of younger consultants? If an engagement manager takes too much credit for a younger consultant's ideas, that is a real problem to be addressed at the team level to minimize internal competition and friction.

■ ■ ■

The great firms differentiate themselves from other firms in the remarkable excellence of their support staffs. Goldman Sachs, McKinsey, Mayo Clinic, and Capital all enjoy unusual strength in the quality and commitment of the people who serve as members of their staffs, often for long careers. The messages about how to achieve staff excellence are similar—careful recruiting, rigorous training, discipline, deep respect, superior compensation, and caring management. As at other great firms, Cravath's nonprofessionals are treated with genuine respect, are devoted to the firm, and are as committed to doing superior work for the firm's professionals as the leading professionals are committed to serving clients. Explains a former associate, "You just can't understand the level of support Cravath lawyers get until you go to another firm." Staff are effective "carriers of the faith," passing on cultural norms as well as helping new associates learn quickly how to adapt to the specific working style and pet peeves of the partners they're assigned to work with, as well as simple things such as how to dress for work on Saturdays. Cravath staff get superior pay and are notably loyal; careers of 50 years are not unknown. There's an extra benefit: Staff don't need to make partner to stay at Cravath.

"We function as a team—all of us do, including every member of our staff," Katherine Forrest said.

> Showing real respect for each person is a hallowed norm here. Associates are told how important this is to us. No yelling or scolding can ever be allowed. I know that if I were mugged, my purse and clothes stolen, and I was lost in a city I didn't know, the receptionist on the thirty-eighth floor would get me home safely. Our staff are devoted to doing everything they can for us—so we can serve our clients. They'll go over the wall for us. Our respect for them and the roles they perform for us are what makes the difference when, suddenly on a Friday afternoon, there's a memo to get out. Everyone has two choices: Will I do this quickly so I can go home? *Or* will I do it the best I possibly can and stay late? If you truly value people for who they are and what they do, they know and appreciate that and it directly affects the choices they make.

Executive director Steven Spiess, who supervises the staff organization, illustrated the respect partners show to Cravath staff with a simple example:

> Sam Butler, then presiding partner, called me on my first day and said he'd like to see me. I told him I'd be right up. He said no, he'd like to come to me. But I was working in a sub-basement where, when you got off the elevator, there were just locked doors. You had to have a special key to get in. Sam insisted, came down, and spent 30 minutes. I'll never forget it. He's a great teacher of how to be a good person.

Staff pay is consistently on the high side, plus a pension fund, a 401(k) plan, a cafeteria offering a fine lunch for just $4.00, a gym, an award-winning daycare center, and a department for secretarial and word processing training. Cravath has never had staff layoffs. It offers confidential assistance through an outside firm for anyone with family problems or drinking. One day each year, the firm takes over the Big Apple Circus for employees and their families, and on the day before Thanksgiving it serves a Thanksgiving dinner with all the trimmings at 2:00 P.M. In these ways, Cravath engenders a small-firm family feeling and environment.

During New York City's 2003 blackout, more than 800 Cravath people were ensured safe rides home. For others who had reasons to stay, cots were set up in the lobby. Bottled water was brought in immediately. During that blackout, a client pleaded for help with finding *any* temporary space. While the other organizations the client called said it would take several days to arrange anything, Cravath had half an entire floor—phones, IT, word processors, desks—set up and ready for the client's use in less than 24 hours. The firm has a staff unit that specializes in setting up remote branch offices so when an out-of-town facility is needed the lawyers can concentrate entirely on practicing law and working with clients.

Along with another law firm, Cravath was once retained to defend a client in a junk bond lawsuit. When the lawyers from the other firm came to visit the temporary offices Cravath set up in Columbus, Ohio, for this one case, they were impressed by the word-processing and data-processing equipment, the number of data lines and phone lines, the desks, conference tables, and other facilities of an obviously well-settled-in operation fully staffed with very busy people. "How long have you been here?"

"Four days."

"Four *days!* It looks like four *months!*"

Spiess explained: "We want this done by our own people, not by Hessians. We have certain standards, and as Ben Franklin once said, 'If you want something done right, do it yourself.'"

The commitment to developing capabilities and effectiveness continues throughout each person's career. The same long-term focus is applied to developing relationships with clients.

Chapter 5

Client Relationships

Developing Ties That Last

For obviously different reasons, the quality of the professional–client relationship matters greatly to both client and professional. The great firms aspire to be not only better than any competitor at serving clients' interests, but better than any competitor could be and better than clients expect. The professionalism that pervades their relationships with their clients starts with their conviction that if they never compromise professional standards, never vacillate on matters of integrity, and act consistently in clients' long-term interests, the economics will take care of themselves. Of course, strict adherence to principles comes more comfortably to already successful firms, but this truism misses the salient reality that, as the histories of superb professional firms repeatedly show, long-term success begins with integrity. Great clients are always looking for the few firms that are both superbly skillful and absolute on matters of integrity.

■ ■ ■

Capital Group has often presented itself conscientiously as "the firm that can't do," pointing out what neither it nor any other money manager can deliver. It explains that to have the best performing mutual fund, the manager must be smart, do lots of things right, take big investment risks—and have lots of luck. And it gives examples: If an investor could pick a series of stocks that would each go up 50 percent—from $10 to $15—every six months, and he started with $10,000 at age 30, he would have over $1 million at age 36. He would have nearly $1 billion at age 44, and then the value equivalent of the whole New York Stock Exchange by age 56—and all the wealth in the whole world by age 60! Obviously it can't happen and it won't happen—all the way back to the uncertainty of the first six-month move from $10 to $15 in a single stock.*

Clarity on what a firm won't do can cement client relationships. Capital's history of putting clients first—including deferring introduction of profitable types of mutual funds until frothy markets subside—has paid off. The firm's decisions protect investors and the stockbrokers who sell to them and, among both groups, have built long-term confidence and trust in Capital. That's why Capital's redemption rate (the withdrawal of assets by mutual fund shareholders) has usually been only half the industry average—a win for both the firm and its clients. Lower redemptions make Capital's American Funds more profitable to manage and indirectly lift investors' returns.

Capital's integrity shows in many ways that reassure clients. In an industry still notorious for packing mutual fund boards of directors with "safe" friends of the management company, Capital insists that all directors of its mutual funds be chosen not by management but by outside board members who are clearly charged with being independent. To ensure their independence, Capital keeps fund directors unusually well-informed, including advice by outside counsel on regulatory matters.

The firm has been a leader in reducing management fees even when other fund groups were raising theirs. Capital pioneered the use

---

*Of course, if an investor does get lucky, he'll think he's a lot better than he really is and will be tempted to try again, even harder. This can put him in real danger.

of multiple managers for each major portfolio. This system of portfolio management accommodates very large fund size. Since percentage fees decline as portfolios pass certain size milestones, Capital's average fee per thousand dollars managed is far below industry norms. Its expense ratios, as mutual fund fees are called, are about one-third lower than industry norms in various types of funds, as this table shows:

	American Funds	Industry Average
Growth	0.82%	1.35%
Global equity	1.01	1.55
Balanced	0.67	1.19
Bonds	0.72	1.01

As well as keeping fees down, Capital is an industry leader in saving taxes for investors by managing portfolios to minimize short-term capital gains. When combined and compounded over 10 or 20 years, these differences matter significantly to investors' long-term returns. Furthermore, while most competitors and most investors pay little attention to minimizing investment risk, Capital correctly considers investors' risk-adjusted return the only true measure of success.

■ ■ ■

Refusing to do what competitors did was instrumental in Goldman Sachs's rise from a middle-market investment bank barely in Wall Street's top 10 to its recent preeminence. "Our clients' interests always come first," declared the first of the firm's vaunted Business Principles. For years this principle was visibly manifested in the firm's declared policy of not advising on hostile corporate takeovers. All the leading investment banks had had similar policies—until Morgan Stanley broke out as a highly paid adviser to International Nickel when it made a hostile takeover bid for Electronic Storage Battery in 1974. For Wall Street's major investment banks, this example and the high fee involved converted advising on "hostiles" from taboo to must-do. The major firms began aggressively competing with each other for the raiders' lucrative business.

All but one: Goldman Sachs. One of Wall Street's most aggressive firms deliberately chose *not* to compete with all the other major investment banks. Instead, it went the other way—and that soon made all the difference.

As well-known companies suddenly got taken over, many managements worried about "Saturday night special" raids—so called because if a hostile tender offer was launched during a weekend, by law only five days were available for a defense. For Goldman Sachs, this presented a major opportunity to capitalize on years of developing relationships with thousands of companies. The firm's business development focus had historically been on helping smaller companies find a buyer on favorable terms, but now it focused on protecting midsize and larger corporations from hostile takeovers.

Assuring corporations that as a matter of policy it would not advise raiders, it developed a new "tender defense" service to show corporations how to protect themselves against being taken over. While the fee per client was moderate—less than $100,000 a year—total income was consistent and substantial because the service was easy to sell and the same service could be sold to hundreds of corporations that would continue to pay the annual fee for several years. And that was only the beginning. By protecting managements from being thrown out, the tender defense service positioned Goldman Sachs for many years as the trusted friend of corporate America. This gained it favorable access to boards of directors at hundreds of corporations, a unique opportunity to showcase its various transaction capabilities. Subscribers to the tender defense service not only gave Goldman Sachs a superb opportunity to court new business on favorable terms, the prospects effectively paid the firm to come sell its other services. For an expansion-hungry investment bank with many services to offer, this was the classic fox in the chicken coop.

The opportunities for the firm to earn fees on transactions were many. If the client corporation was raided, Goldman Sachs might bring in a "white knight" for a large fee, or at least extract a higher takeover price and so earn an incentive fee. Moreover, the advice on takeover defense usually led to preemptive divestitures of noncore businesses that a previous management had acquired and that had not been successfully integrated into the corporation's main operations—business units that any raider would surely sell off to help finance the target company's own takeover. Many of those preemptive divestiture sales were arranged, for a fee, by Goldman Sachs, which might also get a fee from another corporation that was the buyer, so the firm might develop yet another relationship as a trusted adviser to that other corporation. Moreover, because takeover defense brought all areas of the firm to bear on each corporate client's needs, it helped integrate formerly separated fiefdoms into a one-firm firm; this became a core strength. With all the direct and indirect business it was able to develop from tender defense, its annual M&A fees went up like a skyrocket from only $3 million to $2 *billion.*

The benefits that can flow from letting potential clients know what a firm *won't* do have rarely been clearer. John Whitehead appreciated the vital extra dimension of this strategy: Committing to defending corporate boards of directors and top management, and so becoming the trusted friend of management, set Goldman Sachs apart as all the other Wall Street firms went for the lush current fees from raiders, showing they were all for sale to the highest bidder and could no longer be truly trusted. Whitehead's commitment fit perfectly with the behavior expected of a corporation's lead investment banker and with the firm's first Business Principle. That was the magic carpet that took Goldman Sachs from behind Morgan Stanley, First Boston, and Lehman Brothers to undisputed leadership in investment banking.

■ ■ ■

McKinsey, too, has told clients what it could not or would not do. Marvin Bower turned down Howard Hughes five different times because he was sure Hughes could not be relied upon to take action on the firm's recommendations. And he refused to work for Textron's super-acquisitive CEO, Royal Little, saying: "The problem with this company, Mr. Little, is you!"

Bower and Don Waite met with the head of a client bank to explain that McKinsey felt obliged to terminate their large and lucrative relationship because the CEO was not stepping up to address the major strategic issue facing the organization. "I'm not yet ready to take on that one," pleaded the CEO. Bower said McKinsey felt it could not in good conscience continue the engagement. "Bower was splendid. Clear and direct," Waite later recalled, "and absolutely committed to the professional discipline. You only know what you really stand for and who you really are when you adhere to a principle that you know is costing you serious money." (When, two and a half years later, circumstances forced the CEO to act, he had lost the initiative and the cost to his company was far greater.)

Jon Katzenbach tells of another encounter with Bower. "I was explaining how I lost an opportunity to obtain a major piece of work with Memorex's CEO, Larry Spitters. I was simply unable to figure out how to help him organize his senior leadership group without first gaining an understanding of the economics and strategy of his business, but he told me that would involve unnecessary extra work and turned down my proposal. Since I sounded a bit disappointed, Marvin was quick to point out why I should have been proud of realizing that I did not really have the capability to advise the CEO in the abstract without hard facts. Marvin always thought we should be proud of turning down work when we lacked distinctive capability."

While Bower believed McKinsey should not take any assignment the firm was not certain it knew how to do, one of his successors, Fred Gluck, judged that "this was unnecessarily self-limiting." With in-depth industry expertise, Gluck believed, McKinsey's consultant teams could and should take prudent chances so they could figure out solutions for undefined problems. Eventually—and successfully—Gluck's bolder strategy prevailed and met important client needs.

■ ■ ■

Great firms want clients to think always and with confidence of the firm, not of individual partners. "If a firm has stars," explained Cravath's Bob Joffe, "that comes at a cost to other partners *and* to the firm. Clients queue up for the star and she or he gets the best cases and the best clients, which of course tends to perpetuate the star culture." That limits a firm's capacity for client work because when "the star is too busy to help you today," the firm's reputation and morale suffer.

Cravath partners see themselves as tenants and stewards, not owners. The firm has continued for more than a century and will continue long after they are gone. To institutionalize relationships with long-term clients, the firm makes a point of introducing young partners early and will change the contact partner to a younger partner sooner than other firms would. For example, Bruce Bromley passed responsibility for IBM to Tom Barr, who passed it to Evan Chesler, who passed the relationship to a younger partner—each making the change long before his own retirement.

Every client relationship requires diligent attention. Otherwise, as both sides go through changes, shared understanding will get diffused and attractive opportunities may be missed. Cravath partners meet annually with each client to review the work done—case by case and sometimes item by item. They also review the alignment between the client's legal needs and the firm's capabilities. Clients are asked to be rigorous in evaluating the quality of work done and the service delivered. A few years ago, as the new deputy presiding partner, Chesler met with clients to request: "If you ever have a problem with our services—no matter how small—please call me."

Cravath partners believe they are responsible to clients for seeing legal issues that are developing, explaining how the law is moving or changing, *and* seeing how each client's business is changing and therefore how the two might intersect. When Chesler urged a major technology client to consider the firm for work in intellectual property, the client was surprised to learn that Cravath had been making itself a leader in the field. Chesler did three things. He took responsibility, saying to the client, "That's my fault for not making sure you knew of our strong development in IP." He took the initiative: "Next time you have an interesting problem in IP, please call me so we can show you our capabilities." And since training never ends, he admonished his young partner who worked with that client to be more alert: "I took the heat, but they should have known. Even though your work for them is in very different areas, that's part of your responsibilities—to the client *and* to the firm. There is an art to knowing how and when to look for business: You have to navigate between the Scylla and Charybdis of asking too much and asking too little."

Superb service on major issues results in an unusually high level of client loyalty. Of Cravath's top-ten clients, half were also in the top ten 20 years ago and a few were in the top ten 40 years ago. (Nothing's perfect: Bethlehem Steel and Kuhn Loeb, both now out of business, were each Cravath's largest client at one time.) The firm's 20 largest clients consistently represent two-thirds of total billings. It aims to have no client paying over 10 percent of the total, having learned a hard lesson when Campeau Corp., a Canadian real estate outfit, went from zero to $48 million in fees from 1986 to 1988—and then back to zero when unsuccessful acquisitions bankrupted it. IBM usually averages less than 10 percent. Of course, Cravath is happy to see a relationship grow. Chemical Bank, a longtime client, expanded through acquisitions of Manufacturers Hanover, Chase Manhattan, Bank One, and J.P. Morgan into today's JPMorgan Chase—and is now nearly six times as large in fees. In another case, "the Oneida Tribe came to us initially as a *pro bono* client," recalled partner Richard Clary, "but now, with a booming gambling casino, they are a regular fee-paying client. Their in-house counsel is a Harvard Law School graduate who has organized things to recycle money from the casino into long-term wealth for the tribe. They started with just twelve acres of land and now have over 100,000 acres."

Cravath wants clients who say: *This case is so important, we want Cravath.* "We want Cravath to be better than the best on the toughest cases," said Joffe. "We want to do lawyering that is profitable to our firm *and* economical for our client." Because there's a thrill in solving a major problem that saves a lot of money and delights a client, Cravath prefers to avoid routine matters. As partner Julie North put it, "We want to work on problems where the best solution will be flavorful, new, and unorthodox."

The firm is less concerned with whether long-term clients are right or wrong on a particular business decision. As Sam Butler explained, "We get paid to help our clients achieve *their* objectives, to help them accomplish what *they* want to do. My job as a lawyer is to get the deal done the way my client wants—even if it fails as a business deal. We don't do marriages; we do weddings." Realism about the lawyer's role is balanced with responsibility to help clients consider unforeseen consequences. "We try never to make a decision that solves a current problem if it's not also right for the long term," said Katherine Forrest (who, for recreation, studies military strategy). "We need to have both a rigorous focus on the current specific issue and on the big picture."

At larger companies, having in-house general counsel has become the norm, so Cravath lawyers do not have the same access to chief executives that they used to enjoy. The typical large corporation will have 100 in-house lawyers, who are used for advisory work on deals and transactions but not for major litigation. Litigation now involves such large settlements that it commands the CEO's attention. As a result, the vast majority of new clients come to Cravath via litigation. "We do, occasionally, do 'beauty parades,'" allowed Chesler, "but most of our new work comes in as the result of happy client recommendations. We also get new clients by representing the other side really well in major disputes."

With 85 percent of the firm's practice capacity already booked by longstanding clients, business development is less important at Cravath than at other major law firms. As Richard Clary noted, "We do whatever work comes in the door. This leads to a variety in our practice, protects us against burnout, and causes us to be profoundly happy." Partners smile almost apologetically as they make statements like, "Marketing at Cravath was, for many years, answering the phones on two rings rather than four. Prospects call us." In trust and estates work, most clients come via recommendations from other clients, although some are reluctant to recommend Cravath for fear the firm will get too busy to do the best work for them. In one example of unintended but charming innocence, George Gillespie once asked Dan Mosley to join with him in an initial meeting with a major prospective client—the Walton family. Gillespie's explanation: "They're from Arkansas and you're from Alabama so you should have a good understanding together."

In billing clients, Cravath starts with accurate records of hours and preset hourly rates, then adjusts these up or down by 10 to 15 percent—and sometimes more—based on a judgment of the firm's ability to deliver value to the particular client and the client's capacity to pay. A partner recalled, "One client felt our fee was high, but we didn't want to negotiate so we found a novel win-win solution: We offered to take on a small trial case for nothing and gave the work to an associate who was thrilled to have his own trial responsibilities."

North acknowledged that "we think our rates should be somewhat higher than other firms," but added, "Because we staff leanly, our total charges are usually lower. We believe we deliver a higher value.

'Better' means absolute consistency in work quality and figuring out how to make clients' lives better." As an example, Cravath's bill for a major merger was $1.5 million while another firm's bill for work for the other side on the same merger was $10 million. The other firm got paid but lost the long-term client relationship to Cravath. As the new client explained, "You did most of the work and they took most of the pay."

Market power, the ability to set prices within a defined market, is shifting away from law firms to their clients. In the past, clients rarely asked for an item-by-time breakdown of hours and rates, but with the proliferation of in-house general counsel, specificity has become the norm. Some clients are aiming to reduce bills, others are aiming for greater predictability. Another factor is a new legal bill monitoring service that promises to cut clients' costs by 5 to 10 percent—and charges 50 percent of the savings realized.

No professional loves accumulating and having to justify numerous 15-minute units of hourly cost. Leading law firms are moving toward more "value" billing—charging by the importance and difficulty of the assignment. To clarify the issues, Chesler wrote an article for *Forbes* in 2009: "Kill the Billable Hour." Value-based fees at Cravath have increased from 3 percent a few years ago to 15 to 30 percent of total fees paid by large corporations.*

Still, the focus of some clients is always on cost. Even though GE's in-house lawyers said they saw the extra value in Cravath's work and hated to ask, GE Capital was required by former CEO Jack Welch to insist on a discount on fees. Cravath almost never negotiates fees but did offer lower fees in exchange for GE's promising to give the firm more work *and* pay its bills more promptly. But those promises weren't kept. So when GE Capital pressed for even more fee discounts, the firm refused. GE considerably reduced its work

---

*Cravath agonized over taking a contingency fee from the FDIC in its 1990 litigation against Michael and Lowell Milken of Drexel Burnham Lambert. The partnership rejected the original FDIC proposal for a strict percentage fee even though it would have produced more than the $11.5 million that was eventually paid. After sometimes heated discussions, a complex fee based on levels of recovery was worked out. Looking ahead, Cravath believes there will be more FDIC-like fee arrangements.

with Cravath. When GE again asked for discounts, Cravath stood fast, and GE Capital went to other law firms. Other clients absorbed the available time at Cravath.*

■　■　■

Developing new or expanded client relationships is important for the long-term success of all professional firms. While McKinsey, as a matter of policy, does not engage in "selling" services, it is certainly interested in building up its business. In a typical year, 80 percent of the firm's revenue comes from regularly repeating clients and 70 percent comes from Fortune 100 companies; the firm serves 80 of the 100. Several clients pay over $100 million in annual fees and more than 100 clients pay over $50 million. McKinsey's reputation for charging—and earning—high fees got linked with the firm's prestige over 50 years ago when the CEO of Aluminum Co. of Canada told consultant Everett Smith, "Your fees are *twice* as high as your competitor's!" Smith never blinked as he replied: "Well, I should certainly *hope* so!" Alcan accepted the proposed fees.

Every client decision maker goes through a series of stages in his thinking: He realizes he has a problem; then he realizes he needs outside help; then he realizes he needs a firm like McKinsey; then he negotiates with the firm the nature of the problem, the best way to approach understanding and solving it, and what follow-on help may be needed. Cost is the last thing a prospective client worries about and negotiates. If the problem seems large and the strategy of attack promises highly valuable results, the fee compared to the defined benefits will be "affordable," no matter how large the fee.

McKinsey established two basic pricing policies: It would not do fixed-fee work on major projects—it does on small projects—and

---

*Fred Gluck at McKinsey was also keen to link fees to value instead of cost. Gluck led an internal reorientation in the concept of pricing, away from the value of the inputs over to that of the output—the value of the problem and its solution. "Client service is not the same as client impact," he argued, "where the ideal is to change the way the client thinks and acts because a new way has been internalized."

the firm would not compete on price. After winning an assignment for a major international bank in competition with Booz Allen and Boston Consulting Group, partner Charles Shaw asked, "Please tell me, why did you select McKinsey?" The answers were encouraging: BCG was too theoretical and abstract. It focused exclusively on top management. Booz Allen clearly knew the banking industry, but its proposal was too off-the-shelf standard. McKinsey had recognized that the client considered the problem important and developed a custom-tailored approach that would involve McKinsey consultants and the client's own people in both analysis and implementation. It also included an explicit commitment to continue working with the bank in the future.

When fees are raised to increase the profits of the business simply so it can increase payouts to the owners, the consequences are significantly different from actions taken to increase profitability so the firm can excel at its professional work for the clients. As part of his thrust for making McKinsey a "better business," senior partner Al McDonald initiated a campaign years ago to raise fees so partners could be paid more. Later, Ron Daniel also made increasing fees a major commitment, in steady, moderate increments. Importantly, however, where McDonald focused on raising fees to make the firm more profitable for its senior partners, Daniel made clear that McKinsey needed higher fees to be a great firm for clients and that its first priority was finding ways to deliver higher value to clients. "If we deliver 50 percent more consulting value and impact than expected or promised," he explained, "we can charge 30 percent more than other firms."

Being relationship-centered is why, as McKinsey focused on building its leadership position in Europe, senior consultants agreed to work only where the firm had a good chance of both making a major difference through the engagement *and* creating a strong long-term client relationship. Ideally, McKinsey would be working regularly on different issues over two or three decades when a client felt consultants were needed. At the same time, fees were increased steadily and substantially—eventually more than doubled worldwide. Explained Roger Morrison,

> The crucial point was that we became confident that we could and would make a significant difference that was consistent with

the client's own big picture strategy if we were working at the corporate center, not at the margin. Working from this central position, the cost to the client could more easily be fully justified.

Like all consulting firms, McKinsey is critically dependent on getting help from within client organizations, and helping often does not come easily to proud insiders. Clients must voluntarily help identify the real problems and their causes, help gather facts and opinions, and cooperate with the consultants in implementing recommendations. Any lack of trust will constrict the voluntary flow of information, so the consultants must be worthy of trust by personality, skills, and technical competence. Trust is particularly necessary for clients who compete with other clients in the same industry. Expertise in the industry has to be balanced with the firm's traditional "Chinese wall" policy of serving competitors through separate teams of consultants.

McKinsey consultants believe it is their responsibility to persuade clients to become "owners" of the recommendations *during* each engagement, not just when the final recommendations are made. When key client people embrace the analysis and recommendations, they will be agents of change, not silent resisters, thus greatly increasing the odds in favor of effective implementation. Implementation is the *sine qua non* of successful change, and success with the client on engagement A is often the key to McKinsey's gaining engagement B. In addition, favorable client referrals lead to a large proportion of annual revenues coming in through "radiating references."

■ ■ ■

Great firms know that the more important their relationship is to the most important people in a client organization, the more valuable that client will be to the firm. For their part, clients need to know that the professionals they work with will use their expertise to advance the client's interests. Fidelity to promises, explicit or implicit, matter because every profession is based on trust. And trust is the difference between *client* and *customer*. When a professional firm says "client" but merely means "customer," the firm deceives the customer in the short run and deceives itself in the long run.

The great firms are determined not only to deliver more value to each client than any other firm delivers, but to deliver as much value as it is possible to deliver. This determination fosters a firm-wide culture of innovation.

Chapter 6

Innovation

Changing How the Game Is Played

Persistent innovation and adaptation to external change are habits of mind for the great firms' leaders at all levels. A culture of innovation encourages active experimentation to find promising new ways to serve each client better. Most innovations are small and specific to a particular transaction or client. But habitually innovative people are alert to the present value of future progress. Innovators know that major innovations will not suddenly reveal themselves in fully developed form, but must be tried, nurtured, and reworked as they evolve, so they look for and often find more opportunities. Disappointment and frustration along the way are accepted as the normal costs of trying to find new and better ways that will pay off—sometimes extraordinarily well.

■ ■ ■

Capital Group's multiple portfolio manager or "multiple counselor" structure has proven a major winner over the half-century since its gradual, experimental beginning. This singular innovation enabled Capital to achieve superior long-term investment results while expanding assets managed to more than $1 trillion. As so often with innovation, it began with a problem: Capital's supposed *growth* fund was actually invested more conservatively than the designated *conservative* fund, and investment results were not particularly good. This had to change.

Self-examination led to several insights. Capital's leading investment professionals had very different personalities and ways of thinking about investments, so they were virtually sure to have strong differences of opinion and difficulty sharing information or analyses or even listening closely. As a result, when they met as an investment committee, cross-sterilization of insights and ideas had become more common than cross-fertilization. Collective decisions about investments were all too often compromises that muddled creative thinking and blunted decisive action. This can be particularly harmful in investing, where the best ideas are fragile—"soft-shelled"—at their earliest and potentially most profitable stage. Successful investing is all about making unusual, unconventional, and even unpopular decisions when they look most dubious to others. Those difficult decisions are best made by individuals who will take direct responsibility for the results of their own judgments.

Capital's leaders agreed that neither of the two alternative organizational structures traditionally used in the mutual fund industry—either separate, independent management of each fund by its own solo portfolio manager or collective management by a committee based on consensus and compromise—would solve the problem. Something new was needed. Instead of compromising or, even worse, combining the two inherently contradictory conventional management structures, Jon Lovelace suggested taking the best of both and combining them in a new way that had never been tried anywhere.

The multiple counselor system began with a decision to divide the problem into parts and then rearrange those parts. Each of Capital's two mutual funds was divided into four separate parts, and the four portfolio managers would each manage part of *both* funds.

Each fund's results would be a blend of all four managers' best efforts. As Jim Rothenberg explained some 50 years later, "In *developing* the concept, Jon played the central role in a father–son arrangement, while *implementing* it was made possible by his father's strong sponsorship. This strong support was needed because, at the time, Jon had not been with Capital very long and several people opposed the idea— some because it was considered heresy and others because they simply thought it just wouldn't work." The new system was not an immediate success. "It took several years of patient nurturing and development before the system was working to everyone's satisfaction," recalled Bob Egelston, who was deeply involved in working out the operational and computational complexities of the system in the years before it was computerized.

Today each of Capital's many portfolios is assigned to several, sometimes as many as a dozen, different managers, each responsible for his or her part of the fund. Portfolio managers concentrate on the kind of investing they do best, manage assets of a comfortable size, and focus on achieving Capital's primary objective: superior long-term investment results. The system ensures that portfolios are diversified across many investments and across the several counselors' differing perspectives on the market and different styles of investing.

The multiple manager system ensures that no fund will ever be dependent on a single star manager. And it effectively copes with a problem endemic to conventional investment organizations: As the size of the fund increases, both market liquidity and the mental agility of the solo portfolio manager become progressively overburdened. Capital can easily accommodate a fund's increasing assets by adding additional portfolio counselors to parts of the whole. Individuals can come into or leave the process without disruption. Explained Rothenberg, "It's really a case of diversity promoting continuity."

The system encourages career growth among Capital's research analysts. They can manage real investments early in their careers, investing in their own best ideas instead of having to convince portfolio counselors to act. Analysts typically begin investing in the industries they cover—buying one or two stocks at first, then more and more. Some analysts eventually manage very large amounts of money, all in the industries they know best.

Portfolio counselors are not individually responsible for achieving optimal portfolio diversification. An investment committee oversees the whole portfolio and coordinates the component sub-portfolios to ensure that all investments remain within the stated objectives of the fund and achieve optimal diversification. The open flow of information and complementary compensation policies encourage portfolio counselors to help each other by sharing ideas and information, but they have no need to compromise or persuade others to agree on a decision; they are expected to act boldly in making their own investment decisions, and each counselor's investment results are measured and reported regularly to all the other portfolio counselors. To work well, the multiple counselor system needs at least one senior sponsor who can smooth over the occasional interpersonal rough spots that are virtually inevitable in any effort to have creative people work interactively. This role was filled for many years by Jon Lovelace and is now provided by several designated senior people.

Surprisingly, almost no other investment organization has chosen to replicate Capital's transformational innovation. This lack of replication is particularly surprising since a large majority of the world's investment managers continue to produce inferior investment results, apparently because the markets are increasingly efficient because they are dominated by experienced professionals, and because each manager's professional capacities are overwhelmed by the volume of assets they gather in as they build their businesses. Replicating the multiple counselor system is difficult, but the evidence continues to accumulate that no other organizational design deals so effectively with the daunting challenges of actively managing large funds.

Some at Capital wanted to keep the system a secret so other organizations wouldn't catch on. But Bob Cody was sanguine: "It's so complex, if any competitor tried it without *really* understanding it, they would sink." Capital associates agree that the concept of the multiple counselor system of portfolio management can be explained briefly in 30 seconds—or in full operational detail over 30 *days*.

When Capital began using the multiple counselor system, total assets under management were only $400 million. Today assets are 3,500 times larger, and more than 200 managers are simultaneously running parts of various funds and portfolios, making decisions to buy and sell specific securities every day.

■ ■ ■

Threatening moves by a competitor can trigger defensive innovation that becomes pervasive. McKinsey's focus on strategy, which today is at the core of its service, began as a necessary response to competition. Marvin Bower had always insisted that McKinsey did not substitute for management but complemented and supplemented management. He believed that any successful long-term strategy had to be based on each client's particular foundational beliefs. He certainly did not believe in predicting the future or imposing an outsider's strategy—even when the outsider was McKinsey. "Marvin thought it terrible to promise what he was not sure could be delivered," recalled Terry Williams. "So, like an outside lawyer, he always wanted to be one step behind." Bower expressed his strong reservations about consulting on strategy: "The problem with strategy is that it's dealing with the future. Since we don't know the future, we cannot be accurate." This may have seemed workable so long as the firm had no large, aggressive competitors, but in the late sixties that condition was changing fast.

In sharp contrast to Bower's deliberately modest conservatism, Bruce Henderson, at Boston Consulting Group, was making an aggressive drive to capture for his new firm the high ground in top-level strategy consulting. In 1966, BCG announced the Experience Curve, which purported to show how accumulating experience always drove down the unit costs of production: "A businessman can predict his normal costs far into the future if he understands their basic relationship to experience."

Henderson launched a fusillade of pocket-size memos to management that he called "Perspectives." Over the next decade BCG produced 400 Perspectives—each just 800 deliberately provocative, attention-gathering words. In 1969, BCG created its now-familiar Growth/Share Matrix with stars, dogs, and cash cows, and boldly declared a series of easily remembered propositions that told executives exactly what to do.

Bower's cautious conservatism fed directly into Henderson's aggressive strategy, which positioned BCG consultants as tough, smart, creative experts focused on strategy and working exclusively for top management. BCG also tried to position McKinsey consultants, along with those of Booz Allen, AT Kearney, and other firms, as implicitly less brilliant—okay for routine, middle management consulting on ordinary problems so long as you didn't expect too much and didn't pay too much. This seemed to justify both high fees for BCG and low fees for McKinsey.

Strategy had not been a top priority at most corporations in the sixties, and consulting on strategy was certainly not important at McKinsey. The firm had to move decisively to catch up. "BCG might not really have been better than McKinsey on strategy, but McKinsey had no overall *theory* of strategy," explained Williams. "So BCG had at least pulled even, by declaration and by taking the initiative."

Leaders can foster innovation by putting the right people in charge of "figuring it out." Ron Daniel became McKinsey's leader in 1976 when earnings were low, the firm was vulnerable, and BCG was a major concern. He asked the firm's best people to work on "thinking about what McKinsey should be thinking about." A memo from one of those people, Fred Gluck, asserted that McKinsey was behind competitors in strategy, operations, and organization. Gluck advocated developing much deeper knowledge and expertise, saying, "If you're not the most advanced, you can't know how far behind you really are." Over the next several years, McKinsey's focus would shift from acquiring existing knowledge to creating new knowledge, building a treasury of intellectual property that consultants would adapt, deliver to, and implement with each client.

Gluck originated a series of easy to read one-page bulletins. When some consultants doubted the bulletins would be accepted as important enough to be worth all the effort, Gluck promptly wrote 10 bulletins himself. His idea was simple: Gather up the best ideas from client work, synthesize them into proprietary knowledge, and apply all that to the work done for other clients. A thick directory of McKinsey consultants' expertise, organized by topic, was soon produced to encourage collaborations.

Gluck favored organizing the firm by industry practice with each team building proprietary knowledge and expertise in areas of greatest interest to clients, such as banking, insurance, electronics, aerospace, energy, consumer businesses, and pharmaceuticals. This would require many consultants spending up to 15 percent of their time on knowledge building. When others said they were reluctant to give up client time, Gluck took the lead by giving up *all* of his client time. Communicating and championing his vision through-out the firm, Gluck defined the benefits: improved work for clients, faster training for new consultants, and more new ideas. Practice development soon became an integral strength of McKinsey.

Bob Waterman, Jim Bennett, and Tom Peters were assigned to lead a working group on the organization practice while Gluck was asked to lead a strategy planning group. Gluck declined, saying, "Words matter. A planning group will produce *plans*. I'm interested in leading the management process that will produce *action*." He agreed to lead a strategic management steering committee to develop an understanding of the subject that would lead to action.

Perhaps inevitably, the two working groups became rivals, each convinced it must show it had found *the* way forward for McKinsey. After all, strategy *included* organization, asserted Gluck's unit—which he dubbed the Super Group—while organization *was* strategy, as the Waterman-Peters group saw the world.* Which was really the most important? Wasn't it crucial to any successful *strategy* to have organization really right? Wasn't the essence of any successful *organization* to have its strategy right? As so often, the real contest between the two groups was for professional recognition and affirmation from their McKinsey colleagues. Both groups agreed on the need for the firm to mobilize all of its capabilities. For example, as a truly multinational organization, McKinsey could commit a winning *international* team—resources that BCG and other consulting firms simply did not have. So, if a New York bank had interests in Asian exporters, McKinsey could call on its own experienced Asian consultants.

Gluck's strategy group decided to position BCG's specialty as a commodity and emphasize that McKinsey had many arrows, not

---

*Their work in the group led to a book, *In Search of Excellence*, which became the business bestseller that made Waterman and Peters high-profile management gurus.

just one, so major clients should take advantage of the firm's size and diversity. McKinsey didn't need cute tricks like dogs and stars; it was a custom *service* organization, not a standard *product* seller. Over the next three years, all 200 McKinsey partners came in groups of a dozen to one-week training sessions on strategy, often at Harvard's conference facility in Vevey, Switzerland. Gluck participated in every session—one every two months—as the firm's strength in strategic thinking kept accumulating.

"Proving McKinsey was very much in the strategy game would require analytical rigor, but early efforts became too analytical with too much rigor," according to Jon Katzenbach. Developing a McKinsey strategy for strategy was sometimes agonizing. A New York consultant offered a four-box matrix, a London partner presented a nine-box matrix, and a German had an even more complex matrix. Each claimed to have The Truth. Gluck finally proposed concentrating on a nine-box matrix that had previously been developed by a McKinsey consultant and that GE would later celebrate widely. An effective framework, such as the matrix, would drive better questions and open consultants' minds to look for better answers.

But in strategy, concept is only 5 percent and execution is always 95 percent of success. While boxes might provide a checklist to guide deep thinking, Gluck believed McKinsey should first understand each client's unique strategic problem and then develop a custom-tailored solution. McKinsey should clarify that BCG had solutions in search of questions, not questions in search of answers; BCG wanted to impose from above its rigidly standardized solution while McKinsey had the flexible creativity— and the respect for each client and its uniqueness—to tailor the optimal solution from the bottom up. McKinsey would marshal its analytical prowess, its fresh eyes, and its reputation for integrity and independent views, as well as its skill at engaging the client company's executives in a well-structured process that would take each consulting engagement all the way from research through analysis to implementation. With this strategy McKinsey steadily built a strong clientele in strategy consulting.

Traditionally, McKinsey consultants had believed they could understand any business in two weeks of analysis, so they treasured the concept of being generalists, not specialists. They had loftily claimed that the essence of a specialist was a consultant who, if someone else would define the problem, would know how to solve it, while the essence of a generalist was the ability to define the real problem. Not being expert in each client's particular business, McKinsey consultants had had to excel sufficiently with their generalist knowledge so the lack of specific industry expertise would not impede success. But with increasing competition from BCG, Bain, and other consulting firms—and with more and more client corporations having numerous MBAs and internal consulting units—McKinsey was meeting skeptics within client organizations who scoffed at any misuse of industry jargon. The old generalist ways were clearly becoming no longer sufficient. Expertise was seen as industry-specific—not fungible. McKinsey would need to change.

The firm's leaders soon recognized that if McKinsey's challenge and opportunity was to move *up* each client's chain of command, the firm must first move *down* and develop deep industry knowledge. The consultants increasingly came to recognize that knowing a lot about an industry was not narrow specialization. As Gluck put it sardonically, "Every McKinsey consultant needs to be a generalist, but it's not necessarily a handicap to know what you're talking about." Consultants began specializing in one major industry like banking or energy while establishing themselves as generalists within that industry. Industry expertise was made into a vital strategic strength, beginning with banking and then insurance. In time, the banking practice would represent one-quarter of the whole firm, and its consultants would be recognized as generalists who specialized in banking.

The specialized industry groups had important organizational impact. Regional offices had been virtual fiefdoms for their office managers, who set the tone, decided which clients to serve, and decided how to staff each engagement. With Daniel's leadership the firm moved toward a matrix organization with geographic location on one axis and industry expertise on another. In a contest, industry expertise would almost always trump geography.

McKinsey's strategy in banking and other industries centered on a major commitment to developing "breakthrough" proprietary intellectual property. The explicit objective: knowing in advance the nature of the strategic issues that banks, for example, would face as a result of major changes such as computerization, deregulation of interest rates, and consolidation. All these issues hit the industry in the seventies, followed by mergers and international competition in the eighties, removal of the Glass-Steagall Act separating commercial and

investment banking in the nineties, and risk management, securitiza-
tion, and loan syndication thereafter. Because McKinsey was ready for
each wave of industry change, it benefited mightily.

■ ■ ■

All innovations need a driving change-maker, a favorable environment, and persistence. John Whitehead successfully developed a
revolutionary new structure for investment banking in the 1960s
that eventually forced Goldman Sachs's competitors to try to follow. Instead of one banker trying to execute all transactions for "his"
cluster of client companies—while also maintaining close relationships with all his clients—Goldman Sachs divided the work into two
coordinated groups. One group specialized in relationship development. Devoting full time to clients and prospective clients, bankers in
the relationship group were in frequent contact with each client or
prospect, always looking for more and better business opportunities.
Meanwhile, each member of the other group specialized in executing
one specific kind of transaction and met clients only when that specialty was wanted and where the specialist would be properly introduced and pre-sold by the relationship manager, who would also do
all the routine follow-up. When well coordinated, this dual system,
with each person doing what he did best, easily proved far more effective than the traditional approach in which one banker was usually
a jack-of-all-transactions, master of none, and could pay attention to
relationship development only when he had no transactions to do.

Whitehead's group began covering 500 corporations, then
expanded to 1,000, and then expanded again to 2,000. By the seventies, 4,000 U.S. corporations were being called on regularly by bankers
from Goldman Sachs. Initially, Whitehead had conceded the 100 largest
corporations to Morgan Stanley and First Boston because they had
such strong, established relationships; but later these, too, were covered
and often became Goldman Sachs clients.*

---

*Even into the late 1970s, elite investment banking firms like Morgan Stanley
and First Boston would send engraved invitations to selected corporations—even
the government of Mexico—informing them that they would now be welcome
to make an appointment to visit the firm at its office to discuss the possibility of
becoming clients.

Few strategic innovations come all at once. Most require lots of experimentation and adjustment before they achieve liftoff. Utilities represented a major opportunity for Goldman Sachs in the 1980s—not because utility companies did over half the total public securities offerings of corporations; not because there were so many utilities sure to continue to be major users of Wall Street in good markets and bad, and not because utilities were important to all the prestigious investment banks. Utilities were a major opportunity because Goldman Sachs had almost zero business with utilities—so the opportunities were unlimited.

The one utility that the firm had done *any* business with in the early 1970s was the right one: telephone. AT&T was a start, but would there be any followers? Assigned by Whitehead to develop the business, Barrie Wigmore had many concerns: Utility stocks were of no interest to most of the firm's important institutional clients. The firm had no small retail customers, the traditional utility-stock buyers, and Ray Young, head of security sales, had declared: "We have no business in selling utility stocks." Every utility already had established stable investment banking relationships that it would be cautious about changing. Wigmore didn't know the complex ins and outs of utility regulation, regulation that differed from state to state and from one type of utility to another, and he didn't know the rating agencies and their work—except that they were important. So were the lawyers of the utility bar—lawyers he did not know. Finally, he didn't know any utility executives, and they didn't know him.

Barrie Wigmore was a long, long way from his family home in Saskatchewan. To win business, he would have to outflank the established firms and be innovative. So he searched for ways to differentiate his business-development initiatives and capitalize on strengths that the firm had not yet applied to utilities. Every Monday morning, Wigmore's team gathered at 8:00 A.M. The agenda was always: What's new and changing? What opportunities might be developing?

"We tried out all sorts of ideas," recalled Wigmore.

Some were nonstarters. Some were crazy. But some of them really worked. It was exciting to be in the hunt and it was really exciting when we developed a winner. Pretty soon we were earning a reputation in the industry for being well informed and imaginative. More and more people wanted to talk with us and hear what we had to say and work with us on developing new ideas.

Here are some of the new ideas that worked:

- The first nuclear-fuel lease with commercial-paper backup. The firm bought nuclear fuel through a special subsidiary, Broad Street Services Corp., financed it with commercial paper, and leased it back to the utilities. This used the firm's strengths in commercial paper and leasing, specialties few competitors knew. A similar opportunity was found in equipment leasing.
- Pollution-control revenue bonds capitalized on the firm's recently developed strength in tax-exempt finance.
- The private placements department opened up new opportunities. When an institutional investor wanted to buy a specific type of bond, Wigmore's team would scour the utilities, asking, "How would you like to borrow $10 million *now* at such and such a rate?" This unorthodox approach soon made Goldman Sachs a go-to intermediary in this fast-growing new segment of the capital market.
- Eurobonds, sold through the Netherlands Antilles, opened another niche market.
- The Saudi Arabian Monetary Authority had huge cash flows to invest and valued credit quality more than high interest rates. The utility group arranged two- to five-year private placements with the Saudis for the highest-grade utilities.

Successful and profitable as these innovations were, they were all concentrated in the debt markets. Common-stock equity financing was the utilities' lifeblood, and determined their choice of investment bankers. Goldman Sachs would need to penetrate the equity market. The firm developed an easy-to-use sales tool that could be run off by computer every day. It showed, in rank order, the deviation in every utility stock's yield from its historic relation to the industry's average yield. Trading off the model, institutions became increasingly active customers, with, of course, Goldman Sachs executing their orders. Since it was the leader in block trading, the next steps were easy for Goldman Sachs:

Offer blocks of new-issue utility stocks to institutions it knew were buyers, enabling the issuer to avoid the cumbersome, expensive, time-consuming process of organizing a "road show" all around the country. Now utilities could raise $50 million to $100 million of low-cost equity capital in just one day with none of the usual market uncertainty. And the cost to the issuing utility was compellingly low: only 0.5 percent versus the customary 3.5 percent underwriting fee.

Next came persuading utilities that doing one big offering every year or so was not as low-cost a source of financing as a "shelf registra-tion" that allowed them to take advantage of market opportunities as they developed. The firm gained respect in equity underwriting and drove to increase its share of each utility's business. This aggressiveness upset the established underwriters, of course, but the strategy worked well for Goldman Sachs: no underwriting risk, no capital tied up, and no disruption to established business relationships because it had none. "The utilities loved it, too," recalled Wigmore, "so they began giving us other business as well. It was great, really great." Parallel progress was made with gas pipelines. Fortunately for Goldman Sachs, White Weld, the traditional pipeline investment banker, was in decline and other firms were slow to specialize in pipeline business. Pretty soon Goldman Sachs went from zero to ranking number one in pipelines' new issues.

In the spring of 1983, Roy Zuckerberg had an idea that got him so excited he simply had to discuss it with someone who could convert his concept into a significant business. Daniel Stanton, then a young associate, was the right person, and the business, though small at the time, appeared ready to take off. Hedge funds were catching on with wealthy investors, new hedge funds were being organized, and hedge funds were starting to attract institutional investors. This business could become huge. And, over the next several years, it certainly did.

Hedge funds manage their assets very intensively, so they need accurate, up-to-the minute reports on their positions during trading hours every day and swift, accurate clearance of all their trades, many of which are complex. Margin lending is important, too, because hedge funds use leverage boldly, and their margin-lending brokers need to know exactly how much good collateral each hedge fund has to support its borrowing. Goldman Sachs was doing this work for one hedge fund, Steinhardt Partners, and Morgan Stanley was working with Julian Robertson's Tiger Fund, but the other securities firms didn't have the people, computer power, business model, or interest to compete effectively.

It made no sense for a hedge fund to work with 50 or 100 brokers and then try to consolidate all their reports into one database when all that work could be done by one "prime" broker who would keep accurate records of everything the hedge fund was doing with all its separate brokers. Because hedge funds traded so actively in all sorts of securities, serving as a hedge fund's prime broker would be operationally exacting and depend on advanced computer technology. Goldman Sachs had that technology. It also knew large numbers of wealthy investors who would want to get introduced to the most promising new hedge funds and would need expert advice on which funds to select. Goldman Sachs had everything that every hedge fund would want or need.

Not only did hedge funds grow faster than anyone had expected, but the business barriers blocking competitors from entering prime brokerage were formidable—including $100 million of costs *every* year to keep up with computer technology. As a result, pricing held up well and volume growth flowed to the bottom line. And it stayed that way for 25 years: a high-margin growth duopoly that became one of Goldman Sachs's biggest and most profitable businesses. As Stanton observed: "It doesn't get any better than this."

■ ■ ■

Long before Goldman Sachs forced its way into the top rank in international investment banking, Mayo Clinic was quietly innovating its way to the top rank in health care. Dr. Charlie Mayo declared that the day he hired Henry Plummer in 1901 to take over the clinical laboratories and x-ray diagnosis was "the best day's work I'd ever done for the Clinic." Believing the clinic should make its records accurate, complete, and readily accessible to all its physicians, Plummer won approval in 1907 to develop a revolutionary new system of record keeping. Traditionally, doctors kept their records separately and chronologically in large ledgers. Over a year of study—particularly including visits to organizations outside medicine—Dr. Plummer developed the clinic's famous dossier system, in which each patient was assigned a number that was put on an envelope. Inside the envelope went all information about that patient: diagnostic history, surgical and hospital records, and all lab data in standardized formats. Each time the patient returned to Mayo Clinic, all new information went into the same file. The files were cross-indexed by disease, surgical technique, pathology findings, or surgical results. Plummer's record-keeping system contributed decisively to Mayo Clinic's development as an integrated, multispecialty group practice and to bringing all the specialists consulting on a particular case onto a virtual team.*

Today the descendant of Plummer's original system is a core competitive advantage for Mayo. Before a patient arrives, that patient's coordinating physician or "champion" can, through a central resource, pre-schedule all the requisite tests and specialists likely to be participating in the diagnosis. If other specialists are needed, they can be added during the patient's first visit. Mayo calls this patient-centered, all-in-one-place, all-at-one-time convenience "single-destination care." To accumulate the same tests and specialist visits elsewhere could take the peripatetic patient a month or longer.

Group practice was a radical approach to medicine 100 years ago. The American Medical Association declared it "soviet medicine." While many academic medical centers now describe themselves as group practices, they tend to divide into medical schools, hospitals, and medical staffs with separate and often financially competing subgroups or departments whose priorities conflict. At Mayo, "all is one," in the words of Stephen Swensen, whose title is director of value. "We are all aligned toward Mayo Clinic, not toward separate departments. If cardiology has any money left over, that money is Mayo Clinic money, not

---

*Henry Plummer was notoriously absentminded. Agreeing to take his wife shopping in Minneapolis, he left work and drove halfway to the Twin Cities before realizing he'd forgotten his wife. On another occasion, Dr. and Mrs. Plummer got lost late one afternoon. As night fell, both were getting hungry, so Plummer stopped and said he would ask directions at a farmhouse he could see from the road. When Mrs. Plummer grew tired of waiting and went to see what was going on, she found her husband sitting near the fireplace—finishing his second piece of pie.

cardiology money. There is no personal financial interest in a patient's gall bladder or an extra imaging exam. And I believe this is a very, very important differentiator." Philosophically, this practice traces back to the Mayo brothers' joint checking account.

Health care is a team sport. Since 1948, a group of systems engineering specialists in the system and procedures group, a unique feature of Mayo Clinic, has been finding ways to increase the efficiency and effectiveness of health-care delivery. Mayo has established a well-funded Center for Innovation—a skunk-works that takes on projects of all sizes in a sustained commitment to continuous improvement. In a typical project, a department found that its surgeons had half a dozen different ways of performing a particular procedure. Wanting to determine best practices, it enlisted the engineers from systems and procedures to help the physicians determine which components of the different procedures were most effective and then formulated a simple composite procedure for all surgeons to follow. Mayo physicians work with the belief that care can be improved only if they measure accurately and search vigorously for ways to standardize improvements.

Change is part of the culture. The clinic's focus is increasingly on prevention and on health maintenance versus just correcting problems. "We are always self-critical," said Jill Ragsdale, the chief human resources officer.

> We are never satisfied. In our regular staff satisfaction surveys, we'll get a lot of concerns expressed by staff about needing to improve in various categories, but then when we ask an overall question like "Where would you want a family member to go for care?" the answer is *always* Mayo Clinic. Our heritage from the Doctors Mayo transcends time. Never being satisfied is a very big deal around Mayo Clinic.

■ ■ ■

Not all innovations are new. Some of the best involve developing an old idea in a way that is new to a particular organization. Long one of the world's most profitable law firms, Cravath is unique among major firms in having 100 percent lockstep compensation. Lockstep, in which all partners rise equally in compensation at a predetermined rate each year, was common among New York law firms in the first half of the twentieth century and is still common among London law firms. Even today, a few American firms use a modified or "topped-up" lockstep. But modern Cravath stands out in its full commitment to pure lockstep.

Lockstep compensation certainly did not originate with Paul Cravath. He had no interest in equality of compensation among the partners. It was his firm. He brought in most of the business directly from Westinghouse Electric, where he was a director, and through Kuhn Loeb, the investment bank, where his love of music brought him into close friendship with its senior partner, Otto Kahn. Cravath—and then Swaine and then Moore—took disproportionately large shares of the firm's earnings. Famously dismissing the concerns of younger partners who hoped earnings could be spread more equitably among the partners, Cravath bellowed: "Do the division any way you wish—with *your* half of the profits!"

Robert Swaine introduced a modified form of lockstep compensation for partners in the 1940s as a way of defusing the main issue marring a strong, collegial environment. (Swaine also established one-partner-one-vote democracy at weekly partners meetings.) The magnitude of difference between the have and the have-not partners faded during the forties and fifties, but the inequities were still quite clear. In 1975, a committee recommended moving to pure lockstep. "The lockstep system is key to the firm, not only for the partners, but also for the clients," said Kris Heinzelman. "It means that a client is *always* a client of the firm, so they receive the best advice from the best lawyers without any bickering over who gets points or credit for work."

Lockstep produces an orderly progression of income that maximizes a partner's compensation in his or her fifties. In their first year, new partners are paid a salary substantially higher than a senior associate's. (Currently, it is over $500,000.) For their second year, partners receive one full point of participation in the partnership pool of profits. Over the next decade, they move up 0.15 point each year, then by 0.10 point a year to a peak of 3.0 full points—three times the percentage of a second-year partner—after 16 years in the partnership. Partners then hold at this level of participation until the age of 62, after which their points decline by 0.5 point a year to 1.5 points and mandatory retirement at 65.

Lockstep compensation is in harmony with Cravath's "all for one and one for all" culture of teamwork, partner interchangeability, and focus on client service and long-term client relationships. Lockstep removes money as an issue and diffuses power because, with compensation pre-resolved, there is less reason to have or need to use power. And this removes the force that can drive the divisiveness, politics, hurt feelings, and wasted time that burden other firms where partners compete or campaign for "more." Other firms invest significant amounts of high-value partners' time working out equitable divisions of their partnership pools, responding to both temporary and sustained changes in productivity and ensuring that partners not only get treated fairly but believe they got treated fairly. As one Cravath partner put it, "With lockstep, there's no bitching, no moaning, and no long, tiring compensation discussions." In other firms, the major client of any individual partner can put excruciating pressure on that one partner to reduce fees and perhaps to compromise on quality—a pressure Cravath partners could not accept. Lockstep clearly puts the firm first. It makes it easy for partners to help partners, even when they're already working harder than hard, and it makes it easier for the presiding partner to ask one partner to help another.

Cravath is, partners agree, a firm of "overdeveloped alpha males"— even those who are actually women. Partners doubt the firm could hold together if there were differential compensation. At Cravath, explained Dan Mosley, "Partners are confident that there's plenty of work and therefore see no need for rainmakers. And on the profession-versus-business teeter-totter, they don't ever feel any need to be 'realistic.'"

Lockstep is good for recruiting in the abstract, but most young lawyers coming to Cravath as associates do not expect or plan to become partners, so the impact is neither near in time nor personal to them. Among partners, the obvious problems with lockstep concern the top 10 to 20 percent and the bottom 10 to 20 percent in revenue generation. Some partners believe their incomes would double if the firm changed entirely to merit compensation. Superstar performers may not be willing to live with "normal" compensation when they know they could make more in other firms or other fields, and some partners have left at the peak of their careers. Lockstep does not encourage partners to launch or sustain the long and often emotionally draining campaigns needed to develop important new clients; Cravath is certainly not aggressive in following up on opportunities to convert one-off engagements into major relationships. Theoretically, an unproductive partner might migrate to a back office and hope to ride out the career-long lockstep bell curve—a reminder of the importance of decisions on who should become a partner. In practice, any such free riders are counseled to retire.

Cravath rejects the organizational devices others firms have used to gain economic leverage, such as acquiring or merging with other firms, often in other cities, or calling lawyers who are less than the best lawyers "partners" because, if paid less, they can appear to be profitable to the other partners. Branches obtained through acquisition often bring problems: They are physically remote so they don't have the personal bonding of a single-office firm; branches often bring unanticipated client conflicts; and both distance and lack of continuous contact make both sharing how best to practice law and quality control difficult.

For Cravath, the "least evil" answer to the challenges of change has been to designate permanent associates and senior attorneys—lawyers somewhat similar to "income partners" in other law firms. Cravath currently has 25 senior attorneys and hopes to encourage more associates who do not make partner to stay with the firm as senior attorneys. It believes 10 percent of its lawyers could be senior attorneys without changing core Cravath. "We know them well, they are Cravath trained, and they have met Cravath standards," explained Chesler, "so they are very good lawyers, but not *quite* Cravath partners." (One senior attorney was made a Cravath partner after three years of impressive performance.) A senior attorney at Cravath earns more than a partner would at most law firms, works on the most interesting cases and issues, and works for what he believes is the best law firm. Still, nothing's perfect. Some who had the ego to seek a Cravath partnership don't have the ego or self-confidence to stay at Cravath after being told they won't be partners. And some spouses can't accept it: *But they* rejected *you! How can you stay in a firm that doesn't really want you?*

Another structural innovation at Cravath began during an airplane trip Chesler took with a young partner. Going over a computer print-out of charges for legal temps, he was struck by how high one of the charges was: A cluster of lawyers had been hired to screen documents for discovery evidence in a particular case. "We were simply billing the client for those costs," recalled Chesler. "We were just a pass-through with no value added. I realized that this was not cost-effective for our client; that the lawyers doing the work had no institutional knowledge of how to do Cravath-quality discovery; and that we would have to retrain each time we brought in a new group, so we had no assurance of consistent quality." He designed a better way for good lawyers with a personal preference for regular hours—typically for a family reason—who still valued the prestige of identifying themselves as Cravath law-yers. To test his concept, Chesler said, "Go hire the three very best you can find and let's experiment." It worked well, with consistent high quality and lower cost than having Cravath associates do the work. Cravath now has 30 discovery associates who graduated from Harvard, NYU, and Stanford law schools. The arrangement is a win for those lawyers, a win for the clients because their work is both first rate and less costly, and a win for Cravath because it is quite profitable.

■ ■ ■

Over and over again, the component policies and practices of each great firm fit snugly together. Cravath's recruiting, training, and cul-ture are in harmony with lockstep compensation in enabling the firm to achieve its mission. Capital's multiple counselor system of portfolio management fits sensibly with its concept of independent research, its "loose-tight" organization of investment professionals, and compensa-tion based objectively on results. Significantly, it also enables Capital to achieve the three-dimensional mission of benefiting associates, owners, and clients by increasing true diversification and reducing both port-folio risk and manager risk. It creates a learning machine for develop-ing superior investment managers able to deliver superior long-term investment results. McKinsey's refocusing on strategy and organi-zation, and its expanding expertise in major industries and particu-lar disciplines, enables it to capitalize on its global structure to serve international clients and provide career opportunities in ways no other consulting firm can match. With compensation based entirely on qualitative appraisals of effective consulting and teamwork, McKinsey is extraordinarily able to form into optimal consulting teams wherever and whenever needed to serve clients. Goldman Sachs could not have been so repeatedly successful at innovation if its culture was not so focused on internal communications and developing better ways to create value and increase profitability. And it was a mutual blessing that Henry Plummer's innovations found such fertile ground to germinate in just as Mayo Clinic entered an era of transformation in the nature of medical practice. Not by accident, the great firms' important innovations almost invariably depend upon and strengthen teamwork.

When changing the way the game is played is not enough to deliver the maximum value to clients, the great firms do not stop. They go on to change the game itself—often with profound strategic consequences.

Chapter 7

Macro Innovation

Changing the Game

The long history of organizational design is full of examples of serious conflicts between structure and strategy. Usually the structure designed for the *past* constricts or even blocks the optimal strategy for the *future*. Sometimes changes in strategy and structure are interdependent: Transforming a firm's strategic effectiveness can depend on making fundamental changes in the structure of the organization. More frequently, as its environment changes, simply sustaining an organization's historic strategy to continue fulfilling its mission depends on adaptive changes in structure.

Major changes in strategy typically generate opposition from those who have been successful and comfortable with the past strategy and the existing structure. They fight the strategy by defending the old structure. And the changes rarely come all at once. So like less sweeping innovations, they take time to muddle through and prove out.

■ ■ ■

McKinsey changed its legal structure defensively by incorporating, so it could stay on mission; changed its organizational structure offensively to become an international firm; and then changed again to match the way its consultants would work together.

Initially, Marvin Bower had opposed incorporation because he treasured the spiritual values he associated with partnership; they complemented his determination to establish McKinsey as a truly professional firm. In the early fifties, Ewing W. "Zip" Reilley and Everett Smith advocated incorporation so McKinsey could establish a tax-sheltered retirement plan. Another increasingly important argument for the change was that the economic claims of retired partners were becoming a serious financial disincentive for younger partners—a problem sure to become more serious as major shareholders with long years of service retired. Incorporation also would make it easier for rising young partners to borrow from banks the money they needed to buy shares in the firm and would limit the personal liability that came with a partnership, a concern that would increase as the firm grew. Yet another reason for incorporation was the need to accumulate capital in the firm to finance growth.

With his financial orientation, Smith was a particularly strong advocate. Starting from the consensus that the firm needed capital equal to at least three months of revenue, Smith showed that partners would be hard pressed to provide that much capital if the firm's growth aspirations were achieved. Personal savings—after tax at the then-prevailing 70 to 90 percent income tax rates—would be inadequate. "Being private meant the needed capital had to come from the partners," Jack Vance pointed out. "In the early years McKinsey recruited people from 'good' families who had money—at least they were not paupers—and many capital contribution checks came from parents."

The three-month minimum capital need would be Smith's fulcrum, and Bower's aspirations to establish a long-lasting firm would eventually be the lever to gain his agreement. As part of his early opposition to incorporation, Bower retained a consultant who reported what he thought Bower wanted to hear—incorporation would be "problematic"—so for a while that had ended that. Then Gil

Clee, a partner who had also been initially opposed to incorporation, wrote a memo separating the legal *form* of incorporation from the managerial *values* of partnership. After resisting for two years, Bower gradually accepted that "partnership values" could be preserved after adopting a corporate structure that would help McKinsey become the perpetual firm he had always wanted. McKinsey incorporated in 1956.

An important corollary of incorporation was Bower's agreement to reduce his ownership share very substantially—from 40 percent to just 5 percent. Smith's persistent logic had persuaded Bower that this limitation would be necessary if McKinsey was ever to become a perpetual professional firm. Bower's selling most of his shares to his partners at book value was decisively different from the decision of other consulting firms' leaders to either sell out or hurt their firms by taking too much out for themselves. Arthur D. Little and Booz Allen both went public, while Cresap, McCormick & Paget sold itself to Citicorp. Bruce Henderson of BCG and then Bill Bain of Bain arranged such outsize payout commitments to fund their retirements that both firms were saddled with seriously burdensome obligations. During the same era, securities firms and advertising agencies were also going public for the first time. The heady opportunities for CEOs of service organizations to monetize their ownership stakes were becoming pervasive.

Bower was not unmindful of what he had given up to keep McKinsey on its pathway to being a professional firm. In later years, he often admonished Smith about how much personal wealth he had forgone.

McKinsey's strategic drive toward becoming a truly global firm began on a vacation trip to Portugal that Bower and his wife, Helen, took—their first outside North America. Bower, as usual on his vacations, thought about McKinsey. He decided the firm should become international to serve U.S. clients that were increasingly expanding in Europe.* Through the fifties, consulting engagements involving international work for U.S. clients were increasing for McKinsey and other consulting firms. Interest in opening abroad was accelerated by a 1957

---

*An alternative view is that Clee was the visionary who saw that the future of the firm had to include Europe while Bower was initially against going to Europe. Clee also predicted accurately that government was sure to have a rapidly increasing impact on business.

Business Week article observing that McKinsey was still only an exporter while Booz Allen Hamilton had established offices in Europe. In 1958, Clee circulated a memo in favor of opening an office in London, emphasizing that the Common Market would cause many corporations to reexamine their operations. Doubters, led by Smith, pointed to the profitable expansion opportunities in America and contended that most European companies, family owned and family run, were not prepared for McKinsey's "top management" approach or its substantial fees. Skeptical partners worried about two kinds of costs: the direct cost of opening a new office to serve a new market and the opportunity cost of consultants sent to London not being in New York where they were sure to be highly profitable. Smith also worried about maintaining McKinsey's standards. He insisted that if the firm ever went international, the same policies that had made McKinsey strong in America must be consistently adhered to abroad: the same quality of work for the same caliber of clients by the same quality of people at the same level of fees and with the same professional approach. Finally, he said McKinsey should not go international until it had a major European client.

Support for the expansion was evident at a partners meeting. When further study was suggested, Bower asked for a show of hands on moving ahead. The decision to launch was made, and Bower announced it publicly the next day. Then he got lucky. To everyone's surprise, Royal Dutch Shell soon became that necessary major client—in Venezuela.

Created in 1907 by combining Royal Dutch Petroleum Co. and Shell Transport and Trading Co., Ltd., Royal Dutch Shell was still operating with its original structure nearly 50 years later. Over time, it had become a complex of 400 operating companies reporting to one of the two headquarters in London and The Hague. Both were staffed with numerous older people who had been transferred home to headquarters in their last leisurely years before retirement. The structure was costly and decision-making far too slow to keep pace with competition.

A top Shell executive, John Loudon, recognized the need for change and knew that change would be internally resisted, so he would need outside help. Since the Dutch would resist a British consultant and the British would resist a Dutch consultant, Loudon decided to turn to an American firm. He had learned of McKinsey's and Bower's capabilities from Gus Long, CEO of Texaco. As a test, Loudon asked Bower to do an

organization study of Shell's operations in Venezuela, its largest single operation, where he had previously worked. The Venezuelan operations were
a microcosm of the corporation's global business: 13 operating companies
split between Dutch and English managements.

Bower led a team of four associates for three weeks in a preliminary examination. They began by tracking how decisions were
made, particularly at the production camps around Lake Maracaibo.[*]
Bower, deeply engaged, continued to visit Venezuela for a week each
month and was a stickler about the reports produced. Loudon also
went several times and spoke frequently by phone with Bower. In
the end, the McKinsey team's recommendations for Venezuela were
accepted and adopted.

Soon after, as expected, Loudon was appointed chairman and
promptly asked McKinsey to study the corporation's headquarters
operation—but *not* to suggest combining London and The Hague.
Bower again led the team, which included three Shell executives. The
main conclusion from field interviews was that operations were far too
centralized. Initially, Shell's managing directors resisted, but after six
more weeks of collecting 50 specific examples, some quite hilarious,
the McKinsey team was able to win them over.

McKinsey suggested a series of geographic and functional (for
example, refining and marketing) coordinators and recommended
establishing a staff services organization to advise operating companies
and developing training programs to nurture Shell's culture and share
experience. Loudon announced that Royal Dutch Shell had adopted
McKinsey's recommendations and published a major article in the
Director, the U.K.'s status business publication. The matrix organizational structure McKinsey recommended—a first in Europe—would
not be changed for 30 years. All in all, the work with Shell was a great
way to begin McKinsey's internationalization.

While the intended strategy was to serve the European subsidiar-
ies of expansionist American corporations, the major demand was soon
coming instead from European corporations that wanted American

---

[*]Surrounded by the wild Monteleone Indians, who could shoot four foot-long
arrows 100 yards using their feet, the workers were protected by heavy fencing
placed 200 yards from the wells. Still, several wanderers had been killed.

consulting on top management strategy, usually involving decentralization. Success with Shell led to a breakthrough at ICI, the chemical company that was the largest industrial corporation in the U.K. with a gigantic headquarters building in London. By 1966, the London office had grown to be McKinsey's busiest outside New York.

"Have you been McKinseyed?" became a common question among executives at major British corporations as one after another retained the firm. Lord Kindersley at Lazard introduced McKinsey to Dunlop, where the chairman of Vickers was on the board. That got the firm into Vickers, a giant conglomerate, which led to Rolls-Royce, which led to the Bank of England and the BBC, which led to the Post Office. Anthony Wedgwood Benn, Postmaster General in Harold Wilson's Cabinet, set out to determine whether the price of stamps should be raised one penny. McKinsey was called in. Michael Allen, a new consultant, decided to spend a night at a mail-sorting office and found that the men on the night shift started at 10:00, left at 10:30, went home and slept, and returned at 5:30 to work until 6:00. They were hardly working at all! McKinsey was soon engaged to organize the separation of mail handling from telecommunications.

"We then began identifying the clients we most wanted to serve," recalled Norman Sanson. "We were deliberate and determined to be the international consultants of choice. Our strategy was to bring the worldwide organization of McKinsey to the U.K., and we focused on U.K. corporations with international expansion plans. In the U.K. we were perceived as a British firm. But we did not do all that work just with those of us in London; we engaged the whole McKinsey organization."

While McKinsey was enjoying teaching British clients lessons on management, the firm was about to learn a painful lesson itself. As the number of major corporations wanting McKinsey's help mushroomed, the firm's major challenge seemed to be merely managing the queue to serve as many clients as possible. This overly optimistic perception led to problems. The first was a drop-off in the quality and customization of engagements. Consultants were spread too thin so work devolved to less experienced people, while a drive for speed to completion eclipsed paying attention to each client's needs. When clients were disappointed, they didn't come back and certainly didn't recommend McKinsey to others. The second problem took McKinsey by surprise. With that seemingly endless queue of interested prospective clients, the firm failed to focus on its golden opportunity to develop a strong relationship with each client. When the decentralizing work was done, there was little or no follow-on or new-problem work with those same clients. And the U.K. had only so many large corporations interested in major studies that could help them move toward decentralization. As a result, said a partner, "One day we looked out the front door and found nobody there." Fortunately, important work came from Africa and kept the firm busy for a year, giving it time to reorganize business development in the U.K. Then it launched its expansion onto the European Continent.

When McKinsey decided to go international, it sent over its best people. "That seems obvious now," observed Jon Katzenbach, "but only in retrospect." Then, soon after starting, the firm recognized that to be really significant, it had to recruit, nurture, and establish nationals as the McKinsey consultants in each country. Recruited nationals and those initial American consultants were then transferred back to the United States as "internationals"—the key to being a one-firm firm.

As usual, McKinsey's success with its transformational strategy to become international was 95 percent implementation. The strategy was implemented by opening offices in one country after another. As a driven entrepreneur, Herbert Henzler set up McKinsey offices in Moscow, Istanbul, Stuttgart, Cologne, Vienna, Berlin, Warsaw, Budapest—and Brazil. The outposts were not always successful, particularly in their early years. When the firm opened a Tokyo office after a couple of false starts, except for Mitsubishi Heavy Industries there were almost no clients. Thanks to all the overhead costs, the breakeven was a daunting 50 percent of the office's consulting capacity. Tokyo was incurring losses of nearly half a million dollars a year. A painful major reorganization was imperative, but Japanese employment regulations made terminating employees difficult and costly. In addition, McKinsey had made a mistake in selecting the early consultants for Tokyo by sending Western consultants with a "Japanese connection."

Developing new offices in new countries was not the only strategic thrust for growth. Several times, McKinsey consultants proposed initiatives to get into new lines of business. *McKinsey has the best brains*, was the thinking; *we can do anything—so let's do things that make more money.* Fred Gluck wanted to expand the information technology group and thought he had found the way to do this in October 1989: Acquire Information Consulting Group, a firm started just a few years before by people from Andersen Consulting and Bain Capital with backing from Saatchi & Saatchi PLC. ICG put together a proposal on how it could fit with McKinsey by doing the detailed IT implementation work with clients after McKinsey developed the macro strategy. While Marvin Bower spoke at length against the acquisition at a meeting in Paris, the younger advocates made and won their case.

When the acquisition was completed, ICG's leaders were made McKinsey directors or principals as an accommodation. This offended numerous consultants who had labored long to earn those ranks. The values of ICG soon proved in conflict with the culture of McKinsey. Few of the ICG staff remained at McKinsey more than a few years. Gluck later made the analogy of a transplanted organ being rejected by a patient to describe the failure of the acquisition. Another explanation—one that is often the reason "strategic innovations" fail— is that when the motivation and justification are dominated by expectations of easy profits, the acquiring organization may not be careful to ensure there is a good long-term fit with culture and mission.

■ ■ ■

When Goldman Sachs sent Gene Fife to London in the mid-eighties to head its intended expansion across Europe from a small, money-losing outpost in London, he didn't know Europe and had no budget, almost no authority, and almost no interest or support from headquarters. Most of the firm's people in London, he knew, would have to be replaced. As he later recalled, "Goldman Sachs was *not* Goldman Sachs in London"—or anywhere else in Europe.

Aiming to reposition his firm as a strong market leader, Fife was determined to make major changes and knew he would need lots of help. He didn't know the movers and shakers in business or government in *any* country, nor did he know anyone who did. And he didn't know the subtle but important inside rules and customs specific to each European country. So he knew the bank needed expertise on social, political, ethical, and cultural matters, and he didn't want the aristocratically titled "ornamentals" other firms were then retaining. Fife wanted advisers who would be rigorously critical of every aspect of Goldman Sachs's business plans in each country, would capably advise on how to develop major relationships for the long term, and would know how to position Goldman Sachs as an important firm with which to do important business.

Knowing that powerful people would be reluctant to be mere advisers, Fife worked with Sullivan & Cromwell to create a new company, Goldman Sachs International. He would be chairman, and advisers would be vice chairmen with base salaries of $150,000 and an opportunity to earn bonuses up to $1 million. They would meet twice a year for two days—one to brief the firm's bankers on important developments in their country and one for the firm's bankers to present their business development strategies to be rigorously critiqued.

Time and again, the international advisers made decisive differences. Jacques Mayoux, country adviser for France, was typically effective. When Total, France's giant oil company, was to be privatized, the CEO had decided to use Morgan Stanley. Informed of this on a Sunday, Mayoux was indignant. "What? Morgan Stanley? This cannot be!" He instructed his driver to take him immediately to the home of Total's CEO, where he sputtered: "You dishonor me! This underwriting will *not* be given to Morgan Stanley! This underwriting will be managed by the one correct firm, which is, of course, Goldman Sachs! See to it *immédiatement!*" Next day it was announced that Total's giant privatization would be managed by Goldman Sachs, and Total's CEO won recognition among France's business elite for his astute judgment. If he had not made that decision, Mayoux had made it clear: He would be marked for life as an incompetent.

Romano Prodi, later the prime minister, became country adviser for Italy. Behind the scenes, he offered advice like, *Don't do this piece of business that way; do it in the following way.* When it appeared that the only way to land one major transaction was to pay the customary bribes, Prodi consulted with Fife, who insisted that Goldman Sachs would never pay bribes. Together they worked out a series of moves that not only boxed in the bribe-seekers politically so they couldn't block Goldman Sachs from getting the business, but also had important observers applauding the decision to award the firm the mandate. Recalls Fife, "After we won that mandate, we did a *ton* of business in Italy."

Goldman Sachs enjoyed so many successes with strategic initiatives that it's instructive to observe the firm's struggle with repetitive self-inflicted failure in what eventually became arguably one of its best and most valuable businesses: investment management. Over the years the scale of its business of managing other people's money would go from modest to magnificently global and from less than $1 billion to well over $1 trillion, but only after many false starts.

In the sixties, a small investment advisory operation was started under Arthur Altschul when he was made a partner largely because he could contribute needed capital to the firm. The omens were discouraging. Fees were low because the business model was only advisory— no trades could be executed unless the client so directed. Customers were wealthy individuals who required lots of hand-holding, were reluctant to sell securities because they hated to pay taxes, and would rather not be bothered with phone calls. Since the mostly elderly customers kept dying off, the business had poor asset-growth prospects. Moreover, partners believed that Goldman Sachs should not compete with its customers. Since it was the leading institutional stockbroker that meant staying out of the booming business of managing investments for pension funds.

Things changed when Gus Levy read the initial public offering prospectus for Donaldson, Lufkin & Jenrette in 1969. He saw how profitable investment management was for that upstart securities firm: Fees were *not* low, they were *high*. Exclaiming "I've gotta get in on *this!*" Levy moved quickly. The partner he put in charge, Bruce McCowan, assembled a team of young go-getters, focused investing on midcap growth stocks, got recommended by investment consultants, and was soon landing accounts. But when midcap growth stocks suffered badly in the bear market of the seventies, the new unit was in trouble and needed to find a strategic breakthrough.

International investing was just starting to attract U.S. institutions' interest. Several American firms had created joint ventures with long-established British firms. For Goldman Sachs, the obvious linkup would be with the London firm it had done business with for 50 years: Kleinwort Benson. Levy made the introduction and a joint venture was soon agreed. But with the conventional problems of neither side actually doing what the other side thought had been promised, the joint venture flopped. Then in 1980 an internal group bought out Kleinwort Benson and, a little later, bought out Goldman Sachs—but continued to fumble. At that point Goldman Sachs was entirely out of investment management and, like Aesop's fox with the sour grapes, declared it had no interest in ever getting back into the business.

In 1981, John Whitehead got a call from an acquaintance who was a trustee of a money market fund that served only institutional investors and was looking for a new manager. Only someone as senior and powerful as Whitehead could get the firm to accept this opportunity to go back into investment management. Within a decade, the money market fund's assets multiplied 40 times to $20 billion, but even so, it contributed only $12 million of profits, a mere rounding error for Goldman Sachs.

About then, research director Leon Cooperman went to senior partners Robert Rubin and Steve Friedman with a business proposition. Hedge funds charged 20 percent of profits plus a management fee. Twenty percent of 20 percent was 4 percent, so, as Cooperman painted it, if he could produce 20 percent gains on assets of $500 million, that would be $20 million—almost twice the profits of the money market fund. But before a hedge fund could be launched, Goldman Sachs came under public criticism for the activities of its highly profitable Water Street Fund, fairly dubbed a "vulture" fund because it took controlling positions in distressed debt securities and aggressively confronted managements to maximize payoffs. John Weinberg closed down Water Street and ordered Cooperman to change from a hedge fund to mutual funds that could be sold to wealthy individuals through the Private Client Services unit. Hoping to avoid offending institutional investors that were its major stockbrokerage customers, the firm imposed restrictions: no use of the name Goldman Sachs, no poaching portfolio managers or salespeople from institutional customers, and no competing with those customers for new accounts. In sum, Cooperman had only one chance for success: stellar investment performance.

The first mutual fund was launched in 1990. Performance was okay, but disappointing relative to high expectations. Cooperman, feeling strategically constricted, left the firm to organize his own hedge fund in 1991, and Mike Armellino took over what was now called Goldman Sachs Asset Management, or GSAM. Asset gathering was progressing, particularly in fixed income, when partner Michael Smirlock was caught wrongly reassigning bonds to different accounts—reminding skeptics that brokers couldn't be trusted as investment managers. Then poor investment performance struck the equity business. A series of possible acquisitions never materialized. Once again, the firm's investment management business was in trouble.

This operational failure was accompanied by strategic failure. Goldman Sachs' senior partners did not understand the potential of the investment management business. They measured the value of new business only in terms of annual fees, not the cumulative present value of many years of future fees. They didn't appreciate how "sticky" the accounts were. They worried that the key people could hop on an elevator and leave at any time, taking the business with them. They didn't recognize the underlying 5 to 10 percent growth of assets from long-term market appreciation. Worst of all, they didn't recognize that the most powerful force for increasing profitability was Goldman Sachs' distinctive strength in selling.

In 1995, after Hank Paulson sat down with partner John McNulty, GSAM's objective stayed the same—build a major business—but the rules were greatly changed. Results would be measured differently: not on current profits, but on the size of assets managed—that is, on capacity for future earnings. McNulty and Paulson were acting on the lessons learned in investment banking, where a specialty had recently developed in selling investment firms to giant banks and insurance companies; valuations were always based on assets under management. Paulson took the gloves off. McNulty could hire the best people, even from institutions that were important trading customers. He could use the firm's capital to acquire interesting investment firms, and they could compete to win business away from important clients of other divisions of Goldman Sachs. With no constraints, McNulty could now build a major asset management business.

With sardonic Irish humor, McNulty told his GSAM co-head:

Your destiny is clear. You are a pioneer. When nobody can recall your name, they'll build you an anonymous statue to celebrate your fighting the natives, clearing the land, and taking all the risks of disease, mosquitoes, and robbers. Your statue will attract pigeons and your reward will be . . . pigeon shit!

McNulty, David Ford, David Blood, and Suzanne Donahue came up with an ambitious strategy commensurate with Goldman Sachs' global footprint. Their so-called 3 × 3 × 10 strategic plan included three continents; three marketing channels—direct selling to institutional clients, indirect selling to institutions through investment consultants, and direct selling to wealthy individuals; and 10 investment products—stocks and bonds of all types plus hedge funds and private equity funds. This strategy would transform GSAM from a marginal entity into a major worldwide money machine in just 15 years.

At the same time, NcNulty went looking for small investment firms with hot records to acquire. In 1995, GSAM acquired Liberty Asset Management and converted it to the GSAM brand. When acquired for $80 million, Liberty managed $2.5 billion. Ten years later, with GSAM's power in asset gathering, Liberty managed $23 billion and was valued at $1.2 billion—15 times as much as it had cost. More acquisitions would soon follow.

"Did you guys see what I saw in today's *Financial Times*?" asked George Walker in London in the spring of 1995. The British government wanted to privatize the management of the British Coal Board's £25 billion pension fund, but had twice had a failed auction. If GSAM could gain that mandate—even if all it got was a contract to manage that fund for seven or eight years—it would suddenly be on the inside of a closed market, would get good people, and would have control over substantial commissions with which to attract brokers' research on companies, industries, and economies. GSAM paid $75 million for the contract (on which it earned $95 million in fees) and absorbed several years of operating losses to build a major investment management business in the U.K. and across Europe. Assets rapidly multiplied—fortyfold—from £2.5 billion before the Coal Board account to £100 billion.

In 1997, GSAM acquired Commodities Corp., a leader in investment "alternatives," particularly hedge funds. It was losing money because it was weak in marketing, so the purchase price was only

$11 million. A decade later, with GSAM marketing, it managed several billions with wide profit margins.

GSAM lost money in 1999 and 2000, but in 2001 profits were $25 million, in 2003 $250 million, and in 2004 over $1 billion. Then troubles caught up with GSAM again. An asset-gathering business focus, stressing current profitability, was badly misaligned with the professional disciplines of sound investment management. GSAM's investing capabilities were seriously oversold, and investment performance was poor. Assets flowed out and profitability declined. A series of GSAM's top managers had come from banking with no professional credentials in investment management and were changed almost annually. Apparently Goldman Sachs' senior management still did not understand that investment management is a long-term professional service business based on trust. Emphasis on current profitability encourages compromise on professional standards in any profession and is the usual tipping point toward a firm's professional deterioration.

■ ■ ■

Capital Group's major organizational change must, at first, have appeared to outsiders as virtually no change at all: In 1969, Capital became a one-firm holding company. While almost nothing of substance happened at the time of the conversion, Capital freed itself to take a series of initiatives over the next few years, and these initiatives became engines that would drive strategic change.

Capital had been sufficiently successful in its mutual fund business to show signs of structure blocking strategy. One example: The possibility of pursuing the separate business of managing investments for wealthy individuals and institutions was getting no serious attention. Capital's senior investment managers saw no reason they should give up the prestige and compensation of the large, steadily growing business of managing mutual funds to go off into a risky little startup business unit that hoped to win corporate pension business away from big banks that had close, long-term relationships with senior financial executives, strong balance sheets, well-established trust powers—and charged very low fees. Besides, they realized, if the institutional business succeeded, they would have to be out on the road, away from the office and away from home, traveling from city to city to meet with clients whenever and wherever they might require. "Not me!" was the general reaction.

Staying in the center of the well-established business of managing mutual funds was clearly in each individual's self-interest. That was Capital's main business; it provided internal status and prestige. That was where compensation was both largest and most assured. Meanwhile, the mutual funds' independent directors questioned how the firm could fairly allocate such major costs as investment research to the different businesses. Several directors opposed any diversion of people and other resources from Capital's primary mission of managing mutual funds. Pricing was another concern. Many client institutions had begun shifting huge assets from banks to investment counsel firms. Those firms were charging considerably higher fees than Capital was charging to manage the mutual funds. If the new institutional business paid such high fees, how could the directors be sure the mutual funds would still get the best people and the best investment ideas?

Searching for an organizational structure that would enable Capital to develop good answers for these and other questions, Lovelace came up with the idea of a one-company holding company. It took many meetings and discussions before consensus emerged that Capital should indeed change its structure and create a holding company—initially with just one subsidiary, the mutual fund management company. "The long-term consequences and results of creating the holding company have certainly been impressive," Shanahan noted. "But at the 'creation,' we were not focused on ends, just on providing appropriate means."

The process of Capital's creating its own parent organization was, with some humor, dubbed "Project Mutation." The paper holding company that resulted, Capital Group Companies, would become substantive as one after another of the spaces on that paper got filled in with real business developments. Despite several serious internal issues, a new subsidiary, Capital Guardian Trust Co., was organized to focus on large institutional accounts. Over the next 30 years, Capital's institutional business would grow to be larger for a time than its mutual fund business.

Acquisitions have been unusually important over the years to Capital, despite their generally unfavorable record overall. Too often, the price paid is, in retrospect, too high and the presumed strategic synergies are never fully realized. Most "acquisitions" are really *sales* driven by the knowing seller who wants out—not *purchases* originated by an astute, informed buyer. Acquisitions that fail, as most do, are often driven more by emotion than rational judgment. The record of acquisitions in the investment management field has been particularly poor. Still, Capital made several highly successful acquisitions during severe bear markets by being rigorously analytical, having ample resources available so it could buy on favorable terms, and seeing long-term value when others were concentrating on the short-run problems of the early seventies. In addition, Capital made itself the preferred buyer by inspiring trust across the mutual fund industry and confidence that combining into Capital would work out well. Being trusted to serve mutual fund shareholders well, even in the worst of times, proved decisive several times. Finally, Capital's acquisitions had positive attributes: favorable financial terms, modest use of capital, clear strategic business complementarity, and immediate organizational integration.

Taken as a portfolio of long-term decisions, even though some failed, Capital's strategic actions put the organization in a remarkably strong position when the market tide turned. By basing its decisions about long-term investment value on its analysts' expert knowledge of companies, Capital produced superior investment results. Since it always put long-term professional values ahead of current commercial criteria, it developed strong loyalty among investors and brokers. This loyalty resulted in steady incremental sales and low redemptions, fundamental elements of its long-term asset growth and profitability.

■ ■ ■

Adding major new lines of business or expanding into new markets are ways in which great organizations change—sometimes defensively, sometimes offensively. In the late 1970s, the development of "closed panel" health maintenance organizations—particularly in Minnesota—appeared to present a major threat to Mayo Clinic: Why would HMO participants be prepared to pay up for a separate provider's care, even at Mayo? While the HMO threat soon faded, it focused attention on the importance of ensuring access to large, affluent populations. This resulted in a trio of bold strategic initiatives. Mayo opened the Jacksonville, Florida, campus in 1986 and the Phoenix, Arizona, campus in 1987, and developed a stronger presence in its own region. In 1983, 890 physicians and scientists supported by 6,854 staff members and administrators had served 275,800 patients with 30,800 surgeries. By 2007, those numbers multiplied to 2,706 physicians and scientists with 51,000 staff serving 520,000 patients and performing 76,300 operations. Working in teams, Mayo people try to identify the best medical knowledge, identify the single highest-value procedure, standardize it, and distribute it through another important innovation, Ask Mayo's Expert, the clinic's knowledge management system that is available online.

■ ■ ■

Ideally, structure follows strategy and helps an organization fulfill its mission and achieve its objectives. But when conflicts arise between established structure and forward strategy, structure usually prevails. This is not what should be, but what is. And this unfortunate reality has been decisive in preventing numerous good firms from rising to greatness. Structural changes are hard for many reasons, not all of them good. The people in organizations that have been effective naturally strive for stability and seek easy opportunities to use familiar skills to repeat their past successes. Changing organizational structure always involves loss of stature and power for some individuals. If senior and powerful, they often focus on what's best for them rather than what will be best for the organization. That's why structural changes and large-scale innovations almost always get implemented only by stages and always require determined leadership.

Leadership is, of course, crucial to the success—or failure—of every firm that aspires to excel. Leadership must be in tune with the times and the circumstances of each organization. It must nurture the culture; sustain the mission; ensure excellence in recruiting, training, and development; and foster innovation at multiple levels so the firm continually excels at delivering value to clients. Leading is hard and seldom understood by those not "in the center of the ring . . . facing the bull." So it's always lonely at the top.

Chapter 8

Leadership

Bringing the Secrets Together

L eadership is partly conditioned by circumstances: Different opportunities and challenges call for different kinds of leadership. Major external opportunities and challenges create opportunities for great leadership, while internally, leadership depends on the abilities and commitments of both the leaders and the followers who accept their leadership. The ultimate test of a leader is the degree to which he or she achieves change that makes an enduring positive difference.

Candidly, most leaders are merely conventional *transactional* leaders. They focus on the regular, expected work of the organization. They are usually skilled at particular transactions and at developing business relationships. Exceptional transactional leaders can set an inspiring example in the quantity, quality, or complexity of transactions they execute as they engage directly with specific clients. In doing the work of the organization unusually well, they can advance their firm's competitive position, but most transactional leaders do not even consider making important changes in the organization or its work. Transactional leaders may be loved or disliked, admired or feared, but like builders of sand castles on the beach, they usually leave little long-term impact behind.

The next higher level of leader—the *process* leader—adds another dimension by developing improved, repeatable, and teachable processes by which the same or similar transactions can be executed more effectively. Having proven a superior method, the process leader can go on to other improvements. Often the better processes will continue long after the process leader has gone. Sometimes the process improvement is so significant that it has strategic impact, making the organization significantly more effective.

At the next higher level, the *strategic* leader conceives of and convinces others to take up a new strategic initiative and bring it to successful operation as an integral part of the organization and its work. Strategic initiatives come in many sizes, and their impact on the organization can be small or large, short term or long term. The most important strategic initiatives have lasting impact. They change the structure of the organization, the nature of the work done for clients, and the firm's competitive position—its ability to attract major clients or stellar young professionals.

The command-control leadership that prevailed a century ago in rigidly hierarchical organizations—railroads, armies, banks, manufacturing and retailing corporations, insurance companies—cannot compete effectively with today's flexibly entrepreneurial, knowledge-based, market-sensitive service organizations. Senior leaders of these dynamic organizations empower leaders at all levels—decision makers who are close to the market or close to the technology, continuously searching worldwide for creative ways to respond to accelerating change and competition.

Great leaders, often called *servant leaders,** develop process leaders and transactional leaders throughout their organizations. They guide

---

*Robert K. Greenleaf coined the term in *The Servant Leader* (1970) after reflecting on his nearly 40-year career with AT&T and reading Hermann Hesse's *Journey to the East*. Servant leaders get results in an organization by attending first to the needs of their colleagues. The concept is ancient. Muhammad, for instance, is quoted as saying: "On a journey the leader of a people is their servant."

those leaders with broad objectives, major concepts, and high standards. They inspire them to change the transactional capabilities of the organization, to multiply its ability to formulate successful strategies, to develop effective new processes, to execute more difficult transactions in greater volume, and to develop future leaders. These transformational leaders—often quite modest as individuals—concentrate on nurturing significant, persistent improvement in the quality of their organizations.

A great servant leader will ensure the organization is strong in each of the vital elements of organizational excellence and decisively excels in several. A familiar analogy explains the internal focus of a true servant leader. Good parents—who have no idea what work their kids will do during their adult lives, whom they'll marry, or where they'll live—devote many years to facilitating the healthy development of each child's values, strengths, and skills, and then, when appropriate, defer silently to the maturing child's own decisions on all the important choices. Similarly, the focus of an organization's servant leader is primarily internal: recruiting, training, and developing talented people; nurturing culture, climate, and commitment; ensuring teamwork and self-discipline; fostering internal communications; keeping the organization's structure aligned with its strategy and its strategy in harmony with its long-term mission; and developing future leaders at all levels. Everything servant leaders do in the short and intermediate term is determined by their best understanding of what will be really right for the organization over the long term.

■ ■ ■

Not all great leaders are servants to their organization. For Paul Cravath, his firm was there to serve *him*. "Cravath believed that a law firm, like any other successful organization, must have strong executive direction," recounted Robert Swaine. "Until the mid-1930s, his firm was under a dictatorship in his person. Cravath never delegated to anyone ultimate determination of office policy or evaluation of associates and partners." He was "not so much a great lawyer as he was a brilliant businessman and promoter endowed with a legal mind," and he had, as a senior partner remembered, "no overarching, overriding morality beyond serving clients effectively."

In diagnosing a practical corporate law problem, Cravath had no superior among his contemporaries. Recognized as a master of the difficult art of delegation, he would work only with associates already trained by other partners. If an associate displeased him, second chances were rare. Inscribing brief marginal notes such as "vague" or "recast" on an associate's draft, he would command a revised draft be delivered in too little time for much more than retyping. Meeting with associates at his apartment after a concert or dinner party, often well past midnight, he would expect a completed revision on his desk by 9:00 A.M.

One associate, given brief instructions and believing those instructions incorrect, returned to the office at 2:00 A.M., checked law books, drafted what he thought was correct, and left it on Cravath's desk. Next morning, Cravath was livid. He refused to listen to the associate's protestations, threw a law book at him, and tore up the draft, shouting: "I've practiced law long enough not to have to be told by *you* what I want—and if you can't give me what I want, you can get out!" A new draft, obedient to the original instructions, was soon presented. Cravath was pleased: "I knew you could do it."

Quietly, the associate persisted: "I'm still sure you're wrong. I wish you'd look at those cases." After studying the cases, Cravath realized he *was* wrong and called the associate. He gave no apology and offered no explanation, saying only, "Send up the draft you prepared last night." He never mentioned it again.

Clearly, compliments were not his way. When he was once out for surgery for two months, a young partner handled a complex matter skillfully and the clients said how pleased they were. When Cravath said, "You did a good job; the clients liked it," the partner replied: "I appreciate your saying that. It's the first time you ever told me that a job I did was good." To this Cravath coldly replied, "Good work doesn't call for comment; it's expected."

By 1960, the time when one dictatorial partner could run the Cravath firm had passed. The firm was then led by four senior partners. It would never again have a single, dominating leader, but it would have a servant leader who was focused on guiding the firm to sustaining excellence. In September 1980, Sam Butler was asked to be Cravath's presiding partner. "I didn't want to do it," recalled Butler, "but since I didn't want anyone else, either, I took it." In selecting Butler as presiding partner, his predecessor reached over several seniors to a man of 50 who would clearly be serving as leader for a long time: over 18 years. Today's partners value Butler's servant leadership during those years, in which Cravath adapted successfully and almost effortlessly as the profession experienced increasing economic pressures and change. As one partner said, "Sam Butler didn't need Cravath as much as Cravath needed Sam Butler."

At today's Cravath, the presiding partner, after consulting with others, presents his choice of successor to the partnership for approval. No objection has ever been raised. The successor presiding partner is elected a year before he or she will become presiding partner and serves during that year as deputy presiding partner. With retirement now at 65 (reduced from 70) the incumbent will relinquish the position at 63, two years before retirement. When Butler was to retire at 70, he relinquished the presiding partner role at 68. At the first weekly meeting after his 18 years as presiding partner, Butler quite matter-of-factly sat with the other retired partners and, like all the others, followed the norm of saying nothing unless asked a direct question.

Cravath, Swaine & Moore is a much better and stronger firm than it was when Paul Cravath died at 79 in 1940. It has since had many much more collegial leaders. But without his protean leadership, his remarkable organizational innovation—still admiringly called the Cravath System—and the corporate clientele he developed, the firm would never have become today's Cravath. Nor could it have become today's Cravath had it stayed pretty much as he left it. Paul Cravath was a great transactional leader and a strong process leader—with powerful and enduring consequences for his firm. He was certainly not interested in being a servant leader.

■ ■ ■

Perhaps appropriately for a firm whose focus is management, McKinsey has had a succession of leaders of practically every stripe. All its consultants are considered potential leaders, just as all Marines are considered potential leaders. Today hundreds of strong strategic leaders are recognized within the firm and more than 1,000 consultants are transactional leaders for specific client engagements.

Despite all his extraordinary contributions to McKinsey, at the end of his long tenure in 1967 Marvin Bower's McKinsey was good but not great as a professional firm. It was only moderately profitable, was unable to pay its best consultants particularly well, had no strong leadership successor, and was about to face formidable competition. To facilitate the selection of a successor, an interim executive group was set up, composed of Bower and the three directors most likely to be chosen as the next managing director. Bower chose Ev Smith, Gil Clee, and Dick Neuschel. After a few ballots, Clee was elected "unanimously" and Bower stepped aside. He continued as "of counsel" well into the eighties, with no salary but, on the basis of an objective evaluation, an annual bonus.

Clee sought to create a working environment in which "the individual has a maximum opportunity for innovation, freedom within the disciplines of teamwork, and fairly rigid quality control." Just one year later, the firm was shocked by Clee's death from lung cancer. "Gil's untimely death really pushed the firm back," recalled Jack Vance. "Gil was the only one who could offset Marvin and mediate. He had great empathy and kindness. Broke us all up to beat hell."

Lee Walton, elected managing director after Clee's sudden death, was a compromise candidate and not a classic McKinsey man. (He was short and had no graduate degrees.) The firm had expanded rapidly, but McKinsey's financial model was not working and the firm was on the defensive professionally. Partners tried to encourage one another by saying things like, "If we go without bonuses and keep paying only base salaries, we'll be okay." At a meeting in Puerto Rico, the partners were told that they should prepare their personal finances to be able to respond to a capital call. Fortunately, that call never came, but Walton began complaining openly about the burdens of leadership. After completing two years of Clee's term and one more three-year term, he had had enough and left for Texas, where he led the successful development of offices in Dallas and Houston.

Ron Daniel was asked to join Al McDonald and Jack Cardwell in standing for managing director after Walton. Daniel declined. He had had only three years as head of the New York office and believed he had too much more to do there to change roles so soon. McDonald, a commanding personality who had been a sales manager at Westinghouse before joining McKinsey, boldly made his case for being elected managing director: "I'm tough and know how to run the firm in a businesslike way. I can deal with this difficult reality." McDonald's record in Paris, where client activity had seemed strong as London's revenues collapsed, appeared to validate his emphasis on tight cost management to improve the business economics of the firm.

Elected managing director in a close vote after several ballots, McDonald proceeded to change half the office managers, stop residual payments to the retired Zip Reilley—which others thought was wrong—and announce that the firm had "essentially completed its expansion." Consultants feared for the future of the Paris office without his strong leadership. Actually, a steady falloff in repeat work for major clients would later demonstrate that McDonald's aggressive drive for more business had caused the Paris office to grow too fast, milking the firm's franchise in France. Clients were overloaded with too many studies and could not absorb and implement all the action recommendations they had received. For a while, the problem was hidden by offsetting work for clients in Spain, Portugal, and Algeria. But in 1973–1974, the Paris office's volume virtually collapsed.

McDonald saw himself as a top-down CEO who brought a corporate discipline to the firm. Some saw this as necessary. But others felt he moved too fast with too much pressure and grated on too many people. Marvin Bower later said, "Al McDonald has one fatal flaw. He was all for Al McDonald." At a partners conference in the Bahamas, McDonald was making a presentation showing revenues rising nicely, costs falling, and profit margins expanding. He was obviously proud of this record. But in the back rows, four senior consultants were whispering snide comments and ridiculing the presentation and its focus on commercialism. Among their concerns: Business disciplines were overshadowing the firm's commitment to professional excellence. For example, McDonald had significantly increased the ratio of associates to principals to get more "economic leverage." The change left far too little time for mentoring each junior consultant. Soon the ratio had to be reduced back.

Symbols mattered, too. Where Bower had always taken the regular commuter train to and from his home in Bronxville, New York, McDonald organized a limousine to drive him to and from work and at noon each day to take him just five blocks up Park Avenue to the Racquet Club for lunch—and then five blocks back to the office. He installed his chauffeur in an adjoining office so he would always be ready. One day, coming out of the club after lunch with a colleague, McDonald said, "Hop in—I'll give you a ride," and got this reply: "No thanks, Al. I'd rather walk."

There were other irritants. Bower had always used blue type on blue paper to distinguish his memos from all other paperwork so they would be seen and read by everyone. McDonald would do much the same, but to be clearly different, his paper color would be gold. Gene Zelazney, the firm's brilliant graphics designer, was instructed to produce four different versions of gold paper so McDonald could select the best one. To dramatize his contacts with the king of Saudi Arabia or the chancellor of West Germany, McDonald had the highlights of his travel itinerary printed in each issue of the firm's internal newsletter. The unintended consequence was an increasing distance between McDonald and his partners. "In many ways," recalled Shaw, "Al prepared the way for Ron Daniel and his warm, personal way."

At the next triennial election in 1976, McDonald was clearly determined to run again. Daniel and Cardwell agreed that only one should run, and Cardwell said, "It's your turn, Ron. Last time, I ran. Besides, I'm leaving McKinsey to be president of Sara Lee." Daniel was elected with well over 50 percent on the first ballot and would prove to be a great servant leader for McKinsey.

In his first formal talk to the firm, at a meeting in Monte Carlo, Daniel outlined his commitment to Bower's values. Those values were reinforced by repetition and amplification, by practical application, and by individuals challenging even slight deviations. Recalled Norman Sanson, "Ron always advocated our going the extra mile for a client to be sure we delivered solid value or, if we didn't, to make amends." Even today, questions like "Is this really in the client's long-term interest?" or "What would Marvin Bower do?" are effective ways of focusing attention on core values. When Daniel finished his talk at Monte Carlo, Bower went up to him, put his arm around his shoulder, and said, "Now we'll be okay!"

Where Bower was demanding and forceful, Daniel did what Bower could never have done: He brought all the consultants together into a genuine one-firm firm. Daniel celebrated Bower's values and with his graceful style made them attractive and easy for members of the firm to commit to—and stay committed. Daniel was never confrontational, while Bower often was. In real ways, Daniel institutionalized Bower's values and reputation at McKinsey. He not only brought Bower's ideals and principles back to the firm, he brought Marvin Bower back as a personal symbol of those values and commitments—partly by placing Bower's black-and-white photograph in the reception area of every McKinsey office. He also encouraged Bower to be visible as a regular presence in the office and gave him special status. As a result, Bower would have major impact on the firm's values and language ("never a . . . a . . . *business* system!") for 25 years *after* he had retired. "Ron was magic," recalled Terry Williams. "He made Marvin Bower's firm successful and institutionalized Marvin as an individual and made those values into a compelling, meaningful, guiding vision of McKinsey as a professional firm."

Servant leaders understand that informal leadership is more powerful and more respected than formal leadership. Charles Shaw recalled,

> Ron was charming and a beloved "older brother" to many McKinsey consultants. A very clever guy, he had run the New York office's recruiting program and then ran the firm through a group of followers he had mentored in prior years. In effect, he had a partnership within the partnership. Ron always had thirty or more pink telephone slips on his desk as people he had delegated tasks to were calling to keep him informed.

Daniel would serve as managing director for 12 years. "In his first term, he showed how good he was at selecting young future leaders and taking smart risks on empowering young leaders," recalled Mike Bulkin, a former director. Daniel launched major initiatives in strategy and organization, establishing a committee structure of governance and making it operate well. He raised the firm's quality standards, closed down its boring work on compensation policies and practices, and expanded recruiting. He led the firm through a series of significant fee increases, saying: "We *can* do this and we *must* do this both for the firm and for those clients who really want McKinsey to be first rate." He identified the firm's best thinkers and leaders, steadily bringing them together from wherever they might be and engaging them in a series of strategic initiatives.

A key feature of McKinsey's strategic success during Daniel's leadership was the foresight to go beyond internationalizing to "localize" the firm in each country. While the initial group of consultants in a particular office were often Americans, the strategy in each country was always to serve local clients—often large, international corporations—with local consultants who typically had had a significant part of their training in the United States.

Daniel shifted the firm's leadership from his own contemporaries to a younger generation. Because their power within the firm was tied to their positions as heads of McKinsey's major offices, he saw that his peers had been independent rivals too long. They did not and could not work closely together. Office manager roles had been long-tenure positions. At Daniel's initiative, McKinsey did a two-year internal study of its strategy and an 18-month study of governance and concluded that to open up leadership opportunities, rotation of leadership was important: Office manager tenure should average five years, within a range of three to seven years. Since then, rotating leaders has worked well. "There are no perpetual roles or positions at McKinsey," observed Don Waite. "Nobody stays in charge of anything for very long."

Daniel pushed leadership responsibilities down into the middle of the partnership by celebrating the importance of industry expertise. Skillful selection of future leaders was crucial. Daniel could do this well partly because he had long invested personal time in lunches and dinners getting to know the younger consultants. He understood their individual strengths and weaknesses. During his tenure he doubled the number of consultants identified as leaders.

For McKinsey to succeed, Daniel knew that the whole firm had to become one large collaborative. The New York office had to learn that it would have to give resource support to Germany; the Los Angeles office would have to send its star consultant to Amsterdam. Fortunately, there would be little internal resistance to these transfers based on economics because in McKinsey's performance evaluation process, qualitative factors clearly trumped revenues, cost allocations, or arguments over who got credit for doing what.

Daniel's successor was Fred Gluck, whose intellectually power-ful and disruptive style of leadership took others by surprise. "Fred Gluck would ask you your view on something and then, after hear-ing your views, start arguing that you were *wrong!*" said one con-sultant. When a colleague warned Gluck, "Fred, the firm is out of control!" Gluck smiled and replied: "Agreed! It's deliberate—part of the plan. We want energized talent taking lots of creative initiatives, not control."

After Gluck came Rajat Gupta, who as an Indian was seen as a natural leader of McKinsey's expansion in Asia. Next came Ian Davis, an Englishman and a thoughtful spokesman *for* the firm *to* the firm, particularly in his extensive travels around the world visiting the many offices, articulating core values, and, in his gracious, thoughtful way, listening deeply. Dominic Barton, a Canadian, was elected in 2010. He had been based in Korea and was particularly active in the firm's expansion in China. Barton demonstrated great leadership during the crisis created by Gupta in 2011. (See Chapter 10.)

As McKinsey has grown substantially and institutionalized the "McKinsey way" of managing itself objectively, the managing direc-tor's relative impact as a leader has surely declined proportionately, but he continues to set overall tone and direction. Two factors other than size are particularly important. As a remarkably analytical organization, McKinsey has developed rigorous processes in every area: recruiting, training, managing engagements, determining compensation, and pro-moting consultants to principal and then to director. In addition, with over 400 directors—all chosen and proven as leaders—strong leader-ship is widely dispersed.

■ ■ ■

As a firm matures into a great firm, servant leadership grows increas-ingly vital. At Goldman Sachs, Sidney Weinberg had no more interest in management, planning, or organization than Paul Cravath had across town. The firm was there to assist Weinberg on transactions—*his* trans-actions for *his* clients. He was a big man on Wall Street, but his firm was small and not powerful. The corporate clients were almost all Weinberg's clients, and Goldman Sachs was Weinberg's firm—a proprietorship.

Only a leader as strong and driven as Gus Levy could have succeeded Weinberg. While Weinberg respected Levy's drive and capabilities, he did not trust him because Levy was a trader. His commercial focus threatened to lead Goldman Sachs away from Weinberg's focus on investment banking and the reputation for integrity he treasured. So even after ceding the role of senior partner to Levy in 1969, Weinberg kept sole control over admission to the partnership and partnership percentages. Before moving his office uptown, he established a management committee to control operational decisions and gave Levy only a 49 percent vote, so he would have to get at least one other member's agreement. Then Weinberg stacked the committee with loyalists he knew would report everything to him so he could instruct them on just how to vote.

Levy might have appeared to conform to Weinberg's controls, but he regularly undercut the committee in various ways. Meetings were short, had no agenda, and were held in Levy's seldom-used office. There were no chairs for members to sit on, and Levy spent most of the abbreviated meeting time taking phone calls and doing transactions.

When most of Wall Street arrived around 9:30 A.M. and went home around 5:00, Levy got to his office by 7:00 A.M. to start making phone calls—brief, factual, and cordial, but often leaving the recipient wondering exactly *why* he had been called. Soon everyone at Goldman Sachs was in by 7:00, two or three hours ahead of any competitor. Levy answered his own phone and expected everyone to do the same. He kept two secretaries busy all day placing calls and typing letters, and every night took clients to dinner—often two dinners. He not only added six more hours to an eight-hour day, he accelerated the pace of everything during those hours. When he asked questions, Levy wanted answers that were short and specific. He abhorred ambivalence and uncertainty. When one of his colleagues offered tentatively, "We may be able to do something that may help," Levy cut him short: "*May* is just a month between April and June. It has *no* place here at Goldman Sachs."

A superb transactional leader and often a strategic leader, but never a servant leader, Levy would become, in the late sixties and early seventies, the most powerful man on Wall Street: the chairman of the New York Stock Exchange, the head of Mount Sinai Hospital, a power in the Republican party, the "best" director of numerous corporations, the center of action in New York City philanthropic fund-raising, the go-to man at the hub of booming conglomerate finance, and the unquestioned leader of Goldman Sachs. He was *the* recognized moneymaker.

In October 1976, after a May Department Stores board meeting, Levy took the red-eye flight from Los Angeles to New York for a full day at Goldman Sachs followed by a board meeting of the Port Authority of New York and New Jersey. There he had a stroke, and he died a few days later at 66. His successors, "the Two Johns"—John Whitehead and John Weinberg, Sidney Weinberg's second son—agreed to co-lead the firm. Friends for more than 25 years, they had become partners on the same day and held the same partnership participations throughout their careers. They agreed that Goldman Sachs had the potential to become the leading firm on Wall Street and worked closely together to make it happen. Their decision to co-lead the firm became a decisive strength and set a pattern that would proliferate at all levels of leadership throughout the firm. Whitehead and Weinberg always put the interests of the firm ahead of their own, a priority that was not so clear with their successors. John Weinberg was an effective transactional leader with such strong values and high standards that they had strategic impact. Whitehead was a transformational strategist and a demanding servant leader focused intently on building the firm. During his era, Whitehead had more long-term positive impact on his organization than any other leader on Wall Street.

John Weinberg, ever the Marine, led from the front. For any proposal coming before the management committee, he required all materials 48 hours ahead. Warning there would be no "presentation"—the meeting would begin with questions—Weinberg would always ask the first question. His approach to dispute resolution was simple and effective. He would take the antagonists aside, lower his voice and move in close to say:

Now I'm going to decide this thing once and for all—by noon tomorrow. So each of you should think *very* carefully about what you really want most included in my final decision and then tell me by memo today the exact decision you'd like me to make—a decision you can and you will live with. Make it just as fair as you can to the other guy because he'll be giving me his best and fairest

final decision, too. I'm going to pick just one of those recommendations and that will be that—and we'll all get back to work.

Where Weinberg was instinctive, intuitive, and well liked, Whitehead
was cerebral, deliberate, and respected. He wasn't concerned about hurt
feelings when commanding others in his smoothly rational way. "John
was almost regal in the way he acted," said Roy Smith.

I never met anyone else like that in my life. It's really quite amazing. He tells you exactly what he wants you to do; gives you the
clear understanding you have no alternative and *must* do it; then
proceeds to encourage you to believe you might very well be *able*
to do it; and continues on to give you the feeling you might even
enjoy doing it, particularly if you commit your every effort to be
sure you'll succeed.

As market growth opened opportunities, Whitehead and Weinberg
continued to increase the pace. They made recruiting a firm-wide priority, made teamwork and discipline an even stronger part of the culture, expanded substantially in investment banking, and strengthened
their organization in people, process, and discipline. Most advances
were carefully based on a low-risk, fast-follower strategy of "feed
the winners and starve the laggards." A business centered on serving
wealthy families was built up to nearly rival in profitability the firm's
vaunted institutional business—but without the need for risking capital
in block trading. It later led directly to a superbly profitable business
duopoly with Morgan Stanley as prime brokers to hedge funds.

In October 1981, Goldman Sachs made a bold strategic move: It
acquired the commodities firm J. Aron at, it soon realized, the unsus-
tainable peak of that firm's reported profitability. The acquisition was a
major mistake. J. Aron's risk-averse business model was so badly out of
date that during its first year as a unit of Goldman Sachs it lost money.
Whitehead and Weinberg held intensive weekly meetings to find a
way to convert a blunder into a moneymaker. A major change in strategy was needed. It came when Mark Winkelman, working under Bob
Rubin's supervision, switched J. Aron from cautious agency brokerage
to bold principal trading and took the unit massively into currency

trading with the firm's capital at risk. This led to terminating 130 of its 230 employees, a clear conflict with Goldman Sachs's tradition of long-term employment. (An exception was made to keep one promising young salesman: Lloyd Blankfein.) In its third year with Goldman Sachs, J. Aron made over $100 million. A few years later, with the addition of oil trading and currency options, it made well over $1 billion.

Goldman Sachs's London outpost had been a marginal "outsider" unit unable to break through the tight circle of established firms in the City. Whitehead had long argued that since the firm was now the leading investment bank in New York, the world's largest and most advanced capital market, it could and should make itself the leading firm in the world, starting with London. The decision was made in late 1986 to build, not buy, and to build as quickly as possible a major market-leading operation.

As Wall Street roared through the bull market of the 1980s, Goldman Sachs was in a period of accelerating transformation. Part of the transformation came externally, with growth in institutional block trading and merger and acquisition activity driven by the emergence of acquisitive conglomerates and a deliberate reduction in federal antitrust activity. Part of the transformation came from within the firm, as recruiting brought in increasing numbers of people who were too skilled, well trained, and ambitious to wait very long for things to happen. Part of the transformation came with the soaring compensation that could be earned by combining creativity, capital, risk taking, and entrepreneurial determination. Part came with serial successes leading to increasing self-confidence, which led to still more successes. And part came from the Two Johns' confidence that hard work, intensive client service, and discipline would make Goldman Sachs preeminent.

When Steve Friedman and Bob Rubin became co-heads, the two friends drove for greater coordination across the whole firm by centralizing control of the performance appraisals and compensation that had traditionally been left to the different unit heads. Made more rigorous, these evaluations singled out unusually effective people who were impatient for advancement *and* those who were not. Anyone ranked in the fourth quartile was likely to get fired; anyone in the fourth quartile for two years—called "the fifth quartile"—was *sure* to get fired. The firm's "family" traditions were being squeezed out.

As the focus of Friedman and Rubin shifted from building a great firm—with the assumption that good financial compensation would naturally follow as a secondary benefit—to a far greater focus on making money, the change got expressed in business strategy and in compensation. In business strategy, the firm would continue its agency business—executing transactions for others—with even more profit discipline. But it also committed to making money with money, bringing in a group of bond traders from Salomon Brothers to displace the service-based concepts that were failing to keep the firm competitive in a rapidly changing debt market.

Gus Levy had seen that the once-moribund bond business was changing and could be highly profitable, so he decided to get into it. Still, strength and real profitability in taxable bond dealing came only when Friedman and Rubin took over the division, hired experienced capital-at-risk bond traders, and changed strategies from risk-avoiding sales and service to risk-embracing proprietary trading. Fixed-income dealing, bond arbitrage, and proprietary trading would steadily become the firm's largest moneymakers and thereby the center of power.

Comparable change was brought to individual compensation: increasingly quantifying individual contributions and paying bigger and bigger bonuses based on individual, current-year performance. This, of course, was happening at other firms, too. The dominating reality shifted from abstractions like *integrity* and "clients' interests come first" to a direct focus on making money. As one partner explained, "It's all about the money."

Other changes were coming, and Goldman Sachs wanted to be a leader in most if not all of them. In the early nineties, Friedman enlisted investment banker Hank Paulson to help him develop a private equity investing business. This would be a major breaking away from the firm's traditional clients-first agency business and from its avoidance of competition with clients. The increasingly massive capital-at-risk exposures of trading in all sorts of bonds, commodities, and currencies not only changed the business of Goldman Sachs, they changed Goldman Sachs. So did its expansion into virtually all global markets, its growth to over 30,000 employees—10 times its size 20 years before—and, at the end of the nineties, becoming a public company with huge permanent capital. Increasingly, the profits were made by traders, so more and more partners came from trading. The business, the leadership, and the values would shift from investment bankers' persistent striving to develop long-term client service relationships to traders' drive for mega-profit transactions.

A change in leadership came with Bob Rubin's departure to join the Clinton administration, where he soon became a widely admired Treasury Secretary. Rubin's departure left Steve Friedman alone in an increasingly difficult role as volume surged. While others urged him to appoint an effective co-head to share the burdens, he would not do it. The pressures mounted as he centralized decisions and became an increasingly serious bottleneck for the firm and a burden on himself. In September 1994, saying he was exhausted by the unrelenting pressures of the job, Friedman stunned the management committee with an abrupt announcement of his decision to retire almost immediately. Partners, noting the firm's heavy trading losses in bonds that year, said Friedman hurt the firm by leaving in the wrong way at the wrong time.* John Weinberg, in his Marine mode, called him a "yellow-bellied coward" for abandoning his post under fire.

Friedman's departure required the small management committee to select from their number the firm's new leader in less than a week. Such speed to decision on leadership was foreign to Goldman Sachs. Leadership succession at all levels had traditionally been methodical, so everyone would have ample time to adjust and keep personal ambitions under control. Having no time to prepare and only five days to decide on succession—during an unusually bad loss-making year in the bond markets—was terribly fast. Adding to the pressures, in the weeks that followed, the firm suffered further large losses in a severe bear market. A record 45 partners withdrew, many in fear for the firm and for their own net worth, thinking, *What does Steve know that's causing him to leave that he's not telling the rest of us?*

The leadership consensus settled on Jon Corzine, a quietly charismatic "people person" and successful bond trader. Corzine, alone among the candidates, was at least acceptable to everyone. Observed Mark Winkelman, who had had to find a way to get along with Corzine as co-head of fixed income, "What we didn't recognize at the time was

---

*Six months before he told the management committee, Friedman had told Rubin and the firm's in-house general counsel, on condition they not say a word.

that Jon had always wanted to be senior partner of Goldman Sachs and that his ambition had defined the way he built alliances and loyalties inside the firm. As a natural politician, it was in his blood." A strong transactional leader, Corzine would prove unable to succeed as the strategic leader he wanted to be and thought he was.

Corzine was clear about his immediate priorities: Cut costs by $1 billion—mostly by firing people, a major departure from the firm's traditional practice—work out of toxic bond positions, and then take the firm public. He hoped to get a vote in favor of an initial public offering in 1995. But then, recognizing the strength of opposition within the partnership, he declared the IPO a "nonstarter." Still, he had made an IPO discussable and could bring it up again later. Meanwhile he tried several times to arrange a merger with a major commercial bank without getting prior approval from the management committee. This infuriated his partners. So did his committing $300 million—$50 million more than the maximum his partners had only reluctantly approved—to the rescue of Long Term Capital Management, the highly leveraged hedge fund whose near-collapse threatened a major market crisis. So did the public embarrassment, after finally gaining partners' approval for an IPO in 1999, of having to abort the offering just three months after announcing it. Corzine was increasingly ridiculed as "Uncle Approximate" because he was so often indirect or dissembling.

When John Thornton joined the management committee, only four votes were needed to take out Corzine—not out of his position as managing partner, but right out of the partnership. Corzine was popular: If the whole partnership had voted on whether to remove or keep him as managing partner he would almost certainly have won. But only the management committee had authority to decide who was in or out of the partnership. Paulson made a deal with Thornton and John Thain to oust him and the deed was done. Corzine would be forced out—after the rescheduled IPO—and Paulson would be sole CEO.

Denying that there had been a palace coup—which it certainly was—and blithely calling such stories "inaccurate in every respect," Paulson went on to blandly claim to the press, "This is an evolutionary transition in management and governance." The IPO was completed on May 9, 1999, and by May 18 Corzine was gone. He went on to become a U.S. senator, governor of New Jersey, and head of MF Global Holdings, a securities firm that collapsed spectacularly in 2011.

The IPO—and the great wealth that was going to some and *not* to others—divided the partnership into winners and losers in explicit and highly personal ways. While efforts were made to be fair, "fairness" would really be all about power and position at the IPO moment. Whitehead, Weinberg, and others who had made extraordinary value-adding contributions that were essential to the firm's current strength and profitability were no longer in power, so they got little. The big money—$200 million or more apiece—went to those on the management committee. Their decisions made the reality clear: As many had increasingly feared, the meaning of *partnership* had changed completely.

Paulson aborted a carefully developed plan to merge with J.P. Morgan at the last possible moment, saying he was concerned about massive lay-offs of redundant employees and believed Goldman Sachs would soon be stronger on its own. Shrewdly, Paulson drove hard to build the private equity business and supported an aggressive buildup in asset management. He also made big mistakes like acquiring the largest NYSE specialist, Spear, Leeds & Kellogg, shortly before the implosion of the specialist function. And in one of many steps toward a singular, aggressive pursuit of profit, Paulson decided the firm should abandon its vaunted "no hostile takeovers" policy.

As compensation continued to skyrocket, the focus on the money increased at least as rapidly, making it harder and harder to justify honoring the "old-fashioned" values. As more and more partners came up from trading, the internal center of gravity moved, too. Since the late 1980s, a majority of partners have been traders. Traders don't have clients; they have *counterparties*. Investment bankers develop a trust-based client relationship over many years of entirely visible services, documented ideas, and extensive discussions. Traders are invisible: They can enter or leave the market whenever they like and nobody knows they were even there, much less what transactions they did or with whom or with what result. Increasingly, the "mission" of Goldman Sachs narrowed down to making maximum profits.

Goldman Sachs and other firms were heavily fined in 2003 for violating the rules of the National Association of Securities Dealers, the industry's self-regulatory organization, and the New York Stock

Exchange in an action brought before federal district judge William H. Pauley. The essential issue was whether research analysts, while presenting their work as unbiased, were in fact distorting their recommendations to help their firms win investment banking business during the dot-com bubble. Judge Pauley found that Goldman Sachs and the other firms knew about the conflicts and failed to establish policies and procedures to detect and prevent them. Detection would have been easy. In their individual business plans, analysts had been expected to tell how they would support investment banking in getting and doing deals. Ever the pragmatist, Paulson called Bob Steel, vice chairman and head of the equities division: "Bob, your job is to get a settlement that makes Goldman Sachs look okay—okay compared to Morgan Stanley. It may well be that our analysts did worse things than theirs did, so your job is clear: Make sure our firm fares no worse than their firm." Steel "won." Goldman Sachs was fined "only" $110 million. Morgan Stanley paid $125 million.

In jointly ousting Corzine, Paulson had made a political deal with Thain and Thornton that he would be CEO for just two years and then pass the baton to them. But he grew to like his position and decided to stay on. While it's not clear whether Thornton really chose to leave or was pushed, he did leave in July 2003. Then, on the day Lloyd Blankfein was made co-president, Thain, who had seen Blankfein's various rivals over the years suddenly "sidelined," quickly accepted an invitation to head the New York Stock Exchange. As a result, Blankfein was the obvious successor when Paulson went to Treasury in 2006.

Blankfein recognized that the powerful position Goldman Sachs had achieved—in market stature, proprietary information, and established relationships in virtually every area of global finance—meant that within the limits set by the competitive marketplace, major corporations, central banks, wealthy families, and investing institutions really *had* to do business with the firm—and on terms largely set by Goldman Sachs. While agency-business profit margins were shrinking, principal-investing activity was growing in volume and profitability. Only if the firm exploited its best opportunities could it continue to attract and hold the best people. And it needed to have the best people to stay on top.

Blankfein had no trouble with the change from an all-agency business to an increasingly principal business: It was the new reality. Every major competitor was changing, too, and the best competitors were changing the most and the fastest. Sure, the firm would continue to nurture strong relationships with corporations, governments, and institutions all around the world. They gave it great strength in both sourcing and distributing transactions. But relationships were only the means to the end of maximizing profits.

While the firm's many businesses would certainly incur conflicts of interest, Blankfein's answer was not to pull back from those conflicts, as other banks would, but to master them and assertively manage them. So just as Goldman Sachs had embraced market risk and learned how to manage risk profitably while others pulled back, it would now embrace conflicts and decide for itself how best to manage them. The firm was making itself judge and jury of its own activities. This created a new kind of risk, particularly when decision-making power was so widely dispersed to individuals, at least a few of whom would be moving from self-assurance toward self-centered arrogance. Controlling that risk demanded tougher, more visionary leadership than the firm was able to muster. Sidney Weinberg, John Whitehead, and John Weinberg might have seen troubles coming, but they were gone.

■ ■ ■

Challenging as they are, most of the ingredients required to excel can be attained by astute, disciplined organizational and individual commitments over the long term. But the great firms all know that sustained success requires something more.

Chapter 9

. . . and Luck

Sometimes It Really Matters

Every successful person, every successful organization, and most happily married couples can cite those pivotal instances when luck entered in and made a decisive difference. Every great firm can find moments in its history when, no matter how inevitable the rise to triumph may appear in retrospect, a decisive factor along the way was . . . good luck. Some instances of luck make delightful stories but are not particularly important. Others matter greatly. As Pasteur observed, "Chance favors the prepared mind." And as golfing great Ben Hogan said when asked about lucky breaks after winning a major tournament, "You know, the harder I work, the luckier I get."

■ ■ ■

If Marvin Bower had not been initially rejected by Jones Day when he graduated from Harvard Law School, he would not have gone on to

Harvard Business School and so would never have met Ewing W. "Zip" Reilley at the HBS Club in New York. As a result, he would not have been able to organize the capital needed in 1939 to buy the McKinsey firm from James O McKinsey's estate.

If Bower, when ultimately hired by Jones Day, had not been assigned to serve on bankruptcy trusteeship committees because he had gone to business school, he would not have met James O. McKinsey.

Bower would never have earned the MBA that enabled him to leave the law to join McKinsey if he had not met Arthur M. Anderson, a J.P. Morgan partner. After a year at the Harvard Business School, Bower called on Anderson, without an appointment and only because he had found him listed first, alphabetically, on a list of Morgan partners in HBS's Baker Library. Still, Bower was quickly admitted when he said he wanted to talk about Harvard Business School. As he sat down, Bower said, "Mr. Anderson, I've finished one year at the Harvard Business School and done well. But I want to practice law and don't know that it's worthwhile spending that extra year and extra money to complete the second year."

"Well, young man," came the reply, "if you *don't* finish that year, you'll spend the rest of your life explaining that you didn't flunk out."

Then and there, Bower resolved to go back to Harvard Business School—and became so deeply interested in business management that he was ready to leave his expected career in law when invited to do so by James O. McKinsey. Without Bower's driving commitment and sense of mission, there would be no McKinsey today.

■ ■ ■

If Rochester, Minnesota, had not suffered a severe tornado in 1883, the Mayo brothers would not have turned for help to the Sisters of Saint Francis—a teaching, not a nursing order—and Mother Alfred Moes would not have been inspired to propose building a hospital, a core component of what would become the Mayo Clinic.

■ ■ ■

Capital Group's becoming by far the largest manager of emerging-market investments—larger than the next 10 managers combined—got started only because of a long sequence of improbable developments, some of them clever moves and some clearly lucky breaks.

- When Antoine von Agtmael graduated from Yale, he went to Bankers Trust, where he did well in the training program and so got his choice of a posting—in sophisticated Paris or in remote Bangkok. He surprised everyone by opting for Thailand. During the next four years, he realized that there were some great companies in "underdeveloped" economies. Returning to the United States, he transferred to the World Bank's International Finance Corporation (IFC), a unit devoted to promoting private sector capital investments in developing economies.
- Agtmael joined an after-hours study group to develop an index of the stock market performance of such companies. Despite resistance from old hands, the study group became convinced that a fund that would invest in the best of such companies should be created.
- For credibility, the IFC decided to go outside the World Bank and retain a private sector investment manager. At a promotional meeting intended to attract possible managers, the term *underdeveloped* was dismissed as discouraging and, as a result, two days later, a more attractive new term was chosen: *emerging markets*.
- When a list of possible investment managers was made up, Capital was not on it. Fortunately for Capital, TIAA-CREF decided not to participate in the competition, so a disappointed employee, apparently hoping to get a job with Capital, recommended that Capital's name be added. Since it had a record of at least some international investing, including some investments in the emerging markets, Capital was invited to compete for the mandate.
- Despite his initial skepticism, Capital's David Fisher decided to take a look at the whole proposition. He liked what he thought he saw, but he was almost alone. Others at Capital, including those who'd gotten badly burned on much the same concept several years before, argued forcefully that the emerging markets had been trying unsuccessfully to "emerge" for a long time and would probably continue to disappoint hopeful investors. Accounting was unreliable, stock markets were neither open nor transparent, and local insiders would always get any important information first. Worse, taxes were onerous and in those days money could not be moved

out of most underdeveloped countries. Currency devaluations were common, inflation was rampant, and corruption extensive. Those markets were sure to blow up again in ways no outsiders could ever anticipate, and those blowups would do serious damage to Capital's reputation. But Fisher remained optimistic.

- Fortunately, he got enough support from Jon Lovelace to take his proposal to Capital's board of directors. The board was divided, so Lovelace deferred the question to give Fisher time to lobby his case for offering a loss-making proposal to the IFC. He "won."

- Despite its best efforts, the IFC couldn't raise enough investor money for the new fund to get the NYSE listing it wanted. This was actually fortunate because closed-end international funds were then selling at serious discounts to their net asset value. That would surely have cut demand before the business of international investing at Capital could achieve breakeven scale.

- To get enough commitments from investors to cover its large new costs, Capital went after corporate pension funds. This led to the next consecutive lucky break: The Bell telephone companies had begun using Professor Roger Murray of Columbia as a consultant on investing, and he documented and vigorously recommended the diversification benefits of emerging-markets investing. Several Bell companies hired Capital.

Ten years later, emerging market assets managed by Capital were $13 billion. Another five years later, Capital's emerging market assets were $25 billion, with clients in 29 countries. The improbable ugly duckling had become one of Capital's greatest strengths.

■ ■ ■

Cravath's files were complete back to 1818. When Robert Swaine launched his project to produce the history of the firm in the 1940s, every partner was dragooned into the project. Each partner was to go through a big stack of files and record a description of the contents. "They all hated it," said Sam Butler, "but we found two handwritten letters by a lawyer working for the firm as a correspondent in Illinois. His name was A. Lincoln. They are now, of course, priceless."

■ ■ ■

If Judge Bruce Bromley had not joined with the majority of judges in deciding against a minority group complaint in the politically fraught Bedford-Stuyvesant area of Brooklyn, he would not have lost the upcoming election, and would have remained on the bench and not returned to Cravath. As a Court of Appeals judge, he could not have become a director of IBM, and so IBM would probably not have chosen Cravath to lead its defense in the great antitrust suit. That victory established Cravath as the leader in "bet your company" litigation, and that changed the nature of the firm and its practices.

■ ■ ■

In the dot-com bubble market, Jack Grubman, who shortly after became the poster boy for investment banking abuses by securities analysts, was being courted by Hank Paulson and other investment bankers at Goldman Sachs as a lateral hire to cover telecom companies and do deals in that fast-changing industry. Although an analyst, Grubman had a strong deals focus and a detached view of compliance with rules and regulations. Moreover, he insisted on being free to operate independently of, and not accountable to, the research director. Research director Steve Einhorn recalled, "Bringing him in over our existing analyst in the telecom sector, instead of advancing the man we had trained for the position, seemed unfair to me. Besides, he was *not* nice to work with."

Paulson and others insisted that the firm should absolutely hire Grubman. Jon Corzine didn't want to confront the issue, so he withdrew from the recruiting process, making it possible for Einhorn to block an offer. But the second time around, Paulson insisted, Einhorn was overruled, and the firm made Grubman a big offer: $25 million.

Luckily for Goldman Sachs, Citigroup's CEO, Sanford Weill, topped that offer significantly, and Grubman stayed where he was. Soon after, his employer paid a civil penalty of $400 million—by far the largest penalty paid by any firm in the "analysts case" where serious conflict-of-interest transgressions were uncovered.

■ ■ ■

John Weinberg and John Whitehead's service as co-chairmen of
Goldman Sachs had many dimensions. One of their most important contributions to their firm's success would prove extraordinarily
lucky—but only after they had both retired.

One day in the late 1970s, Whitehead learned of an exciting real
estate opportunity. Through his work with the Port Authority of New
York and New Jersey, he found an unusually attractive opportunity to
get a long-term lease on connecting floors in an iconic new building.
The firm would be able to consolidate all operations, which were then
divided among six buildings, into one location. Importantly, each floor
in the new space was wide open—ideal for the firm's increasing need
for large trading rooms—and the long-term rental was low. Since the
time had come for Goldman Sachs to rise up from its past custom of
having somewhat shabby offices, moving to occupy floors high up in
this major building would be a subtle declaration of the reality that
Goldman Sachs had become the international market leader.

As Whitehead began explaining to his friend and partner the
superb benefits of making this major commitment, he could see that
Weinberg was somehow not interested, so he turned to other subjects.
He could come back to the new office space a week later.

When Whitehead brought the space opportunity up again, he got
even less interest from Weinberg—so he again went on to other items
on their agenda.

The third time he raised the matter, Weinberg said, "John, you keep
bringing this up, but I'll never be able to support such a move."

"Why not, John?"

"I could never work that high up in a building with sealed win-
dows that I can't open. I'd get claustrophobia 90 stories up in the air.
Please don't ask. I couldn't do it."

"Okay, John. If that's the way you feel, we'll look for space in
other buildings."

Except for this fortunate act of friendship, most of Goldman Sachs's
people in New York City and almost all its senior executives would
have been near the top of the World Trade Center on 9/11.

II

SUSTAINING
EXCELLENCE

Chapter 10

Trouble

Excellence Challenged

The best indicator of great leadership—and of an organization's long-term intellectual and spiritual strength—is the ability to do three things at once: adapt to external change, sustain commitment to its long-term mission and values, and correct internal problems. Organizations are, after all, living human organisms, and even the best encounter troubles, as have all those celebrated in this book.* Great organizations spot troubles early and act against them decisively. Accurate, candid self-diagnosis and disciplined self-correction are often

---

*Even the idealistic, nonprofit Mayo Clinic occasionally encounters misbehavior. In 2009, suspicions of falsifying results centered on a Mayo research associate who had published 17 papers on his work with a molecule that appeared to show promise in treating certain cancers. Since results of experiments differed when the research associate was involved and when he was not, he was excluded from further tests. When the tests all confirmed the original suspicion, he was dismissed.

the hardest and surely the most important parts of sustaining excellence. "The key for managers and leaders," observed Capital's Tim Armour, "is to keep looking for the problems, striving to catch them at their early stages and taking preemptive action to reduce the pressure by making changes. But you do have to be good at figuring out what particular changes to make and how to make them."

The worst troubles are usually subtle, develop gradually over a long time, and, like termites, can be invisible to those absorbed in the compelling daily decisions of management. And of course, the easiest short-term response to problems is to put decisions off until "tomorrow." Leaders must have the will to manage for long-term results and the courage to decide on corrective action long before conclusive evidence has accumulated. So leaders must always be looking for trouble, particularly as the organization becomes larger, more complex, and has more competitors in more different nations, cultures, and markets where the vital expertise is always local.

■ ■ ■

The most startling news in McKinsey's recent history broke on March 15, 2011, when several hundred senior partners from around the world were meeting in Washington, D.C. They had already been concerned by reports of an SEC investigation of insider trading accusations against their respected friend and former managing director, Rajat Gupta. Now came reports that converted the accusations, which Gupta and his lawyer vigorously denied, from generalities to specifics. Worse, it was now clear that Gupta had known for nearly two years, but had said nothing to the firm, about $1 million a year in payments by the Galleon Group hedge fund to a McKinsey partner and Gupta favorite, Anil Kumar. While it was not clear Gupta knew whether Kumar had been providing insider information obtained while consulting with McKinsey clients, the payments contravened McKinsey's longstanding policy against any consultant taking money from a firm other than McKinsey.

Gupta had blatantly violated the firm's core value of absolute professional integrity—essential to its business practice of consulting to multiple clients in the same industry while assuring clients it would always protect confidential information. While he no longer did consulting work for McKinsey, Gupta had continued to use McKinsey offices and support services, was receiving substantial payouts from the firm as a former managing director,[*] and regularly identified himself as the former head of McKinsey.

Federal prosecutors accused Gupta of six counts of insider trading shortly after Raj Rajaratnam, head of Galleon, was convicted on 14 counts and sentenced to 11 years in prison, a $10 million fine, and a $53 million forfeiture of illegal gains. Among the allegations: Immediately after leaving a Goldman Sachs board meeting during the 2008 financial crisis, Gupta, then a director, had called Rajaratnam about Warren Buffett's still secret decision to invest $5 billion in the investment bank. Galleon quickly bought 217,000 Goldman Sachs shares, for a trading profit of $840,000. In another call, prosecutors said, Gupta had tipped Rajaratnam that Goldman Sachs would report a per-share loss of $2, not the $2.50 profit the Street had been expecting. This enabled Galleon to sell before the news and get out before the stock fell. While a director of Procter & Gamble, Gupta also told Rajaratnam in advance about P&G's sale of Folgers to Smuckers. Convicted on three counts of securities fraud and one count of conspiracy, Gupta was sentenced to two years in prison and ordered to pay a $5 million fine.[†]

Gupta had a substantial personal economic interest in Galleon Group: $35 million he had invested with Rajaratnam. (An economic interest is needed to make disclosure of insider information illegal.) He was also negotiating for a 15 percent participation as a general partner in Galleon International and had participated in fund-raising in the United Arab Emirates as chairman of a prospective Galleon fund.

---

[*]Gupta received $6 million from McKinsey in 2008 and was to receive $2.5 million in each of 2009, 2010, and 2011. He also received $700,000 as a Goldman Sachs director.

[†]Judge Jed Rakoff, before announcing sentence, described the 63-year-old Gupta's tip on Berkshire Hathaway's investment as "disgusting in its implications" and "a terrible breach of trust." Acknowledging that Gupta was a "good man"— letters of admiration from over 400 prominent people including Bill Gates, Kofi Annan, Deepak Chopra, and others had been orchestrated in a vigorous campaign by Gupta's friends—Rakoff continued, "But the history of this country and the world, I'm afraid, is full of examples of good men who do bad things." Gupta had refused to cooperate with prosecutors' requests for information and, refusing to plead guilty, had vigorously fought the charges.

The trial record showed that at 3:15 P.M. on September 23, 2008, Byron Trott, then a partner of Goldman Sachs and a favorite investment banker of Warren Buffett's, had received a call from the firm's co-president that Goldman Sachs intended to raise $10 billion of equity to signal strength to the capital markets. Trott advocated Buffett's Berkshire Hathaway as a "cornerstone investor" and flew to New York City to press his idea on how "highly credentialing" it would be. Buffett offered to buy $5 billion of preferred stock with a 10 percent interest yield and an option to buy $5 billion in common stock at $115 a share. (In late 2012 the stock was selling above $120.) Such a massive commitment by the world's most admired investor was sure to be, as Trott said, "a major, major event to Goldman Sachs and to the markets." Goldman Sachs's board of directors would have to approve, so a conference call was quickly arranged. The call ended at 3:53. Gupta immediately phoned Rajaratnam to tell him the secret.

Once it takes hold, an exceptionally talented person's compulsion that he or she needs "more" can be compelling beyond any reason, and destructive—self-destructive to the individual and destructive to an organization. As one anguished McKinsey partner said, Gupta was "acting in total breach of what everyone expected of him."

McKinsey promptly took three actions. First, the same day it heard the nightmare news, a senior McKinsey director went to the firm's office in Stamford, Connecticut, to tell Gupta that he could no longer use the firm's offices, facilities, car service, or e-mail or identify himself with McKinsey. Gupta was not contrite.

"*You* are out of line!" he exclaimed angrily. "The partners of the firm would *never* support you in this. You are *wrong!*"

Replied the emissary quietly and firmly, "The decision has been made and will be enforced."

Second, as soon as it learned of the allegations against Kumar, the firm initiated a rigorous law-firm review of its policies and practices that led to certain changes in policies, training, and compliance.

Third, Dominic Barton, the firm's current leader, spoke one-on-one—and usually in person—with the CEOs of over 100 McKinsey clients to tell them in detail what the firm was doing to rededicate itself to its core value of professionalism.

On reflection, McKinsey's leaders recognized that Gupta had gone through a series of changes over his many years with the firm. As an associate and then head of McKinsey's operations in Scandinavia and in his first term as senior partner, Gupta had been modest, comfortable with moderate affluence—and recognized as a leader on moral issues. But in his second term he had apparently bought into several younger directors' strategy of increasing profitability and making even larger payouts to the most economically productive consultants. In his third term, the drive for profits and additional payouts had become so strong that Fred Gluck, Don Waite, and Ron Daniel took him to task at a meeting in Hong Kong and insisted that it was hurting the firm. Gupta was not persuaded to change his focus on profits.

After Ian Davis succeeded Gupta as senior partner, most of the directors who had persuaded Gupta to pursue greater profitability were quietly eased out of the firm, and its traditional focus on professionalism has been steadily reaffirmed.

■ ■ ■

McKinsey had faced a major test of its client relationships in 2002 when Swissair, a core client in the firm's disproportionately large Swiss office, went bankrupt. While overconfident management was a major factor in the failure, McKinsey concluded that its lead consultant to the airline, because he was unwilling to ruffle his most important client, had contributed to the airline's demise by failing to state misgivings that Swissair's actions were not conforming with its strategy and by failing to propose convincing strategic alternatives. The consultant was such a strong solo operator and this one client was so important to him that none of his team members would dare act on their "obligation to dissent" or "speak truth to power." The firm could have let the blame fall on the airline's CEO, but McKinsey would not do that. Ian Davis, having led the firm's self-examination as managing director, ruefully recognized McKinsey's management failure in letting even a well-established senior consultant operate solo instead of as a member of a team. Business in Switzerland fell off so greatly that the firm had to reassign 100 of its consultants there to German clients to keep them busy. Fortunately, the Swiss business establishment recognized the firm's professional integrity in its refusal to blame, and in a few years the office's client base was rebuilt.

■ ■ ■

Sometimes problems are systemic and hard for insiders to identify or recognize as truly serious. In the first decade of this century, Capital's institutional division—Capital Guardian Trust, which serves pension funds, endowments, and other large clients—faced a perfect storm of simultaneous leadership challenges. Ironically, some of the troubles came from Capital's traditional strengths: absence of hierarchy and distributed decision-making power, respect for long-serving investment managers, and patient tolerance for relatively long periods of underperformance. Capital has traditionally favored contrarian investment positions, and the uncertain nature of long-term investment management often includes long fallow periods. So the firm focuses on the long term and cuts lots of slack for its senior analysts and proven portfolio managers. While investment results are measured frequently, the firm is deliberately slow to make judgments or take action.

For a group of hardworking, competitive people, gaining agreement that something fundamental is not working and has to be changed can be painfully slow. And flat organizations, run as partnerships of strong, independent thinkers, change their consensus slowly, particularly if people are in different locations, have many years of success behind them, and are busy with their own responsibilities. All these factors were part of Capital's leadership challenge—but only part. Another part was recent history.

Capital had produced clearly superior investment results in the late nineties. In a classic illustration of success leading to trouble, the institutional portfolio managers, who had recently been beating the market by a sensational three percentage points annually, made the all-too-human mistake of accepting the admiring reports of their prowess from investment consultants and enjoying the applause of happy clients. Also, bonuses at Capital are paid for superior long-term investment results. So since the two-, three- and four-year numbers were superb, large bonuses were paid out. With major increases in assets under management—attracted by the same strong investment performance—Capital's earnings surged. In investment management, as assets increase, incremental profitability can be extraordinary. At Capital, as a private company with widely distributed share ownership, shares and pay-outs to senior investment managers increased dramatically and led to a dangerous brew of complacency and overconfidence. All this made it easy for everyone at Capital not to see that the traditional disciplined process with which the firm managed its mutual funds wasn't being applied rigorously on the institutional side.

Major new accounts had been coming in from international institutions at a phenomenal rate—which should have been a warning signal but was seen only as good news. Business in Europe and the U.K. was particularly strong. Delighted, Capital's institutional investment managers complicated the always challenging work of establishing many new accounts by making a series of mistakes: accepting new accounts too quickly, relying on outside investment consultants to explain Capital's unique culture and unusual core concepts, not developing a strong professional relationship with each new client, and not making sure every client fully understood what to expect. To help with the need for more client communications, a new group of "investment specialists" were put in position, but institutional clients saw them as a weak substitute for direct, regular access to senior decision-making portfolio managers. Nor did Capital explain exactly why its recent investment results had been so strong, leaving the impression that future results would be at least as strong.

In an effort to accommodate large new clients—and their consultants—Capital's portfolio managers agreed to customize many new clients' portfolios. This soon led to a daunting array of individualized investment mandates for institutional clients: Europe without the U.K. for one client, *only* U.K. for another, only Switzerland or only Mexico or only North America for other clients, only Canada or North America without Canada and, in one case, a curious mix of Hong Kong, Spain, and Portugal. Customization exploded into over three dozen different mandate definitions. Everything may have looked fine as business expanded, but trouble was certainly brewing.

As Paul Haaga, vice chairman of Capital Research and Management, recently recounted,

Mandates proliferated as customers told us what we should do for them. Now, that *sounds* right—Marketing 101 says sell what the customer wants to buy—but for a professional service as difficult to perform as investment management, that's *wrong*. As mandates proliferated, we had "one-off" mandates all over the place. If you commit to doing just one kind of investing and you do the same work that you do best for each of forty different clients, that's easy compared to having forty different custom-tailored portfolios.

With a product line so varied, complexity multiplied and supervision—which should have been increased—got diluted. With managers increasingly called away from Capital to meet with prospects, clients, and selection consultants, internal communications on investments got attenuated. Administrative details and custom-tailoring the different portfolios distracted portfolio managers from their main job of making major investment decisions. Investment results were virtually destined to disappoint, but the booming business and compensation hid the underlying problems.

"Trouble creeps in slowly and stealthily," ruefully observed Jim Rothenberg. "In the complex world of investing, trouble is initially hard to recognize and in the very short run, very hard to prove. From 2000 to 2005, we were slow to recognize the seriousness of the problem." At first, underperformance was accepted as the inevitable "give some back" complement to several years of superior results. But as more months of poor performance went by, it became increasingly clear that Capital's institutional investment organization had serious problems that had to be diagnosed carefully and addressed directly. A painful series of lost accounts—combined with the stock market's sharp drop during the global financial crisis—also focused attention. That made it possible, even in Capital's decentralized organization, for strong leaders from other units to take up the diagnostic-remediation process and get significant changes accepted.

Several actions were quietly taken. Capital consolidated the wide array of different investment mandates considerably. Senior portfolio managers were retired—of course, with warm celebrations of their many past contributions—and executive responsibilities were restructured. Several analysts who had not been succeeding in Capital's loose-tight organization were terminated, and strong young leaders from the mutual fund unit were quietly moved over into positions of major responsibility in the institutional division. Operational disciplines were refreshed and enforced so the whole organization got the message that accountability would again be rigorous.

In any group of people, acceptance of change in the short run does not guarantee a deeper acceptance in the long run. Leaders have to be sure their followers fully understand why the change was made as it was and the expected benefits of the change. Changing the product line and changing people was matched with a refocus of the investment process, which had drifted away from Capital's traditional disciplines. Investment consultants and their institutional clients habitually monitor managers by comparing their portfolio's structure to the composition of the particular portfolio benchmark they are using. Excessive benchmark comparisons can cause portfolio managers to pay too much attention to the scoreboard instead of the game on the field. Over and over again, institutional clients and their consultants concentrated on how their funds compared to the overall market in returns and in portfolio structure (but, curiously, not in risk or volatility). They said things like, "Your portfolio is light on energy stocks and that's why it lagged behind the market." Almost inevitably, portfolio managers began looking at and even thinking about how their portfolios did or did not match the market or benchmark instead of always focusing on distinctive investment value.

In Capital's mutual fund group, there were no consultants digging into the details of how results were achieved, so only the actual investment results mattered, and the mutual funds continued to perform well. But institutional portfolio managers, trying to accommodate the consultants, were buying and owning securities that the mutual fund managers would shun. "I'm overweight chemicals and underweight oils," said a young institutional portfolio manager in an internal investment review session. He was stopped cold by a senior mutual fund manager.

Time out! Wrong answer—to the wrong *question*. That's not the way great investing is done. You either *like* a company's stock or you do *not* like it. Ignore the damn benchmark! Never "underweight"

a stock or industry and think that that's an investment decision. If
you're not positive on a company, don't own it at *all!*

That confrontation was the beginning of the end of the malaise that
had been spreading through the firm's institutional investing organization. From then on, managers were reminded to focus on the basics of
real businesses and companies, not the benchmark—and certainly not
on what investment consultants might be monitoring. Another "creep"
problem: In the mutual fund business, because of taxes, it's *not* okay to
take short-term profits. But in the institutional business—whose main
clients pay no taxes—it was okay. So annual turnover had been going
up from Capital's normal 20 to 30 percent of the portfolio to as high
as 100 percent, increasing the number of decisions fourfold. While not
unusual in the investment industry, that pace of turnover is *not* long-
term investing. This problem was externally invisible, but internally it
was considered unacceptable.

Capital's management is now grappling with questions about why
past troubles were allowed to develop. While no one at the firm would
declare victory yet, there is confidence that superior institutional investment results will again be achieved because the corrective tasks of leadership have been dealt with and the central importance of Capital's culture
and mission reaffirmed with appropriate discipline. Internal indicators are
signaling that Capital's institutional operation is back on track.

However, many outsiders have been slow to see it that way. They
remained in doubt because they were conflating other problems into
an overall picture of Capital's perceived troubles. Some were real but
not systemic. Some were indicators of past, not current, problems. And
some were reminders of the increasing difficulty of achieving better-
than-market returns.

For example, a 32-year-old fixed-income analyst had figured out
in the middle of the decade that the carelessly underwritten packages
of subprime mortgages being sold aggressively by Wall Street were
being incorrectly rated AAA. So Capital avoided them. "He put out
a clear, blunt memo on that stuff and we all stayed out of them. But,"
acknowledged Rothenberg with a wince of professional anguish, "we
did not take that insight to the next step. We did not search out the
second derivative consequences to examine all the other ways toxic

mortgage-backed bonds could cause harm." Since Capital did not go that extra step, it did not avoid investing in the banks that were so heavily exposed to those same securities.

In a simultaneous but unrelated problem, Capital's senior management will be challenged by important changes in the structure of the markets it relies on for mutual fund distribution. Brokerage firms like Smith Barney and A.G. Edwards have been acquired and merged into much larger organizations—Morgan Stanley and Wells Fargo, respectively—that have their own proprietary mutual funds. The new owners naturally want their sales forces selling their own funds. They also have different concepts of mutual fund distribution. After the market collapse in 2008, the banks' focus shifted to "model portfolios" designed by headquarters and containing a wide variety of mutual funds, exchange-traded funds, commodities, and other securities. As a result, American Funds' share of the business from its traditional stalwarts for mutual fund sales got sharply reduced—in some cases from a 70 percent share to just 20 percent. Simultaneously, high-volume individual stockbrokers split off from the major firms to go independent as financial advisers. They, too, cut back on their use of the funds managed by Capital.

Broader market trends also worked against the firm. Index funds and exchange-traded funds (ETFs) have been gaining significant market share in response to the accumulating evidence that the securities markets are increasingly difficult for active managers—even Capital—to beat. In addition to this long-term trend, investors have responded to near-term economic uncertainties by moving out of equity funds and into bond funds, which disadvantages Capital's American Funds, which are largely equity funds. While the overall mutual fund industry had returned to positive inflows in 2011, Capital's funds—even after outperforming two-thirds of its competitors—still have not.

Despite the important business problems presented by the changing industry structure, the firm's leaders' strategic priority has been on solving the professional challenges so Capital will stay centered on its long-term mission. Once again, it is acting on the belief that if the professional commitments are well met, the business problems will get worked out.

■ ■ ■

The multiple recent crises of Goldman Sachs were at least several decades in the making. Even further back—before the Great Crash of 1929—the mission of the Goldmans and the Sachses was to have their small firm accepted by the powers of Wall Street and to prosper by serving corporate clients with great care. All their aspirations were shattered in 1929 by the horrific failure of Goldman Sachs Trading Corporation. So, for Sidney Weinberg, the mission of Goldman Sachs began as a desperate struggle for survival in the thirties and early forties. The mission changed after World War II to gaining acceptance as a major firm in financing American business in the postwar industrial boom. Irreverent as he so often was, Weinberg cared deeply about integrity, ran a tightly disciplined ship, and was devoted to serving his corporate clients as the way to advance the stature of his still small firm.

For Gus Levy in the sixties and early seventies, the mission shifted, causing Sidney Weinberg to worry. It was still important to become a major investment banking firm, but Levy put increasing emphasis on profits from arbitrage, institutional brokerage, and block trading. And Levy had no fear of making extra profits through astute trading for the firm on market opportunities he discovered while doing business for customers. He increasingly focused investment banking on acquisitive conglomerates: Their dealings fit well with his strengths in arbitrage and block trading.

In the seventies and eighties, John Whitehead and John Weinberg brought the mission back toward Sidney Weinberg's focus on investment banking for corporations and building Goldman Sachs into a leading Wall Street and eventually international firm. Their mission was to serve clients so well that Goldman Sachs would rise to a leading position at each client organization *and* win more and better corporate clients.[*]

---

[*]One private aspect of Goldman Sachs's mission began with the Sachs family and was invigorated by Gus Levy and institutionalized under the Two Johns: philanthropy. Year after year, the partners of Goldman Sachs, as a group, quietly gave more in personal contributions and time for nonprofit board service and fund-raising than all other Wall Street firms combined. Those who aspired to partnership knew, or were told, that generous philanthropy was not an option; it was expected at Goldman Sachs. Today philanthropy continues to be important to many individual partners, and with such global initiatives as "10,000 Women" to help female entrepreneurs, "10,000 Businesses" to help small businesses, and "Goldman Sachs Gives" to organize substantial philanthropy, the firm continues to lead the financial community in this area—by far.

The firm's aspirations and standards encountered no sudden "light-switch" change. Before they left, Whitehead and Weinberg may have quite unintentionally launched the firm into businesses that were by nature destined (if successful) to be incompatible with the service-intensive, risk-averse concept of the business on which their kind of Goldman Sachs had flourished. They had committed the firm to becoming the global leader in finance, acquired J. Aron's commodities business, built up the bond dealing business, launched investment management, and increased profitability, capital, and the firm's prowess in capital-at-risk trading.

Bob Rubin and Steve Friedman differed from the Two Johns in significant ways. Both saw being senior partner as a job, not as a career or a calling. The firm was a vehicle, not a destination. To increasing numbers of partners, Goldman Sachs was important, but not *that* important. As Friedman later said, "There *is* life after Goldman Sachs." Impatient to increase profitability, they accelerated the pace of activity and empowered those with the drive and determination to make it happen.

Rubin and Friedman focused increasingly on changing the mix and pace of the firm's many businesses to increase profits and payouts to partners. Serving clients more intensively was still considered important as a means of augmenting profits, but client service was increasingly matched and even superseded by trading skills and capital commitments—deliberately taking market risks in bonds, foreign exchange, oil, and other commodities—and increasingly gathering and applying proprietary information. Numerous accomplished people were hired in from other firms and never learned to treasure the iconic values of the Whitehead-Weinberg era. Rubin was primarily a *strategic* leader and Friedman primarily a *transactional* leader. Friedman's leaving abruptly—during a loss-making bond market and without a plan in place for leadership succession—went a major step further in putting personal interests ahead of the firm's. Trading and transactional leadership—and increasingly visible and forceful power politics—were becoming dominant at Goldman Sachs.

For Jon Corzine, the initial goal was stark: Save the firm by terminating enough people to cut out a billion dollars in bloated costs—and trading out of money-losing bond positions. Later, seeing the investment banking agency business—doing transactions for others—as slow-growth, low-margin, and passé, his objectives became to expand proprietary trading for the firm's own account, make acquisitions, and go public. As Corzine twisted arms in the drive to get votes for the initial public offering, politics flourished and prospects for individuals to get huge payoffs magnified everyone's focus on self-interest. Even for those who had been almost romantic about the mission of serving clients, the real purpose had become clear: It was all about the money. Far too little attention was given to the "soft" values and protecting the primacy of the firm's culture.

Hank Paulson, a former relationship banker and a forceful, pragmatic CEO, kept the focus on increasing the independent strength of the firm as an aggressive, profit-maximizing global capitalist. He built up private equity investing, joined in hostile takeovers (a major change), and expanded asset management, technology, and trading while making more than 70 trips to establish the firm in China. Paulson's ability to play hardball showed in his leading the putsch of Corzine and later dismissing his promise to pass the baton of leadership to the others.

Lloyd Blankfein, skilled in sales, trading, and politics, had thrived in this era of transformation and was a creature of the new kind of firm that Goldman Sachs—and all its major competitors—was fast becoming: a profit-focused trading powerhouse that also did banking.* Blankfein's mission began with further increasing the firm's profitability and power à la the great J.P. Morgan—until the global crisis required refocusing his attention on defending the firm politically, legally, and in the court of public opinion.

It might have appeared that Goldman Sachs's mission in Blankfein's era had come full circle to the mission in Weinberg's era, but there had been a fundamental change. Weinberg had wanted to serve prestigious corporate clients and develop a strong business with profit as the *means* to the end of building a great firm. In his era, payouts to partners came later and were modest. Well before Blankfein's era, those two

---

*Blankfein's COO, Gary Cohen, had come up through trading with Blankfein, with similar experiences and values, so the firm's leadership did not have the advantages of balance at the top that it could have had with a banker as number two.

had been reversed: Build a powerful firm in order to maximize profits paid out to the partners. What insiders saw as a spectacular success,
as measured by competitive rankings, profits, and payouts to partners,
would increasingly be seen by customers, regulators, and government
leaders—and by the press and the public—as excessive and suspicious.

By stages, committing capital and taking risks in trading transactions had eclipsed long-term service-based client relationships at
Goldman Sachs and among its competitors. By stages, too, Goldman
Sachs and its major competitors had transformed themselves from
midsize national contenders to global behemoths striving to succeed
in every market in every country. To be fully competitive, decision
authority had to be dispersed from headquarters to the specialists who
knew each market best, greatly weakening enforcement of past standards by central management.

The dispersal to the distant perimeter of power—the authority to
make decisions, to commit capital, and take risks—was one of the most
important and least recognized changes in the structure of Goldman
Sachs (and of its competitors). In over 300 unique markets—in commodities, currencies, stocks, bonds, real estate, and private equity, and in
sophisticated arbitrage operations as a prime broker to hedge funds—
only "the man in the arena" could be sufficiently expert on all the
competitors, customers, regulations, and customs *and* on the capabilities of each person on his team to make the instantaneous decisions
needed to become the most profitable market leader. All these markets
are more competitive, more dynamic, and faster paced than ever before
and require more specialized expertise and capital. Goldman Sachs was
closer to being several hundred firms than one integrated firm. The
common denominators increasingly became not qualitative and "all
about people," but quantitative and "all about numbers": capital, risk,
and profit—particularly profit. The focus on profit kept increasing.

Taken together, the firm's complex, fast-moving businesses form
an extraordinary network of activities that enable Goldman Sachs to
gather and deliver to the point of decision a plethora of proprietary
information the firm can and does act on to make profits. The time
horizon for conducting business moved from years—even decades to
develop a primary relationship with a major corporation—down
to hours, even minutes to do a trade. The language of Goldman Sachs

changed: In the past, it was all about clients; now it was about accounts and counterparties, and the terminology turned toward locker-room crudeness.

Power within the firm had always moved toward those divisions that made the most profit, so power moved away from banking to trading. Partnerships and compensation shifted from the bankers to the traders. The identification of profits with particular trades made it easier for specific individuals to insist on being paid for the reported profit of specific transactions. And this reality had the inevitable consequence of shifting the focus from firm to individual—from *we* to *me*. Twenty-five years ago, 85 percent of the partners were bankers and 75 percent of the profits came from banking. Today banking is less than 10 percent of the profits, and a large majority of the partners—and both the CEO and the COO—are from trading.

Trading businesses are friendless. Success depends primarily on the individual traders. So moneymaking traders are free agents, while individual investment bankers or research analysts or securities salespeople are almost captives of the complex organizations they depend on and represent. They cannot easily leave and take the firm's clients with them. But traders can move overnight to new firms. So the competition for traders has become a "spot" market, and compensation for top traders has soared.

Trading, taking risks, and committing capital to make more profit became the driving forces within Goldman Sachs. Observers began to define the firm as an aggressive, highly leveraged hedge fund with an appendage in investment banking. Major transformational changes gained momentum: Geographically, the firm went from a New York-Chicago-London concentration to a dispersed global organization of several hundred different "market-facing," entrepreneurial business units connected by a powerful, centralized, level-by-level risk management and reporting system—so formidable it was dubbed "The Federation." The securities business was changing rapidly and Goldman Sachs was changing even more rapidly so its skillful, driven people could stay ahead of the curve of change and excel at making money.

Insiders knew the market risks taken, the many kinds of expertise required, the networks of information developed, the capital committed, the intensity of personal commitments, and the capabilities of the people engaged in every transaction. They *knew* that in the hyper-competitive markets of the world, they fought intensely for each and every million dollars. So sure and certain were the leaders of their self-perceptions, they could not give credence to the skeptics or challengers, particularly when they were consistently hostile.

As a business strategy, the firm's massive move away from exposure to subprime mortgages was both brilliant and lucrative. Of course it was silly to describe the firm as "a giant vampire squid," as *Rolling Stone* famously did, but absurd as the charge was, it resonated throughout the media and with the public. During and after the global financial crisis, angry Americans, having been badly hurt, were looking for someone to blame for severe unemployment, collapsing house prices, credit card debts, huge federal deficits, giant bank reserves—and no end in sight.

For all his extraordinary learning capacity, Blankfein's rise to leadership came without a personal need to fully understand the specific nature of each of the firm's many client-based businesses. At J. Aron and in Goldman Sachs, he had come up rapidly through trading and had learned to manage businesses internally and by the numbers, not through building long-term organization-to-organization relationships. He knew the securities industry was changing on many dimensions and principal trading businesses were rising rapidly—and even more rapidly in profitability—so he had recentered the securities business on the lucrative hedge funds and private equity funds. They were the largest and most profitable customers—and swift to take action on creative ideas. Blankfein had no great enthusiasm for the "old-fashioned hand-holders" in securities sales or research or investment banking. He preferred to work with executives who had come up with him and would agree with his priorities and his management practices.

Compared with the Goldman Sachs of 20 or 30 years ago, Blankfein's Goldman Sachs is huge, with 33,000 people and a trillion-dollar balance sheet. As the firm has grown in scale and complexity, the time horizon for management decisions has gotten shorter and shorter. As Goldman Sachs got much more aggressive and hard-dealing in its pursuit of maximum profit, it often appeared too aggressive *and* too profitable.

During the global financial crisis, Blankfein—one of the most capable transactional leaders the firm has ever had—had the toughest job any Goldman Sachs CEO had ever faced as a strategic leader. The firm made that job much tougher by not recognizing that when you're the world's leading financial organization with a reputation for exceptional talent, skill, and expertise, much more is expected—not on the hard, quantitative metrics on which the firm focused, but on the softer, qualitative dimensions on which clients, customers, regulators, the media, and the public focused. No matter how skilled and powerful it is, no firm can expect to continue being the leading firm unless it is the firm with the most well-deserved client and customer trust and public goodwill and respect.

People had long admired the firm's oft-declared values and its repeated best-of-class achievements and even its ability to create wealth—partly because the firm was and is known to be an absolute meritocracy and partly because Goldman Sachs people never flaunted their wealth. But the firm stretched and broke the covenant that all true leaders must accept: to be better in values lived by, in standards, and in integrity *always*—even when nobody is looking. While most Goldman Sachs insiders say they believe in the firm's first Business Principle, "Our clients' interests always come first," all too many customers, competitors, regulators—and past partners—wonder whether it is no longer a core commitment but has become just a principle of convenience. Of course, Goldman Sachs's long-term focus has always been on maximizing profitability, but the short-term focus on trading for "profits today" conflicts with "clients first."

As Goldman Sachs repeatedly demonstrated its ability to make money for itself, clients could react in two ways: one negative and one positive. The *negative* reaction would be: Goldman Sachs is good at making money for itself because that's its whole focus—but that's not always good for us, so we should try to avoid them. The positive reaction could be: Goldman Sachs is a superb moneymaker, so we should align ourselves with them and make money, too. Senior people at Goldman Sachs were confident that the positive view would prevail because that's how they themselves would have reasoned. But those with regular business dealings with the firm, still widely recognized as the most capable of all its competitors, judge Goldman Sachs not by what it says, but by what it does and what they see day after day. All too often, they experience tough "firm first" behavior. As Wall

Street cynics said, "If Goldman Sachs wants to buy, you don't want to sell, and if Goldman Sachs wants to sell, you don't want to buy."

The firm's senior executives were new to the disciplines of public ownership, the challenges of "retail" public relations, and the reality of public perceptions. Unsurprisingly, public opinion did not wait for complex explanations, particularly when snap judgments and sound bites dominated the media. While tolerated in less important firms, Goldman Sachs was pilloried for its inability to appreciate that its aggressive pursuit of profits and its extraordinarily high—and highly visible—bonuses were definitely not okay when so many other people were out of work or losing homes and believed Wall Street had been bailed out by American taxpayers.

The complexity of the global financial crisis was greater than any other market event in scale, intensity, speed, and impact. As a trading "machine," Goldman Sachs's operations for its own account were coordinated, aggressive, and successful at both controlling risk and staying close to fast-changing markets. As a result, it made more profit, took less overall risk, maintained more internal discipline and control, and suffered far less harm than competitors. (Only JPMorgan Chase came close in overall economic performance.) Yet no firm suffered so much loss of esteem.

When the firm had its first public stock offering in 1999, it somehow did not recognize fully how large a change this was from previous equity investments in it by outside institutions—Sumitomo Bank and the Hamakamea Trust. Many partners had thought of the change as primarily a way to raise more permanent capital so the firm could compete effectively with the huge universal banks that were increasingly coming into the securities business and throwing around their elephantine balance sheets. A second major objective was to be so strong financially that the firm could withstand major unexpected losses as it engaged more frequently in large-scale capital-at-risk commitments. Of course, a third interest among the decision-makers was personal: to become very rich.

Goldman Sachs found it difficult to be "public." Few partners had ever been directors of publicly owned corporations so they had little interest in or understanding of the potential importance of good governance. While the firm had taken in public capital and its shares were publicly traded and quoted, it did not reconceive itself as a firm owned by outside shareholders and accountable to the public. It was still run as a private firm to which public investors had provided extra equity capital. Initially, the firm was far from transparent in its reporting to shareholders, who legally owned the company. Its financial reporting was "innovative" in its restrained disclosures. In discussions leading up to the IPO, partners had been correctly assured that disclosure of information as a public firm would be far less detailed than was then being required by the partners. Goldman Sachs would tell its own story in its own words and numbers—the way the firm wanted to be seen.

Investment analysts found it difficult to understand how much of the firm's reported earnings came from which businesses, and this made it hard for them to forecast future earnings. In addition, institutional investors complained that too much of the total profits were being paid to insiders as bonuses rather than to shareholders. The board of directors was widely considered weak for a publicly owned firm, particularly one as complex as Goldman Sachs, and observers worried about the lack of a clear plan of leadership succession. And, like a private firm, Goldman Sachs continued to take care of its own people in its own way. When a top executive got into a major financial jam by borrowing heavily against illiquid investment positions before the 2008 market plunge, he was allowed to sell supposedly unsalable "lock-up" positions to escape a personal investment disaster.

Whether it recognized the nonfinancial consequences of its new reality or not, when Goldman Sachs went public financially it also "went public" in other ways, particularly in reputation. Press coverage and public awareness increased substantially—initially in tones that were close to hero worship. The firm's triumphs and successes had made good copy. Adulatory public and press attention that had increased as more and more of the firm's alumni took senior positions in government service flipped, in just a few years, from positives to negatives. Conspiracy theorists coined the term "Government Sachs" and columnists wondered in print whether the firm had too much power. Simultaneously, as the roaring bull market continued, payouts to top executives zoomed to record amounts—in some cases, more in a *day* than the average worker earned in a *year*. Outsiders increasingly wondered: Was it right for the people of Goldman Sachs to be paid so very much?

Then the global crisis hit. In the midst of all the misery, people on Wall Street—those at the center of the storm—got paid huge bonuses, particularly those at Goldman Sachs. With a series of transactions that, while legal, did not seem right, Goldman Sachs put itself on the defensive—and then mishandled its press communications, making suspicions much worse. The firm's explanations were either too arcane or too dismissive and sounded suspiciously protective.

Nobody was interested in hearing how much worse the crisis would have been for small businesses, families, and individuals if, instead of making the necessary markets, JPMorgan Chase and Goldman Sachs had retreated to the sidelines as did Merrill Lynch, Morgan Stanley, Citigroup, Deutsche Bank, UBS, and Credit Suisse. In the crisis, corporations, banks, investing institutions, and governments had compelling reasons to make major changes in their large portfolios and urgently needed to trade. So, for a bold, skillful trading organization willing to take risks and make markets, with almost no aggressive competitors, profit-making opportunities in the world's disruptive capital markets were extraordinary.

Many people found it difficult to accept that the Treasury's bold actions to prevent the collapse of AIG, once the nation's leading insurance company, had not been at least partly motivated by a determination to save Goldman Sachs, which was a major AIG counterparty. Conspiracy theories abounded, particularly since Treasury Secretary Henry Paulson—so recently CEO of Goldman Sachs—had made the major bailout decision. Even as suspicions of special dealing with AIG continued to surface, the government of Greece skidded toward a financial collapse. Reporters cited a deceptive series of complex derivatives maneuvers linked to a series of bond offerings that had been orchestrated for a multimillion-dollar fee by Goldman Sachs.

The mortgage meltdown did several things. It demonstrated how disciplined, objective, tough, and independent-minded Goldman Sachs was in its operating decisions when it got out of a large exposure to mortgages well ahead of the market's collapse. This astute move also showed how profitable the firm could be, particularly in comparison to its competitors. But it deeply offended the press, public opinion, regulators, and politicians that Goldman Sachs, having sold mortgage-backed securities to investors, traded against those same securities for its own account without telling investors. The firm argued accurately that each of its businesses was run separately and that it had no fiduciary responsibility to tell mortgage investors in one area of its business about its proprietary traders' later negative expectations for the mortgage market in another area of its business. Reporters didn't buy that. Nor did the public or politicians. The hostility escalated rapidly. Goldman Sachs had swiftly gone from an enviable position as the world's most admired, most respected, and most trusted investment bank to being hammered by political leaders and ridiculed in the media. Major corporations, institutions, and governments, while recognizing that no other firm has as much capability, increasingly indicated privately that they would prefer to do more business with other firms if they could. It got worse—and worse.

In organizations, the odds of someone misbehaving rise exponentially with increasing size, distributed decision power, and novelty of products, markets, and people. This was well known by Goldman Sachs senior management—Blankfein once observed, "I spend 98 percent of my time on 2 percent probabilities." The firm had to know from its own experience where to be particularly wary: new products like synthetic collateralized debt obligations or new people with new powers. The firm must have known that very bright, all-too-clever, self-centered fast-trackers were high-risk people needing extra-close supervision. But it didn't do what it should have done.

On April 16, 2010, the SEC charged Goldman Sachs and a 31-year-old vice president, Fabrice Tourre—a math whiz who called himself Fabulous Fab—with civil fraud for their roles in the offering of an issue of mortgages called Abacus 2007-ACI. The issue was backed by packages of marginal, almost sure to fail mortgages. The SEC cited "materially misleading statements and omissions" in the offering documents—in particular, not explaining that the portfolio had been jointly created by a hedge fund that wanted to sell the portfolio short while the firm deliberately gave the impression in the offering documents that the portfolio of mortgages had been selected by ACA Capital, a third party experienced in judging the credit risks of mortgages. In the transaction's "pitch book," 37 out of 65 pages were almost entirely about ACA and its role, capabilities, and organization. In reality, ACA's role was modest; the hedge fund performed the dominant role—and was *never* mentioned. The structure of the deal was highly complex, but the concept was simple: If the mortgages continued to pay off, the security would keep its value. If, on the other hand and as the short-selling hedge fund expected, homeowners started default-ing on their mortgages, the security would quickly lose value. Within just six months of the sale, 83 percent of the securities involved had been downgraded. Abacus was intended to be a house of cards and it certainly was.

Goldman Sachs denied the SEC's fraud charges and argued, among other things, that it had *offered*, but didn't *sell*, Abacus. But salespeople at the firm told friends that in truth there had been internal pressure to sell Abacus, and the reason sales were not made was that institution after institution refused to buy. In its submission, Goldman Sachs insisted it had conducted every aspect of its offering correctly and, apparently to overwhelm the SEC staff, submitted nearly eight *million* pages of docu-ments. Once again reminding observers that it was still run like a private firm, executives in the chain of command above Tourre were quietly terminated or transferred. There were no public hangings, and the firm insisted publicly that it had done nothing wrong.

Members of Congress were indignant and Wall Street competitors expressed surprise that Goldman Sachs had sponsored such an obvi-ously unsavory deal. Press coverage was extensive and unforgiving. Even if the Abacus saga wasn't technically fraud, and the SEC's case would have been hard to prove in court, was it in any way okay for a leading securities firm to be doing that sort of thing? To settle the issue so it could focus on future business, Goldman Sachs agreed to pay a record $550 million settlement to the SEC.

But the bad news didn't stop:

- Complex multibillion-dollar dealings with Libya's cruel dictator were yet another unseemly revelation. Driss Ben-Brahim, a Moroccan, had made partner and collected a bonus of £30 million in 2004 when he was key to the Libyan sovereign wealth fund's $1.3 billion invest-ment with Goldman Sachs Asset Management—an investment that was nearly wiped out during the financial crisis. (A $50 million fee to one of Qaddafi's sons, which some said was really a bribe, was appar-ently never paid.) Ben-Brahim left the firm in 2008.

- Goldman Sachs agreed to pay the SEC a $10 million fine and stop conducting investment decision "huddles"—meetings of analysts and traders gathered together to identify short-term trading opportunities in stocks that had a Goldman Sachs research recommendation for long-term investment. The settlement said that Goldman Sachs "engaged in dishonorable or dishonest conduct"—but added that this was not to be construed as a finding or admission of fraud.
- In a private placement of stock in Facebook, Goldman Sachs did as it had done before on other deals, taking better terms for itself than were later offered to outside investors. (On the subsequent IPO, the firm made a quick profit.)
- In September 2011, newspapers reported that Goldman Sachs had sent a long, well-documented bearish report on the stock market to hedge fund clients two weeks before that same report's existence became known to the firm's traditional institutional clients. This was blatant customer favoritism. The firm's explanation was at least artful: The report had not come from the firm's research department. Somehow, someone near the top of Goldman Sachs had decided that it was okay to have an important analysis go to some clients but not to others—and that it was up to the clients either to ask exactly the right question or to accept others' being favored by one part of the firm while they were left dealing with another part.
- In a Delaware court, the firm was criticized in 2012 for its role in advising Kinder Morgan, the biggest U.S. pipeline operator, on its acquisition of El Paso Corp. Later Goldman Sachs gave back its $20 million fee.
- While factually wrong in his accusation that Goldman Sachs went "massively short" in residential mortgages, Senator Carl Levin captured headlines at the televised hearing of the Senate permanent subcommittee on investigations. As the *New York Times* gingerly acknowledged later, "This isn't meant to say that part of the firm didn't go short—it did and the firm has repeatedly said so. But the suggestion that the short was a huge directional bet by the firm to profit off a real estate collapse may not completely stand up." The Senate report stated: "The problem isn't that Goldman went short and reduced risk—it's how this was done. To establish many of its

short positions, Goldman created new securities, backed them with its good name, and then strung together misleading statements to its customers about what it was actually doing. By shorting the way it did, the bank perverted the market instead of correcting it."

Like the famous monkeys, insiders saw no evil and heard no evil. And the firm continued to play hardball with the press—a game it was certain not to win. Clients and past partners wondered aloud: What's going on at Goldman Sachs? Where are the directors? How long can Blankfein last? When will clients leave the firm?

■ ■ ■

Even with all the missteps and misbehavior, Goldman Sachs remains the largest aggregation of talented, skillful, committed men and women ever combined so effectively into a powerful securities firm. It still recruits the most capable and highly motivated young people; is still the best place to learn the business; still has the strongest culture; still is the market leader in a vast array of specific markets and products; still has the largest number of important relationships with major corporations, investing institutions, central banks, and governments; still has the most effective internal communications; still has the best financial management, operating management, and risk management at all levels and particularly at the top; and still can get more complex deals done faster. And, of course, it still makes more money.

But qualitatively, Goldman Sachs is not considered by clients, customers, and competitors to be as fine a firm as it was 10 years ago. And 10 years ago, it was not as fine as it had been 10 years before that. Part of the change is because the securities business has changed, but even more is because the firm itself has changed. Now the firm would need to change again, and the changes would have to be qualitative and visible.

After nearly two punishing years of being behind the curve, not appearing to recognize the validity of the public furor, Goldman Sachs accepted that the SEC's fraud charges and the record-setting settlement paid by the firm gave substance to the aggressive pieces in the press and the hostile questions posed in the Washington hearings. At the

May 2010 annual meeting, undertaking an initiative larger and more public than any corporation had ever taken before, Lloyd Blankfein announced the creation of a major self-examination by a committee co-chaired by vice chairman Mike Evans, head of Goldman Sachs Asia, and partner Gerald Corrigan, for many years chairman of the powerful firm-wide risk committee. This Business Standards Committee would include 17 of the firm's most senior leaders, plus a distinguished Wall Street attorney and securities industry wise man, Rodgin Cohen of Sullivan & Cromwell, and former SEC chairman Arthur Levitt—but no clients. As part of the committee's extensive exploration effort, more than 100 partners led small study groups in examining every facet of every business for six intense months. In January 2011, the committee presented 39 specific recommendations. All were promptly approved by the board of directors and by senior management.

The committee's 63-page report was made public, an extraordinary, highly visible commitment to action. Its first page was devoted to the iconic Goldman Sachs Business Principles, beginning with "Our clients' interests always come first," and concluding, "Integrity and honesty are at the heart of our business. We expect our people to maintain high ethical standards in everything they do."

For a skeptical audience familiar with spin, the obvious question was whether the report would lead to vigorous corrective actions. Corrigan was determined to see it done. He had come to Goldman Sachs after 25 years in the Federal Reserve System, culminating in nine years as president and CEO of the powerful New York Fed. Genially Irish with a ready smile, he is a tough career public servant who earned a reputation as a man of integrity who gave no quarter even in past negotiations with the U.S. Treasury. Fifteen years before, he and John Thain had designed and installed Goldman Sachs' sophisticated risk management system, and ever since he had co-chaired the powerful, firm-wide risk committee. This position had given him great credibility with the firm's many traders; they knew they depended on that system for every major decision every day.

Recently Corrigan summarized his view of reality: "There is only one word to describe our business today—complex. Risk metrics and the information we need to manage risks are evolving quite rapidly. Over the past five years there has been a major change in our business due to quantification and computers." Then he turned from the industry to focus on Goldman Sachs: "There *has* been culture slippage. The industry *and* the firm are more short-term focused. The orientation is less about clients and more about the firm and current profits." Then he reflected, "All great firms go through difficult periods. The key question is whether a calamity is seen for what it really is and taken as an opportunity to self-evaluate and rebuild."

Phrases throughout the Business Standards Committee's report signaled determination to get things right: "fundamental recommitment," "not just can we, but should we," "making the firm a better institution," "transparency," "strengthen our culture," "focus on serving clients," "we must be clear to ourselves and to our clients about the capacity in which we are acting." The committee's primary organizational recommendation was to change the firm's structure to move mortgage-backed securities product distribution over into investment banking, where due-diligence disciplines were traditionally strong. For reporting purposes, the firm's three major business segments would be made into four with principal investing and lending clearly segregated. Securities services would move from investment management to institutional client services where it belonged.

Mike Evans, a Canadian Olympic oarsman who still looks the part, now chairs the committee tracking the implementation of each of the 39 recommendations.

> We get weekly reports on progress and meet every month for four hours to hear the progress on each recommendation and discuss ways to keep advancing and keep the pressure on. Some are already done, but some—like the new software required for pricing pre- and post-trading—just have to take longer. We intend to complete all 39 actions this year.

Regular reports on progress are made to the Federal Reserve, the firm's regulator that has several of its people full time at Goldman Sachs (as it does with all major banks), as well as to the board of directors and to employees. But no public reports on progress will be made until everything has been accomplished. The firm is not considering going public with progress reports any more than it went public about the quiet removal of those with management responsibilities in mortgages who should have stopped Abacus.

Recentering an enormously complex organization competing in dozens of markets with hundreds of products will be an extreme test of leadership. Regulatory changes will require many stellar individuals to accept significantly lower compensation when hedge funds and private equity firms are paying top dollar and are always looking for proven talent. Exemplary people who could never have been recruited away 10 years ago have been leaving—some promising young future stars and some with 20 or more years of developing expertise and strong relationships with clients. Others say they would leave if it were not for the money.

In publicly endorsing the committee report, Blankfein said, "We believe the recommendations in this report represent a fundamental recommitment of Goldman Sachs to our clients and to reputational excellence in everything the firm does." Setting aside the no-longer-credible assertion that each business of the firm was separate, Blankfein declared, "Goldman Sachs has one reputation. It can be affected by any number of decisions and activities across the firm," and added, "It is important to articulate clearly both to our people and to clients the specific roles we assume in each case." In private conversation, as he was about to leave for another trip to China to conduct a few more of the three dozen Chairman's Forum meetings he has been holding around the world to articulate the firm's commitments, answer questions, and give clients access to the CEO, Blankfein was clear: "This will be my legacy." Given the firm's bad press, he usually opens those sessions with a few self-deprecating jokes to acknowledge the problems the firm continues to have and to encourage people to ask their real questions.

Medical doctors make a clear separation between symptoms and signs. Symptoms are the signals we all recognize: nausea, aches and pains that cause us concern. We go to our doctor, get examined, and sometimes get a prescription. Usually, our doctor comforts us that the problem is not life threatening and we'll feel fine in a week or so— and, happily, we do recover. Signs in medicine are different. You may feel and look good, but if you have early stage brain cancer, oncologists recognize the deadly signs and know that you have only a few months to live. Symptoms for Goldman Sachs include a series of deeply disconcerting reports of past business misbehavior, sound bites from angry senators, innuendos in the press, and, more important, confrontations with regulators. What could be *signs* portending more trouble are a simultaneous loss of confidence by outsiders that Goldman Sachs will always treat clients as clients and the questionable insistence by senior insiders that the commitment to clients is as strong as ever and should be trusted.

Change on the scale that is now needed will not come easily or rapidly: Too many people within the firm have gotten used to and succeeded personally in the culture and with the practices of recent years, and many, many individuals and business units will have to change for Goldman Sachs to change. Yet insiders clearly know real change is needed and point to successes with past challenges—the collapse of Goldman Sachs Trading in the twenties and the firm's embarrassing role in the demise of the Penn Central Railroad in the sixties, its unsavory dealings with rogue publisher Robert Maxwell in the eighties, the analysts case in 2008, and others. Most maintain that the firm has always learned and has always come out stronger.

Goldman Sachs is important to America and the global financial system. The many superbly talented and ambitious professionals who work there will strive to get it right and keep it right—if only for its own benefit. But if insiders do not believe they each need to change and so "just check the boxes," how can Lloyd Blankfein achieve his stated objective? Nothing is more difficult in leadership than sufficiently upgrading the tarnished culture of a large, complex commercial organization to earn back the trust an industry leader always needs.

The firm has recast its public relations strategy and leadership, and the climate has been shifting in its favor. One small indicator in mid-2012 was an admiring report in the *New York Times* of how thoughtfully Goldman Sachs had created a delightfully engaging community of shops, stores, and restaurants around its massive new downtown headquarters building. Another was the report that senior partner Jim O'Neil was being seriously considered to head the Bank of England. Yet another was Lloyd Blankfein's taking a high-profile leadership position in support of the Gay and Lesbian Alliance Against Defamation. In August 2012, the firm got another positive: The Justice Department not only decided to close its examination of the firm's actions during the financial crisis; even better, Justice took the unusual step of saying so publicly. The next month, CFO David Viniar announced his intention to step down at age 57 after 32 years with the firm. To close observers this meant he believed the firm had weathered the storm.

Goldman Sachs continues to perform more skillfully in more areas than any competitor, but much more will be needed to rebuild its reputation. Doing so will first require that no more examples be found of Goldman Sachs breaking the rules or laws. Recognition of such a positive negative can come only with time. Second, the final report on specific actions taken to implement the 39 recommendations of the Business Standards Committee must be convincing. And third, surely the most difficult for a firm that feels a need to believe its own promises, will be to recognize that the iconic statement, "The needs of our clients always come first," can be promised and delivered only to its traditional relationship-based clients in such businesses as investment banking and asset management.

Most of the organizations Goldman Sachs works with are *not* clients. Some are customers—even important customers—but not clients. And still others are not customers but just counterparties. They should all know from experience which they are and what the securities business has become, and the firm should be clear with them—and with itself, too—about its responsibilities, limits, and promises. The most important step toward attaining the respect and trust the market leader must have is to give up unrealistic promises and stop asking for unrealistic credence. The next important step will be to implement the day-to-day behavior that would bring the recommended actions of the Business Practices Committee to life in the real world of transactions with clients, customers, and counterparties. The firm has a lot to prove. Surely it has the resources. Time will tell whether it has the inner values and the discipline to earn again the mantle of unquestioned leadership.

■ ■ ■

If leadership is not up to the challenge, any great firm can slip into the second rank—or much further. A dramatic example of self-inflicted failure of a once-great firm is provided by the many stages of the decline and fall of Arthur Andersen.

Chapter 11

Arthur Andersen

Excellence Lost

In the 1960s, Arthur Andersen & Co. was widely recognized not only as the best of the Big Eight accounting firms but also as arguably the world's most admired professional firm of any kind. Then, over 50 years, Arthur Andersen relentlessly descended through level after level of self-destructive decline to its ultimate death. How and why this serial disaster unfolded illuminates the importance of the essential success factors in developing a great firm and the even greater importance of sustaining excellence.

Andersen was growing more rapidly than any other major auditor. It was attracting the most talented young accountants and the most prestigious clientele because of its relentlessly high professional standards and its unique devotion to client service and continuous professional development. In its charismatic leader, Leonard Spacek, (pronounced *Spah*-chek) it had the most widely respected champion of consistent professional excellence. Spacek coined the concept, later adopted by many others, of the "one-firm firm" that adheres to identical policies and practices wherever it operates. Andersen was the clear industry leader in professional training, enjoyed extraordinary esprit de corps, ensured meritocracy in the distribution of decision-making power and compensation, and repeatedly made bold investments to build the firm. It was ahead of all competitors in showing how computers could improve the speed, accuracy, and usefulness of accounting data as managerial information.

Half a century after its founding in 1913, Arthur Andersen expected to continue to be the best of its kind. Instead, after a long series of compromises and mistakes that were invisible to outsiders, the firm's steadily accelerating self-degradation became increasingly visible. Clients and competitors perceived a series of fundamental shifts in the firm's priorities from leadership in *professional* excellence toward dominance by such *business* priorities as increasing profits and payouts to partners. The Securities and Exchange Commission saw in Arthur Andersen a pattern of unacceptably lax auditing of a variety of misbehaving client corporations and executive arrogance that precluded self-reform. When the management-consulting partners of Arthur Andersen broke away from the auditors in 2000 to form Accenture, they took the main economic strength of the firm with them. But the disturbing truth is that the decline and fall of Arthur Andersen was never necessary, began many years before, and could have been reversed at any of several stages.

Arthur Andersen was indicted by the federal government on March 14, 2002, for obstructing justice by destroying evidence in violation of a permanent injunction. Its remaining business quickly disappeared. Belatedly, the Supreme Court overturned the government's legal case. It didn't matter. As Andersen's decline accelerated, it became almost inevitable. A worldwide firm that had been the profession's gold standard would be destroyed from within, costing 85,000 partners and employees their livelihoods and contributing to billions of dollars of losses by investors. The nightmare decline and fall of Arthur Andersen is a powerful warning: The greatest challenge for every organization of talented people is not to rise to excellence, extraordinarily difficult as that surely is. The greatest challenge is to sustain excellence.

■ ■ ■

The firm had come a long way. As with all professional firms, the beginning was small and personal. In 1907, 22-year-old Arthur E. Andersen decided to leave his well-paid job as assistant to the controller of Fraser & Chalmers, a maker of heavy equipment that later became part of Allis-Chalmers, and take a temporary staff position with Price Waterhouse in Chicago at only $25 a week. His new wife was astounded, but Andersen, as always, was stubborn. By 1908, he became the youngest certified public accountant in Illinois and one of only 2,200 in the nation (now there are more than 360,000 CPAs). Ambitious to advance and seeing opportunity, young Andersen and Clarence M. DeLany agreed in 1913 to leave Price Waterhouse and buy the small Audit Co. of Illinois. It had monthly billings just over $1,000 and a staff of seven, not one of whom was a trained accountant. They renamed it Andersen, DeLany & Co.

Andersen said he wanted his firm "evaluated by the quality of services rendered [rather] than by whether we are making a good living out of it. If it is just a question of making a good living and the creative factors are absent . . . I have no interest in that sort of thing." He proudly spoke of his mother's mantra, "Think straight, talk straight." Bluntness, toughness, and accuracy would be enduring characteristics of the founder and of the firm.

Only months after launching the firm, Andersen had a conflict with an important client, an interurban railway. Andersen said its earnings had been distorted by deferring maintenance and insisted that the true earnings were far below what the company claimed. The autocratic president asserted that it was *his* company and *his* income statement. Well, Andersen insisted, it was *his* certification and there was not enough money in the city of Chicago to get him to change. That client got a new auditor—and in a few months went bankrupt. In another confrontation, a Great Lakes steamship line lost a ship in a February 1915 storm and wanted to use its prior year-end financial statement in a bond-offering circular. Andersen refused; the loss *must* be disclosed.

When the two senior faculty members of Northwestern University's accounting department quit to set up their own school and took with them the course that they had developed and owned, the university asked Andersen to take over and create a new course. He became a full professor in 1915. Believing the best students in his college classes could help him build a different kind of accounting firm, Andersen resolved to recruit only college graduates instead of the high school and commercial-school graduates favored by other firms. He concentrated on recruiting men of lower middle-class backgrounds from small towns who were graduating from leading Midwestern universities and were eager to better themselves by becoming professionals. He resolved to give them better training than competitors so they could deliver better service to clients and aspire to partnership in an open meritocracy. Other firms typically had accounting staff on a separate track from the prospective partners, whom Andersen scoffed at as "stuffy bluebloods."

Demand for tax accounting and advice increased when federal tax rates were revised in 1917 and an excess profits tax was added. In 1918, DeLany quit, and Andersen promptly renamed the firm Arthur Andersen & Co. During the 1920s, the importance of public accounting burgeoned as corporations converted to public ownership, mergers proliferated, the Federal Reserve issued guidelines for public accounting, and more universities taught more courses in accounting. Arthur Andersen & Co. steadily expanded, opening offices in New York, Kansas City, Los Angeles, and San Francisco. By 1928, it had grown to 300 employees.

The young founder disdained being "just another accounting firm" focusing only on audit and tax. "Bookkeeping is mechanical, while accounting is analytical," he said. He was committed to "business consultation," and the firm's services soon included designing and installing new systems of financial and cost accounting. Andersen created an "industrial engineering" group to focus on "investigations to show the strong or weak points in company position or management . . . and seek to . . . correct weak spots." This line of business flourished during the corporate merger boom of the 1920s but came to an end with the 1929 stock market crash. The impulse to help managers manage, however, lived on.

So that the same work would always be done the same way in every office, a Committee on Techniques began deciding in 1929 what the firm's policy should be on any new development in accounting. New hires began their careers with a pioneering three-week training program in downtown Chicago to immerse them in "the exact and only way" to conduct an audit. Consistency included a dress code. Andersen expected his men to eat lunch out so they could be seen as prospering members of the business community, and to wear hats: always felt from Labor Day to Memorial Day, always straw in the summer. While the hats disappeared in the 1960s, the idea continued of dressing to look older—and more like clients. As Leonard Spacek observed,

> [Arthur Andersen] was a great promoter and a very egotistical individual—an ingredient that has to be present in anyone that wants to get things done. He was very good business-wise, but he was very tough on people who violated his principles.

Spacek explained his own unusual ability to get along with Andersen: When we got into a difficult argument, I would say, "I'm from Iowa and can always go back there and plow corn."

■ ■ ■

Early in the Depression, bad news for a major Chicago business created good news for the firm. When the overextended utility empire built by Samuel Insull, head of the company that became Commonwealth Edison,[*] collapsed, Arthur Andersen & Co. was retained by the New York banks to serve as their representative. Because it had no prior relationship with the Insull companies, the auditing challenges were large and so were the firm's fees: almost 20 percent of the firm's revenues, by then above $2 million. This assignment became the engine of Arthur Andersen's great growth and, arguably, the seed of the cancer that decades later culminated in the firm's self-destruction. The Insull business established the firm in the utility industry and led to the development of its information systems practice.

That practice, which eventually grew into the consulting behemoth that transformed the firm, started from Leonard Spacek's recognition that public utilities needed managerial information that was quite different from the statistical data required by regulators. Even

---

[*]And formerly the key assistant of Thomas Edison.

back then, there were occasional tensions between the firm's auditors and its systems consultants. Spacek, then specializing in serving
major utilities, developed a pioneering functional accounting system
for Commonwealth Edison that enabled each manager to manage his
unit for cost-effectiveness. It used punch-card tabulating equipment. As
tabulating later became computerized, the firm would be the leader in
developing computer systems for management.

National developments also helped the firm thrive during the
Depression. The securities acts of 1933 and 1934 raised the stature
of CPAs and greatly expanded the accounting profession's role and
responsibilities. Public accounting's mission was transformed from
checking up on employees to enabling investors to appraise each public
company's earnings and management. In 1935, Andersen spoke publicly about the accounting profession's expanding role:

> Because accountancy is a profession rather than just another line
> of business, it must assume responsibilities which go far beyond
> those imposed by the business function alone, for it has long
> been recognized that the published financial statements of corpo-
> rations are clothed with a public interest and that the accountant
> has a responsibility to the public as well as to his client.

Andersen was an unrelenting taskmaster who worked even harder
himself, a personal value that became a core element of the firm's culture. It was hammered home to every employee that the client *always*
came first, and that it was not enough to put the client first from nine
to five on weekdays. Any firm could do that. "If it weren't for our clients, none of us would be here," said Duane Kullberg, who later rose
to head the firm, "so we never regard it as an imposition when a client
executive calls for assistance at night or on a weekend." While it earned
a reputation as a "hard work" firm, Arthur Andersen was also the first
to pay overtime to its staff, causing a competitor to complain: "Arthur,
you simply have to stop this foolishness. You're spoiling the accounting
profession with this damn-fool system of paying overtime."

Spacek said the hard-work culture was why he got one of the
firm's major clients: United Air Lines. In the 1930s, with airlines
struggling because the government had canceled their mail contracts,

William "Pat" Patterson combined half a dozen of them into United. As Spacek told it,

> Since Pat liked Chicago, he moved his headquarters there. He used Continental Bank as his primary source for financing, hired his lawyers, and walked across the street to our office. He didn't really know much about us, but we were the first firm listed in the telephone directory under "accountants," and the bankers and lawyers had told him we were a good firm.
>
> So Patterson walked into our office one Saturday morning and started strolling down the hall. I spotted him and asked what I could do for him. "Well," he said, "I want to hire an accounting firm. Are you interested in the job?"

Though a manager for only one year, Spacek promptly began working out a general agreement with Patterson. "It was a big job," Spacek said,

> and Arthur Andersen was very much impressed with the idea that our fees on that job were something like $2 million over a three-year period. Arthur always liked to see those fees rise, especially when it was for work that he believed would be of genuine value to the client. And back in the 1930s, $2 million was a lot of money. We did all this work in the off-peak months, and Arthur particularly liked that, too.

To increase its business during the Depression, the firm began a novel practice. In developing new business, it would absorb the costs of the extensive labor involved in evaluating the work of previous auditors and preparing for its own initial audit. "One reason companies didn't change auditors very often," recalled Spacek,

> was that it meant paying the new firm to redo what the company had already paid the old audit firm to do. That was one reason we decided not to charge for the first-time-through work. Another reason was that our standards were higher than those of other firms, and we felt we had to have more and better information. Even way back then, we were known as the highest-priced auditors, so we had to make sure that we provided the very best

service, and all of this time-consuming first-time-through work was one way we achieved that. It also gave us enough knowledge and insight that we were able to keep future costs down and keep our clients happy.

In 1940, the firm established a centralized training program to be sure every new man got the same training at the same time in the same place—a first in a profession where training was largely done on the job in local offices and could vary substantially. "It was a very rigorous program," recalled partner Ed Jenkin. "We had classes virtually all day and then homework assignments every night that could take four hours to complete. It was a great learning experience and by the time you finished, you felt that you could really do an audit."

Centralized training required significant investment by the partners, but as Spacek recalled, "There was no opposition to it because, as a result of that [training], every office got terrific personnel. We believed that fifty percent of the firm's growth came through our investment in training." (In 1970, the firm bought a former Catholic women's college in St. Charles, Illinois, and established the Arthur Andersen Training Campus, which eventually employed over a thousand people to teach more than 60,000 students a year.)

The firm held tenaciously to its insistence on accounting integrity. In 1944, Andersen stopped auditing E.I. du Pont de Nemours in a disagreement over how to report different kinds of surplus. DuPont did not want a "qualified" opinion; Andersen insisted on either a qualification or a change in the corporation's practice. One result was a *New York Times* article with the headline "Arthur Andersen Would Rather Be Right Than Auditors of DuPont." The publicity buffed the firm's reputation nicely.

After World War II, the firm renewed its tentative international expansion. Various previous plans had been put on hold by the 1929 stock market crash and the Depression, although in 1933 Andersen had agreed with a London firm, McAuliffe, Davis & Hope, to provide audit coverage for clients with overseas operations. To build connections in Europe and Latin America, a modest joint venture was arranged with Turquand, Youngs & Co., one of the predecessors of Ernst & Young, and the firm also linked up with a series of smaller, country-specific firms.

■ ■ ■

Arthur E. Andersen, the founder and still dominant owner, died in 1947 at the age of 61 after having been ill for several years. During his 34 years as managing partner, the firm had grown from two partners to 40, from one office to 15, and revenues had increased from $1,000 to over $6 million. But with his domineering personality, Andersen had failed to develop leadership succession. Over the years, he had identified a series of "crown princes" but then trashed each one, often after provoking a fierce argument. He had once hoped his son, Arthur Arnold, would succeed him, but the son said he was not interested. However, after his father's death, Junior tried in vain to claim ownership of the firm "by right of inheritance."

Only 39 years old when he succeeded Andersen, Spacek had a vision centered on professional excellence and growth. He could inspire confidence and commitment in others and was ready to lead energetically. The partners had been ready to liquidate the firm, partly because of persistent disputes between the offices in New York and Chicago. Spacek persuaded them to buy out the Andersen family for $1.7 million. This recapitalization was a major challenge; the firm's net worth then was only $1.5 million. It would take 17 years to complete paying off the Andersens.

To manage the firm, the partners initially agreed on a seven-man senior advisory committee with Spacek as the "administrative partner." Fortunately for the firm, given its many challenges, Spacek increasingly ignored the committee. "I decided it was easier to ask forgiveness than permission . . . and had no intention of letting them get in the way of my doing what had to be done." His first priority was keeping the clients; almost all were suddenly being pursued by competitors. Many had considered themselves clients of Arthur Andersen the man, so Spacek had to convince them to stay with Arthur Andersen the firm. "I can tell you," said Spacek, "those were worrisome times."

Spacek's second major challenge was to build the firm. This would require substantial sums that could come only from the partners' agreeing to accept lower compensation. Inspired by Spacek's vision of becoming a superior professional firm and his tenacious leadership, they did exactly that. (It helped that in those days, partners did not know what partners at other public accounting firms were earning.) Then and there, Spacek put a cap on partners' earnings and poured the rest—once estimated at 30 percent of partners' compensation—into higher pay for younger partners and into developing business. "We made those investments because we thought we had to in order to build the firm. We just kept on pushing." To tighten standards and make them consistent firm-wide, teams of partners and managers were selected to go to other offices and review their audits all the way back to the working papers. In the decade from 1947 to 1956, revenues rose nearly threefold from $6.5 million to $18 million and partners' capital sextupled—from $1 million to over $6 million.

"Even competitors acknowledge that the main reason for Arthur Andersen's success is that it provides superb auditing services," wrote *Fortune*. "The firm's ability to do this is attributed largely to its aggressive recruiting. Each year it sets out to get the finest accounting talent in the colleges and graduate schools. And it generally succeeds, by the simple expedient of offering the choice recruits more money." At the same time, the firm gained economic leverage by having more junior associates per partner than any competitor.

Spacek's specific drive was to get ahead of the firm's main rival, Price Waterhouse. Shortly before taking over, Spacek had substituted for Arthur Andersen at a New York meeting where Price Waterhouse's managing partner, George O. May, had cut him off and dismissed the Andersen firm as just a Midwest regional outfit that was too small to have a serious role in setting policies for the profession; policy would always be set by the major firms. Spacek decided to make Arthur Andersen & Co. a major firm, too. Since Price Waterhouse was proud of having the most NYSE-listed clients, Spacek determined to make Arthur Andersen even larger on exactly that dimension. He kept a personal won–lost list in his pocket until the day, shortly before retiring, he could announce with a grin: "We passed them today." He never realized that this drive for size would, with cruel irony, be a significant contributor to the eventual decline of his beloved firm.

Spacek's philosophy for growing the firm was that everything—the need to serve clients, the need to fulfill the firm's public responsibility, and the need to grow—was tied together. Recalled partner George Catlett, "He believed that you couldn't have the influence you had to have to do what needs to be done unless you had the power, and you couldn't have the power unless you were big."

"I've been asked for years how we planned our growth," said Spacek, "and the fact is we *didn't* plan it. We were very single-minded in those days—the forties and fifties and sixties. We concentrated all our efforts on developing our people, building two-way loyalty between management and staff, and providing whatever service our clients needed whenever they needed it—service that was so good and so responsive that our clients would never think of using another firm. It sounds corny today, but those are the things that really made this firm." Partner Robert Medwick recalled Spacek's summing up: "You do the right things and the profits will take care of themselves."

The spirit of unity and equality that Spacek fostered contributed to his ability to inspire his partners to sacrifice for the good of the firm. "Spacek's philosophy was that every partner of the firm was equal," said partner Robert May. "That inspired a lot of young partners to go out and build the business. The young partners were made to feel that they were a very, very important part of the business and as a result, they behaved that way."

Spacek pressed hard on professional standards, even when the firm lost several clients. He didn't mind losing them over principles he knew were sound. His public campaign for rigor, consistency, and fairness in accounting standards irritated other firms, but he kept at it in speeches and widely distributed publications, always quietly adorned with an image of the dignified double mahogany doors that were the emblem of Arthur Andersen & Co.

Spacek's willingness to shake up his profession was evident in a farsighted speech he made in 1957—16 years before the founding of the rulemaking Financial Accounting Standards Board. "Is our profession so impressed with its ivory tower position in the public mind that we are not hearing basic criticisms of our work?" he demanded. He proposed establishing a Court of Accounting to decide each accounting policy and practice once and for all instead of allowing what he believed were unacceptable differences of interpretation from one accounting firm to another, or even within a firm.

Today there is no place where agreement on basic premises or purposes can be argued. . . . The partners of our firm believe that

the public accounting profession is not in important respects carrying out its public responsibility in the certification of financial
statements at the present time. We believe that the profession's
existence is in peril. Until the profession establishes within its
framework (a) the premise of an accepted accounting principle,
(b) the principles of accounting that meet those premises, and (c)
a public forum through which such principles of accounting may
be determined, our firm is dedicated to airing in public the major
shortcomings of the profession.

Competitors tried to punish Spacek for making comments deroga-
tory to the profession, but without success. The firm became known
as the Marine Corps of accounting: scrappy and aggressive. Again and
again, Spacek insisted on consistent, rigorous professional standards,
and his insistence always began with raising the bar first at Arthur
Andersen & Co. Among numerous illustrations, one was the cost of
depreciating computers. When the firm decided—without asking
or wanting any client's approval or agreement—that while computer
equipment might last physically for 10 years (the "useful life" virtually
all companies were then using to calculate depreciation charges) tech-
nological advancements would make computers obsolete in just five
years. This unilateral decision to cut in half the useful lives of computers doubled the annual depreciation expense charged against clients'
earnings. Clients challenged Andersen auditors: "Who made you God?"
To this there was the one-word answer: "Spacek."
     The boss's intense style was widely accepted within the firm, but
not without some tension—and some amusement, particularly when
he bore down on things others thought all too minor. For example,
Andersen men were expected to wear white shirts and to stay out of
Cadillacs lest clients worry that their fees were too high. In an often-
cited 1954 "walk briskly" memo, Spacek wrote: "Everyone should
make it a habit to be busy all the time and avoid any appearance of
being inactive or unoccupied. When walking in the halls, walk briskly."
     Spacek's leadership had its greatest impact on the firm's two major
strategic commitments: international expansion and an early commitment to computers. Spacek was convinced that computers could be
adapted to business uses, not just scientific projects. Business would use

computers completely differently: a small amount of calculating on lots of data instead of a lot of calculating on a small amount of data as in scientific work. Recalled George Catlett, "Everyone else thought this was ridiculous." Undaunted, Spacek kept advocating computer systems and brought IBM its first major customer, Commonwealth Edison, an auditing client he virtually instructed to buy from IBM.

A major challenge was to convince his partners to put up the capital for the newfangled computers he believed the firm itself would need. He called the builders of the pioneering ENIAC computer. "I told them I had four bright young men whom I wanted to send down to work with them. I assured them that our people would do anything—cook the meals, wash the dishes, mop the floors—just so they could trail them around and learn all there was to know about computers." Those four were the best young professionals he had; he knew to put his best people where he intended to achieve the most significant change. Spacek allocated one-third of partners' earnings to financing the computer commitment known by some as Spacek's Folly.

Spacek explained how the firm got years ahead of other accounting firms in computer systems consulting.

> It grew out of our audit work. To perform an effective audit, you have to comb through a company's financial condition. Of course, the auditor needs in-depth knowledge of the client company's industry to bring any real insight to the job. So the auditor ends up knowing an awful lot about the company and he often sees lots of opportunities for improving the way a company does things. Dealing with those improvements put us in the consulting business in a very logical kind of way.

Spacek understood the risk that the nascent consulting business posed to auditing independence. He repeatedly warned colleagues, "Don't go overboard. Don't do anything that could possibly influence an audit." To prevent the development of "a firm within a firm," Spacek wanted to keep auditing as the controlling professional service of the firm. That was a battle that over the long term would not be won. Not developing a way of accommodating the two areas' different rates of growth or their increasingly different kinds of profitability would allow a relatively small problem to fester and become a major problem.

■ ■ ■

Spacek's strategy for international growth relied on joint ventures and representation agreements that increasingly challenged the "one-firm firm" concept and his aspiration for consistent standards. As he recalled,

> Things came to a head one day when Forrest Mars, chief executive of Mars, Inc., came storming into my office. That's the way he was: He *stormed*. He would also call you every name under the sun—but only if he liked you. One day he was in Chicago and, as I said, he stormed into my office, saying: "I want you to go to London and check on the work your people are doing for my company. . . . The service is lousy."
>
> "Now, wait just a minute," I told him, "it's the same service you get in this country and the same service we give everyone else."
>
> "Well, it's *not* the same," he said, "and it's *lousy*. When was the last time you were in London to check on them?"
>
> "I've never been there, but all of our offices provide the same service."
>
> "That might be the *plan*, but the plan is not working. The service in London is *bad*, and you don't know a damned thing about it!"

Chastened, Spacek agreed to visit the London office, operated by Andersen's British affiliate, to learn firsthand what the problem was. "I went there to see for myself," he said, "and he was right. The service *was* lousy." Spacek was kept waiting for over an hour. He then burst into the manager's office and told him he was fired. "Within twenty-four hours I had canceled a relationship that was more than a quarter-century old."

Spacek convinced his partners that they should build the firm's international organization themselves, characteristically asserting that the long-term survival of the firm was more important than the short-term welfare of the present generation of partners. While other firms grew primarily through mergers, Spacek opposed mergers that might bring in people with different values and practices who might dilute the Andersen culture. (Founder Arthur Andersen had made the point about auditing-firm mergers more colorfully: "They'll knock out the dents, paint over the scratches, and you'll never know exactly what you're getting until it's too late to do anything about it.")

To upgrade the European operation, Spacek concentrated recruiting at Oxford and Cambridge and paid boldly above-market rates. Elsewhere in the world, local nationals were recruited at local universities, trained at the firm's U.S. education center, and promoted on merit, including advancement to partnership as equals, a significant innovation in a profession that still tilted toward headquarters-bred partners. The firm had already been the first to recruit actively at black colleges and universities. In another crucial separation from convention, the whole firm shared in one worldwide profit pool rather than having country-by-country or even office-by-office differences.

After the Korean War, Arthur Andersen affiliated in East Asia with SGV, a 10-year-old firm run by a Filipino who had studied in America and styled his firm as closely as possible after Arthur Andersen. Thirty years later, the two firms would combine. During the sixties, Andersen opened 51 new offices, 31 outside the United States. Looking back, Spacek observed: "We didn't set out to be the biggest firm in the world. All we wanted to do was to make sure our clients who were moving overseas got the same kind of service from us there that they had become accustomed to here."

■ ■ ■

With his solid understanding of what it always takes to succeed in professional services, Spacek said with prescience:

> The day a professional takes his eye off the client and starts worrying about growth and profits and all that is the day he will begin to fail. Do the best you can all the time for every client everywhere, and you're bound to succeed. There's no other way.

Because of his long record of successful leadership, charismatic personality, and client-centered vision of professional excellence, Leonard Spacek could manage the expansion and international dispersion of the firm *and* overcome the inevitable inefficiency of a partnership organizational structure. But he failed to recognize or deal with the firm's inability to continue to excel without him. He had not developed an effective organizational structure to manage successfully the ever-larger, fast-growing firm that Arthur Andersen & Co. had become during his 16 years of leadership. By the end of Spacek's era in 1963, the firm had become too large for any other leader to manage and lead within the traditional partnership structure.

Spacek turned management responsibilities over to Walter Oliphant on December 1, 1963, the golden anniversary of the firm's founding. Wally Oliphant was well liked but could not provide the strong leadership the firm needed. This was the first major step in the firm's long-term decline.

Serious unnoticed differences were soon developing within the firm. The geographic, regulatory, and local business differences within the global enterprise were significant. Differences within the expanding data-processing-systems consulting practice—for example, disputes over tape versus disc storage in the design of computer systems—developed between New York and Chicago and echoed the increasing New York versus Chicago differences in auditing. While major efforts were made to resolve specific issues, the New York–Chicago and the auditing–consulting tensions would morph over time into confrontational territorial divisions within the firm: a major step down.

The firm was simply expanding rather than healthily growing—steadily getting larger and larger but not getting better and better. While Oliphant made adjustments to accommodate the consultants, his defensive moves actually led to still greater divisions. In 1964, the firm had stopped requiring consultants to work for at least two years in auditing. Later, consultants were no longer required to complete audit training—another step down. In 1971, with consulting growing much more rapidly than auditing and developing business with non–audit clients, the tensions were serious enough that the then–managing partner tried to bridge the widening gap by putting an audit partner in charge of consulting. It didn't work. The step-by-step decline of Arthur Andersen was accelerating.

Disruptive external changes came, too. A harbinger of future difficulties suddenly surfaced in 1968: litigation. The first lawsuit was small and settled out of court, but it was disturbing to partners, as well it should have been. Major lawsuits against public accounting firms in America would increase rapidly: 71 in 1970, 140 in 1971, 200 in 1972. Lawsuits always came from disputes over auditing, not consulting. The firm was shamed when one of its audit clients, Four Seasons Nursing Centers of America, collapsed into bankruptcy after perpetrating a massive fraud. Paying out big settlements was embarrassing evidence that Arthur Andersen auditing was no longer the assured gold standard. The firm had been accommodating clients and somehow allowing business "realism" to eclipse auditing professionalism.

In the early 1970s, sales of new computer systems suddenly declined in the United States for the first time, temporarily masking the need to deal with the consulting versus auditing problems in the United States *and* justifying a major international expansion of the systems consulting business. With inadequate attention, the organizational problem of auditing versus consulting became both globalized and more deeply rooted.

During the same period, the environment for public accounting firms continued to change in unfavorable ways. Ambitious young professionals were wooed by competing businesses like management consulting or investment banking, driving compensation costs up. Worse, auditing firms began competing for business primarily on the basis of price since clients increasingly considered audits an undifferentiated commodity service. Arthur Andersen was no longer seen as sufficiently different to warrant premium pricing for its services.

Harvey Kapnick, an organizational "bantam rooster" willing to take on all comers, was elected firm leader in 1972. Three years later he raised eyebrows by taking the "corporate" titles CEO and chairman. Kapnick swiftly opened an office in Moscow, published an annual report on the firm (audited by a competitor), produced a pro forma financial statement of the U.S. government, sued the SEC, and reorganized the firm into a new structure, a Société Cooperative based in Geneva, Switzerland. This structural innovation helped with the problems of being both international and "national" in many different countries, but its high cost coincided with partners' earnings not keeping up with inflation. Kapnick also established a high-profile independent Public Review Board to monitor the firm's professional policies and practices. Anxious to hobnob with famous people, he appointed former British prime minister Edward Heath; William Casey, a former chairman of the SEC and future head of the CIA; and Donald Jacobs, dean of the Kellogg School of Business at Northwestern University.

Obsessed with his need for power, stature, and wealth, Kapnick drove the firm to be "both bigger and better than any competitor" and declared that the "only acceptable criterion is excellence and the only acceptable outcome is success." But his bold initiatives could not overcome the increasing difficulties of maintaining the firm's standards and its one-firm "oneness" as it got larger, more complex, and more diverse. His leadership style added to the problem. His organizational skills were more than offset by what partners saw as self-centered, authoritarian behavior. Among other things, he sometimes commanded partners to cancel complex overseas trips on short notice to work immediately on a specific task described as "vital" and "urgent," and then casually deferred any decision on the matter.

The fast growth of the firm was challenge enough, but Arthur Andersen was also struggling with a serious strategic schism. The systems consulting business that had once required significant cash investment was now gaining strength versus auditing. It was growing more rapidly, earning higher profit margins, and doing more exciting work for more senior executives at client organizations. The firm's size made it all too easy to focus on the economic numbers, not on the traditional professional values, and size magnified the challenges to personal communications and consensus building. The one-firm firm was increasingly dividing into two firms with two very different businesses on two different trajectories in two increasingly different professions with different values, norms, and cultures.

Tensions reflecting the real differences between audit and consulting were exacerbated by the firm's historical structures. Audit and tax partners still dominated the partnership, filling the important positions of office and regional managers and the board of partners where policy, strategy, and compensation were decided. While consulting partners were *earning* more for the firm, auditing partners were *paid* more—a lot more. Audit partners had made all the enabling investments over the years to develop the consulting practice and so felt they deserved good returns on their large past investments. Consulting partners had developed the more successful practice and so felt *they* deserved more of the profits they were producing. What each group saw as fair was seen as very *un*fair by the other—another major step down. At a partners meeting, one of the senior partners rose to observe bluntly: "Relations are bad and getting worse. It has to stop—right now!"

The business-versus-profession tensions worried both partners and regulators. The SEC, as designated watchman over firms that audit public companies, increasingly focused on conflicts of interest: Auditing firms increasingly often had large, lucrative consulting contracts that might impinge upon their independence as auditors. Arthur Andersen was not only the leading auditing firm; it also had by far the largest consulting business.

Wanting to realize the growing market value of the IT consulting unit, Kapnick worked to convince his partners that either government regulation or a mandated separation of auditing from systems consulting—or both—was becoming inevitable. He decided to initiate a meeting with SEC Chairman Harold Williams to prompt the SEC to force a split-off of consulting. While the SEC had no interest in requiring such a separation—and said so—Kapnick reported to his partners that the agency was unequivocally determined to force a separation. After some preliminary discussion of strategic alternatives with a few senior colleagues—but with no advance discussion with the overall partnership that had assembled from offices around the world—he put his idea for a split-up on the agenda for the annual worldwide partners meeting in 1979. Kapnick declared that the firm had only two choices: Drastically shrink the consulting business or separate consulting from tax and audit. Assuming he would have solid support from the leaders in consulting and from his board of partners, Kapnick thought he had the votes. He was wrong.

Kapnick proposed "turning one great firm into two great firms" by spinning off the consulting practice into a "separate but related firm"—with himself as head of both. Partners protested from the floor, and for the first time in the firm's history a secret ballot was called for. The audit and tax partners weren't about to let the consulting business go after all they had invested in building it. Even some consulting partners were opposed.

Kapnick did not appear determined to press his proposal, and later in the meeting he was elected to another four-year term. But appearances were deceiving. The calm lasted only a few weeks. When they realized Kapnick was still determined to split up the firm, powerful auditing partners decided to force him out. Meeting privately in Manhattan, they sent a delegation to Kapnick with a written statement: He no longer had the support of the partners because he was not committed to the combined firm and therefore should resign. "Absolutely not!" declared Kapnick. He quickly sent a telex to all partners saying he had been asked to quit and had refused—and called a special partners meeting for December. The rebellious partners called for a partners meeting to be held even earlier. Soon realizing he had no choice, Kapnick resigned on October 14, 1979. One result of this series of events—and another step down—was the establishment of a rather complex, multistage, several-month process for selecting new firm leaders.

The inherent difficulties of managing a professional partnership expanded geometrically as the number of partners increased. In 1980, Arthur Andersen had over 1,000 partners and a staff of over 18,000. During the next 20 years the scale of the firm increased further by more than three times. New people were added far more rapidly than they could be taught "our way of doing things" or could internalize the firm's values and culture. The partners joked nervously about how many offices they'd never visited and about how many partners they didn't know. In a conflict within audit that became known as Merchants versus Samurais, the auditors divided into two groups: Samurais devoted to high professional standards and protecting the firm's reputation versus Merchants focused on maximizing revenues and profits. When the salience of professional excellence is challenged by commercialism, the "realistic" business arguments are easily made and documented, while fidelity to professional values is abstract and based on a faith that disbelievers often cannot—or say they cannot—understand.

■ ■ ■

All major accounting firms were going through similar stresses for similar reasons, but the partners of Arthur Andersen were more seriously distressed by the pressures of size and the loss of true "partnership." They had higher expectations of themselves and their firm. A culture built on the will to excel *needs* to excel. Inability to compromise, to accept less than the best, is the penalty of professional leadership.

As the problems with size became more severe, the firm attempted to respond by adding new dimensions to its structure. To control the quality of service, to ensure fairness in compensation, and to open the channels of communication so everyone could be heard, coordinating committees, practice committees, compensation committees, operating committees, and strategic planning committees were formed, staffed, and began to meet—adding to the firm's complexity and inviting politics to flourish. Another step down.

Duane Kullberg became managing partner in the winter of 1980 and, trying to recapture the firm's values, changed corporate titles like CEO back to partnership designations; initiated informative meetings for retired partners; created a long-term capital plan to ease the financial burden on young partners; made it possible for senior partners to withdraw capital if dictated by personal circumstances; and worked to develop consensus before taking action. He also led a fee increase, which partners applauded. Kullberg recognized the main challenge to his leadership: "The good news is that we have a large, fast-growing consulting unit; the bad news is that we have a large, fast-growing consulting unit."

In 1985, in a major departure and a further source of difficulties, SGV Group was merged into Arthur Andersen, abruptly adding 3,000 new people, making the firm the leader in Southeast Asia and adding substantially to the firm's scale and to geographic and cultural differences.

With upward pressures on salaries for staff, its main cost, and downward pressure on fees as clients came to see audit services as undifferentiated commodities, auditing's profitability got steadily squeezed. Lawsuits over accounting issues grew more numerous and settlements larger—which encouraged even more lawsuits, increasing the cost of liability insurance. Another increase in costs came with the Supreme Court's decision that lawyers and accountants could advertise.

In contrast to its auditor-dominated organizational power structure, the firm's economics were increasingly driven by consulting's growth and profitability. In systems consulting, the Arthur Andersen name went from a sales asset to a liability as the sober conservatism of auditing the past conflicted with the image of designing innovative computer systems to capitalize on opportunities in the future. Different growth rates and different levels of profitability continued to command attention, particularly among the consultants. As Kapnick observed, "The culture changed. If you were an auditor, you were relegated to second-class status. If you were a consultant, you were on top of the heap."

Senior consulting partners met separately in 1987 and agreed to discard the awkward old name Management Information Consulting Division and rebrand themselves as Andersen Consulting. (They later also discarded the symbolic mahogany doors and adopted an orange globe as their logo.) The following year, partners received and angrily rejected a surprise takeover offer for the consulting business. The former head of Andersen Consulting, Victor Millar, had left the firm in 1986 to join Saatchi & Saatchi and in the winter of 1988 proposed the acquisition. The response from Andersen was magisterial: "Neither the firm nor any segment of the firm is for sale." But the seed had been planted.

Kullberg asked a group of partners to propose a "fair to all" solution to the increasing battle between consulting and auditing. This task force was dominated by audit partners who naturally believed audit should continue to dominate firm leadership. It proposed to set up two separate but revenue-sharing business units—Andersen Consulting and Arthur Andersen—under an umbrella organization called Andersen Worldwide, with two separate strategies and two separate operations. Both sides would report to Kullberg and a new board of 24 partners—8 from consulting and 16 from auditing. Profit participation would be based on the economic performance of each unit, but partners would be guaranteed at least 85 percent of the average of the two units—a proposition that seemed uncontroversial but became increasingly significant as consulting earnings continued to grow much more rapidly.

Kullberg put three strong partners in charge of professional standards, but they never had the absolute authority that had previously resided with a single partner, George Catlett, who had retired in 1980. Later, while the Professional Standards Group remained in Chicago, the managing partner's office moved to New York City. Quick, decisive action on questions of standards was no longer a firm priority.

Three hundred consulting partners met in 1989 to discuss what to do about their big issues: not controlling their own destiny, their problems with an auditing-firm image, and the increasingly large annual transfer payments being made from consulting to auditing. Consulting revenues had grown 33 percent in 1988, more than double auditing's 14 percent gain. Tensions continued to increase. Given the stress and strain of trying to rebuild the firm's structure and culture, it was not surprising that Kullberg resigned two years before the end of his term. He was succeeded by another audit partner, Lawrence A. Weinbach from New York.

Larry Weinbach eliminated the worldwide profit pool—an important bond for partnership because it had put everyone in the same boat—and created profit centers around the world. "It seemed innocuous," said one partner, "but it was most influential because it caused a significant change in the culture." Profit center measurement and rewards encouraged an increasing focus on economics. "The nineties were a go-go period in which the mentality was if you weren't getting rich, you were stupid," observed Kullberg sardonically. "I think that way of thinking had permeated Arthur Andersen." In a drive to increase profits, experienced audit partners were purged and additional revenues were sought by selling clients more services, some of questionable value. Operating costs were cut while fees were increased, producing much higher payouts per partner and the inevitable corollary: dulling down auditing standards. The decline was further accelerating.

In 1992, the Professional Standards Group was, for the first time, overruled in response to pressure from clients: Stock options would *not* need to be expensed. Caving in on this issue was particularly significant because a decade later, regulators and investors, led by Warren Buffett, would agree that options were of course an expense and should be charged against earnings when granted. Spacek would have been amazed by his firm's willingness to compromise professional principles for business benefits, but few then at the firm recognized it for what it was: another major step downward.

An acrid example of reaching for profits was the firm's curious involvement with John DeLorean, the flamboyant ex–GM executive.

Destined for a spectacular failure, DeLorean was dazzling en route: jet-setting with model Christina Ferrare and charging off such personal items as his houseboy and a pair of Mercedes-Benzes he bought for his and her use. Dick Measelle, son of an autoworker, had been in Arthur Andersen's Madrid office for several years before transferring back to Detroit in 1972. When he was called upon to confront DeLorean about those expenses, which DeLorean's own CFO thought were inappropriate, Measelle declared that they were okay—and kept the high-profile account. Later, DeLorean went bankrupt, was charged with (though eventually acquitted of) trying to buy $24 million of cocaine, and tried for fraud and racketeering over a scheme to abscond with $17 million. As DeLorean's auditor, Arthur Andersen settled lawsuits in Britain for $62 million and was barred from auditing British government contracts for 12 years. As another indicator of the loss of firm standards, Measelle's involvement with DeLorean did remarkably little harm to his career at the firm. In 1987, he became head of the U.S. audit practice, and in 1989, CEO of Arthur Andersen & Co.

■ ■ ■

The accelerating change in leadership tone and policies had become pervasive by the 1989 annual meeting, which bore the theme "Keep Raising Revenues." A live tiger was paraded as the hokey symbol of aggressiveness with the admonition that the tiger's eyes "seize opportunity and focus on the kill." The stunt was representative of basic changes increasingly being brought to Arthur Andersen by Measelle and others. Under Spacek and Andersen, subordinates had always been celebrated for *any* accounting error found or questioned, but under Measelle, everybody soon knew that a junior's questioning a partner would be seen as insubordination.

In 1997, the number of partners reached 2,800 and revenues totaled $10 billion. George Shaheen, the charismatic head of Andersen Consulting, was set to head Andersen Worldwide. But at the last minute, the terms were changed to require his acceptance of a CFO and a COO from auditing. He refused. James Wadra, a tax specialist and head of the London office, was then put forward, but he got only 51 percent of the vote, not the required two-thirds.

Shaheen was again nominated, but this time he got only 63 percent, so Wadra was made head of Arthur Andersen and Shaheen continued as head of Andersen Consulting.

Angry, Shaheen got a legal opinion on the ownership of Andersen Consulting. The lawyers said it was owned by auditing partners but with certain obligations to Andersen Worldwide that included rules to keep auditing from competing against consulting. Andersen Consulting partners then voted unanimously to break away. As required in the partnership agreement, they filed for arbitration with the International Chamber of Commerce, asserting that by competing for minor systems-consulting business, Arthur Andersen had nullified the 1977 agreement that would have required consulting to pay 1.5 times its revenues—or $14.6 billion—to gain its independence.

In 2000, Andersen Consulting offered to pay $2 billion to separate—over $1 million to each audit partner—but Wadra turned this down immediately. He estimated the value of Andersen Consulting to be at least $25 billion. The divorce went to arbitration. The arbitrator, Guillermo Gamba of Colombia, who had little experience in such matters, somehow set the breakup valuation of Andersen Consulting at only $1 billion. That was all that the consultants paid to leave and set up their own firm, Accenture.

Meanwhile, at Arthur Andersen, cutting out less productive audit partners and raising fees combined to boost the average partner's earnings from $130,000 in the early 1980s to almost $450,000 in 2000, nearly catching up with the consultants. The driving force was clear: business economics. The firm's annual report stated: "Clients that were either not growing or unprofitable were culled, saw fee increases, or were switched to an alternative service delivery model." Another increasingly common way to increase revenues was for the auditing firm to take on work that clients had previously done themselves, such as internal auditing. This was done with Enron.

■ ■ ■

Serious observers may worry about auditing independence when auditors frequently golf and dine with clients, but the simplest challenge to independence is the most obvious: Auditors' income depends on clients continuing to be clients. Friendships make true independence and objectivity difficult when needed most; economic dependency is much worse. Andersen had been InterNorth Inc.'s auditor when it merged with Houston Natural Gas in 1985 to create Enron. Andersen auditors and Enron executives soon developed unusually close relationships at every level. Together they went skiing, golfing, partying, and to Astros games at Enron Field. Many key people on Enron's financial staff were Andersen alums and many still at Andersen had high hopes for a future job at Enron.

Even more compelling were the fees Enron paid: $58 million in 2000—and sure to increase. Andersen had taken over internal auditing in 1994 as part of a five-year, $18 million contract. If these fees were large for Andersen, they were very large for its Houston office, and very, very large for the partners directly involved, particularly if they put their own interests ahead of the firm's as they increasingly most certainly did.

The Enron–Andersen relationship had become too important, particularly to the Houston office and very particularly to David Duncan, the partner whose position within the firm was being so favorably lifted by all that fast-growing business with Enron. Duncan, who had joined Andersen straight out of Texas A&M, made partner at 37 in 1995 and took over the Enron account in 1997. As a sign of his promise, he was named to Andersen's strategic advisory committee. He worked with Enron's chief accounting officer, an Andersen alumnus and increasingly his companion in and out of the office. Whether or not developing such friendships was premeditated by the Enron executives, they contributed to an inappropriate pattern of influence. Given its importance to Arthur Andersen, the Enron relationship was subject to a periodic "relationship risk" review. The firm's risk reviewers found Enron "aggressive" but maintained that its earnings came from "intelligent gambling," so they okayed continuing as auditor.

To limit the leverage on its balance sheet, Enron used so-called special-purpose entities to borrow the large sums it needed to keep expanding while keeping all that borrowing off its balance sheet. To qualify for this unusual accounting treatment, the special-purpose entities had to be clearly separate, but at Enron they did not meet that requirement—not nearly. Carl Bass, a tough, respected Houston member of Arthur Andersen's professional standards group, began to complain in 2000 about Enron's questionable practices. Enron protested, so Bass was quickly removed from the Enron account. The message was clear: When Enron didn't get cooperation, it would press and get what it wanted.

Enron's stock rose 89 percent in 2000 after a 58 percent gain in 1999. Then, in the summer of 2001, it abruptly fell 50 percent when Enron's president, Jeffrey Skilling, stepped down after serving less than one year "to spend more time with his family." On August 15, Sharon Watkins, an Enron senior accountant formerly with Arthur Andersen, warned CEO Kenneth Lay that certain questions could cause Enron to "implode in a wave of accounting scandals." She hoped they could still be resolved quietly. She also called a pal in Andersen's Houston office, who sent an e-mail to a colleague that began: "Here's the smoking gun you can't extinguish."

As it happened, the special-purpose entities, where the main frauds were committed, were audited by another auditing firm, not Arthur Andersen. In fact, Skilling and Richard Causay, Enron's chief accounting officer, were later indicted on seven counts of defrauding Arthur Andersen & Co. because they had falsely represented a whole series of corrupt deeds. When, months later, the Andersen auditors were taken to trial for alleged professional failures, 9 of 10 were acquitted and the tenth given a light penalty. But the firm's troubles were far from over.

By early October, the inevitable was undeniable: Arthur Andersen had certified earnings that Enron had reported but had *not* been earning. Past "earnings" would need to be substantially restated. But exactly how should they be restated? In a series of conference calls on how to restate Enron earnings, Carl Bass was again included. He was shocked by the scale of the losses. The partner in charge of Andersen's energy industry practice in Houston demanded of Bass: "Who signed off on this?" His tone was clear: It was *wrong* and he was going to find out just who was at fault. Replied Bass sheepishly: "You and I did."

Bass had found improper changes in the accounting for past transactions—made after he had approved a different accounting—and demanded corrections. Junior auditors discovered that Enron itself was reimbursing investors for losses in special-purpose entities. This meant, of course, that the entities were just an accounting gimmick and not at all separate from Enron—but Duncan and other partners had over-ridden them.

■ ■ ■

Partners from around the world were gathering for a million-dollar extravaganza in New Orleans designed to signal that despite the loss of consulting, Arthur Andersen & Co. would carry on. Joseph F. Berardino, who had joined the firm after graduating from Fairfield University and worked his way to the top of the now $19.3 billion organization, would preside over the first worldwide partners meeting in three years. The meeting theme was "The Future Is You."

After Berardino gave his welcome, a partner took him aside to say there were "irregularities" in the reports on Enron. Back in Houston, Andersen auditors were arguing for full disclosure, but Enron rejected that idea and reported on October 16 a single extraordinary charge of over $1 billion—and a loss for the quarter of $638 million. Andersen's auditors cringed. Huge as it was, even $1 billion did not represent the full amount of losses.

On October 23, Duncan told his staff to comply immediately with Andersen's document retention policy, which called for retaining only essential documents such as the "work papers" auditors always keep. (The policy was established to prevent plaintiff lawyers from using the firm's own paperwork against it in the increasingly frequent class-action lawsuits.) While Duncan would later testify that he never meant to obstruct justice, over a ton of documents and 30,000 e-mails were shredded or deleted in just three days. When Arthur Andersen's fraud investigator went to Duncan's office, he was shown an e-mail describing a conversation with Sharon Watkins. Duncan said, "We need to get rid of this," but he quietly nodded in assent when the investigator responded, "Dave, you really need to keep this information. There is a strong likelihood we will need this information."

On November 9, Arthur Andersen & Co. received a federal subpoena. As required by law, shredding stopped. A week later, Enron revealed that it had overstated earnings between 1997 and 2000 by more than $590 million.

By the end of November, Berardino had to know that the problems at Enron gravely endangered Arthur Andersen & Co. But he acted as though Enron's staggering overstatement of earnings was not Andersen's concern or responsibility. First he tried to put the blame on accounting-industry standards. In an op-ed piece for the *Wall Street Journal*, he argued, "Enron's collapse showed that our financial reporting model's emphasis on a single earnings per share number is out of date and unresponsive to today's new business models, complex financial structures, and associated business risks."

Senior staff at the SEC were not pleased. "The op-ed was a disaster," said the agency's chief accountant. "It conveyed the message, 'We've done nothing wrong.'" A week later, Berardino testified to Congress about the need for reforms and, while acknowledging a $172 million error made by the firm's accountants, assured legislators that "Arthur Andersen will not hide from its responsibilities." Later, on *Meet the Press*, he called Enron's failure just a "business problem," suggesting it was not that big a deal and not all that unusual. Federal prosecutors decided the errors were no longer simply negligence and considered criminal prosecution of Arthur Andersen & Co.

On October 16, Enron announced a stunning loss for the third quarter: $638 million, plus a $1.2 billion charge against retained earnings for "certain structured finance arrangements." In the next week, Enron's stock fell 40 percent, and a week later the SEC began a formal investigation. (During all of 2001, Enron stock fell over 99 percent—from $90 a share to 61 cents.) On December 2, Enron filed for bankruptcy—then the largest in U.S. history—and Dynegy Inc., a competitor that had been considering taking over Enron, broke off merger discussions.

Berardino, ever ready to minimize, claimed Enron was an isolated problem and pointed out that botched audits were a tiny percentage of the firm's total. But federal officials saw Enron as part of a repetitive pattern that included faulty Andersen audits of Waste Management, Boston Chicken, the Baptist Foundation, and others. Berardino had been part of the Waste Management settlement a few months earlier in which Andersen agreed to a permanent SEC injunction against any future violation of securities laws.

Berardino tried to protect the firm by scapegoating Duncan as a solo rogue enabled by a few auditors in Houston. Duncan was fired, three Houston partners "placed on leave," and four other senior auditors relieved of management responsibilities. Duncan took the Fifth. He knew it had become him against the firm when the managing partner for business services loftily declared under oath "that [the shredding] was an extreme error in judgment that we as an organization don't support, don't condone, and don't encourage . . . and will not stand for."

But the firm on more than one occasion *had* "condoned" by its loose reviews and increasing emphasis on profits; *had* "encouraged" by driving audit partners to reach for business to boost fees and by not responding to the obvious Enron warning signs; and *had* "stood for" the behavior and the judgments *and* had accepted the fees—until it got caught. A group of Enron directors investigated the collapse and reported the obvious: "Andersen did not fulfill its professional responsibilities."

Clients were leaving Arthur Andersen & Co. in increasing numbers. As one corporation after another departed, other clients felt increasing pressure to quit, too. Each company would have to find another auditor; with only four other major firms, the profession's limited capacity was being taken up rapidly. No company wanted to be too late to make the move to a new auditor.

Desperately, Berardino reached out to Paul Volcker, the former Fed chairman widely admired for integrity. Volcker's response: "If I'm going to get involved, I'm going to have a lot of authority. I'm not going to join a sinking ship just for window dressing." Berardino wasn't willing to go that far, so Volcker said no. Days later, Berardino gave in and agreed to give Volcker greater power to restructure the firm to suit the SEC. A fortnight later, Volcker issued a one-page report: Arthur Andersen & Co. would be redesigned as a model for the accounting profession with strong quality controls in auditing and no consulting at all. Volcker's plan ran into a major problem: Andersen partners wouldn't change the way their firm did business. Before Volcker could persuade key partners of the merits of his plan, they were already moving boldly—and in fear—in other directions.

Merger with Deloitte Touche Tohmatsu was discussed, but then given up because of Arthur Andersen's unknown but surely enormous potential liabilities. Some partners favored Volcker's plan. Others hoped to sell parts of the firm to other firms to save some of their capital value and their retirement funds. Faced with enormous, irreversible, urgent decisions, partners dithered and debated.

Settlement talks with the government were getting nowhere. Volcker chided himself sadly in a later speech: "At seventy-five, I had the romantic notion that I could change things. I thought they would *accept* change because they *needed* change."

On a Sunday, Andersen's lawyers urged on government lawyers the proposition that indicting the firm was unnecessary: Since the firm was cooperating fully, why not indict a few individuals and save the firm? "I'll sleep on it," said Assistant Attorney General Michael Chertoff, "but I'm inclined to indict." He felt the shredding at Enron was the "worst case of corporate obstruction I have ever seen." The next day the government insisted on an admission of guilt. But the firm was unwilling. That would kill it since any remaining clients would terminate.

Even so, Andersen's lawyers were confident that federal prosecutors were "sympathetic," that talks were "progressing," and indeed that they had achieved a deal with the head of the Justice Department's Enron task force, Leslie Caldwell. But 10 minutes after Andersen's lead lawyer got on a plane to Houston feeling elated about that "deal," Caldwell called to say Chertoff would not approve.

On March 2, the phone rang in Berardino's Tokyo hotel room at 2:00 A.M. with news of the firm's indictment. He had just flown in to assure the firm's Japanese partners that things would be okay. After the phone call, he left immediately for Washington, D.C.

Worrying about recidivism, Chertoff decided against compromise. Whereas Duncan had just agreed to plead guilty to one felony count of obstructing justice, Chertoff saw no management commitment to change the firm's behavior. Indeed he detected continuing arrogance. On March 14, with a federal grand jury in Houston ready to hand down a sealed indictment, Chertoff resolved to indict for document destruction.* "An unprecedented exercise of prosecutorial discretion and a gross abuse of governmental power," responded Berardino in a three-page letter to the prosecutor. He may have been accurate, but it didn't matter.

---

*An alternative and informed view is that Ken Lay put pressure on the White House to indict Arthur Andersen to deflect attention away from Enron's management.

Arthur Andersen was then abandoned by all of its partners in Spain and Chile. Still Andersen twitched on. A letter-writing campaign to senators and congressmen was initiated. A large public rally of employees carrying "We Are Andersen" banners was organized in Chicago on March 26. Berardino decided to resign the following day. His announcement made no difference to the accelerating implosion of the firm.

■ ■ ■

The trial of Arthur Andersen began in Houston on May 6. It went badly. Carl Bass testified that documents with his signature had been altered. Duncan testified he had somehow decided that the $1.2 billion accounting error was not material because it totaled "only" 8 percent of stockholders' equity.

The trial outcome was equally bizarre. After 60 hours of deliberation, the jury claimed it was deadlocked. Judge Melinda Harman instructed the jurors to keep trying. A day later, the jury had a question: "If each of us believes that one Andersen agent acted knowingly and with corrupt intent, is it necessary for all of us to believe that it was the *same* agent who acted as 'the corrupt persuader'?" After some quick research, Judge Harmon ruled No.

Andersen's defense lawyers had fleeting hopes of a hung jury, but on June 15 the jury returned with its verdict: guilty. Surprisingly, the jury apparently focused not on the shredding, but on an e-mail to Duncan from Nancy Anne Temple, an Andersen in-house lawyer, urging him to change a draft memo to Enron that originally showed Andersen's disagreement with Enron's plan to characterize its huge write-down as nonrecurring. So Temple was the "corrupt persuader." At the end of the six-week trial, the jury foreman stated: "It's against the law to alter that document with the intent to impair the fact-finding ability of an official proceeding."

That same month, WorldCom, another Andersen audit client, restated revenues by $9 billion. Andersen announced it would stop auditing public companies by August 31.

On October 16, Judge Harman handed down the maximum corporate sentence for obstruction of justice: a $500,000 fine and five years' probation.

Many mid-career partners joined other firms and took their clients with them. Hurt the worst were new partners, who lost their $250,000 mandatory initial investment in the firm; retired partners living on now-vaporized pensions; and older partners who lost both their pensions and their capital in the firm. Many partners felt they had been unfairly treated. They could not or would not see the harm done over many years to Arthur E. Andersen's and Leonard Spacek's firm by accepting the step-by-step shift from the long-term commitment to professional integrity to a short-term focus on commercialism.

■ ■ ■

More than half a century before, on January 13, 1947, the eulogy for Arthur E. Andersen had closed with these thoughts addressed to the partners of the firm:

> Mr. Andersen had great courage. Few are the men who have as much faith in the right as he. And fewer still are those with the courage to live up to their faith as he did. . . . For those of you who worked with him and carry on his company, the meaning is clear. Those principles upon which his business was built, and with which it is synonymous, must be preserved. His name must never be associated with any program or action that is not the highest and the best. I am sure he would rather the doors be closed than that it should continue to exist on principles other than those he established. To you he has left a great name. Your opportunity is tremendous; your responsibility is great.

■ ■ ■

In September 2004, almost two years after the firm's conviction, a petition for a writ of certiorari was filed with the U.S. Supreme Court on behalf of Arthur Andersen LLP, which included this assertion:

> In its zeal to convict Andersen of something in the wake of Enron's collapse, the United States therefore instead charged Andersen with "witness tampering," on the remarkable theory

that it is inherently "corrupt" criminal behavior in this country to attempt to persuade another person to engage in perfectly lawful conduct, if one of the objects of that persuasion is to frustrate the fact-finding ability of a potential future government proceeding. Although it was perfectly lawful for Andersen to have a document retention policy that preserved only the final audit work papers, and perfectly lawful for Andersen's employees and professionals to follow that policy, the United States argued that it was somehow a serious felony for Andersen's in-house attorney and supervisors to remind its employees of the policy—even if they honestly and sincerely believed that their own speech was entirely lawful, and even if there was not the slightest hint of coercion, intimidation, or bribery in their persuasive speech. The Fifth Circuit endorsed that novel theory only by torturing the language of the witness tampering statute.

The Supreme Court ruled unanimously in favor of the writ. The indictment that killed Arthur Andersen & Co. was not valid.

It didn't matter.

By the time of its involvement with Enron, Arthur Andersen was no longer Arthur Andersen. It had already died from within—a stern warning to every professional firm, including the firms celebrated in this book. Attaining professional excellence is not the hardest challenge. Sustaining excellence is the hardest.

Afterword

The pleasure of exploring the great firms and learning their seven secrets of success must, of course, be balanced by the sadness of knowing how few aspiring firms will truly excel. Still, all can strive to be their best. Having devoted a long career to consulting with and studying professional firms, I've learned firsthand how terribly difficult it is for a human organization to go beyond very good and achieve and sustain excellence. Most organizations in law, medicine, finance, investment, auditing, and consulting—and most leadership teams at corporations, universities, schools, museums, hospitals, and the military—may never achieve excellence, and most of those that do will not long sustain excellence. Still, we can all enjoy observing the true exemplars just as we can all learn from them how we can be better.

I've also learned to respect and admire those remarkable organizations of all kinds that—like Olympians who won medals, but not quite the gold—made themselves finalists. Had we more time together, they, too, would warrant study, because they, too, have lessons for all of us who lead organizations large and small— businesses, governments, universities, churches, and military organizations.

In consulting, Booz Allen, Bain, BCG, and AT Kearney have, at different times, been leaders, but none has surpassed or long rivaled McKinsey.

Of 200 or more major investment management organizations, Capital excels, but other strong firms include BlackRock, Dodge & Cox, Pimco, Primecap, T. Rowe Price, Vanguard, and Wellington.

Among 1,000 large law firms, several are excellent. Davis Polk, Debevoise Plimpton, Skadden Arps, O'Melveny & Myers, Sullivan & Cromwell, and Wachtell Lipton are remarkable. Still, most lawyers agree that Cravath is clearly outstanding.

Among several hundred health-care organizations, Johns Hopkins, Mass General, Kaiser Permanente, Intermountain, and Cleveland Clinic are outstanding, but Mayo Clinic is supreme at achieving its chosen mission: "The needs of the patient come first."

Of nearly 100 securities firms that have risen to prominence at one time or another over the past century, only Goldman Sachs is currently recognized as the best of its kind—even as it now faces great challenges, particularly from within. It is also challenged competitively by the formidable JPMorgan Chase.

Of course, many smaller, newer firms aspire to become leaders. But we know from history that only a very few will excel. There is no way to predict which specific newcomers will have the unrelenting combination of inspiring mission, disciplined culture, extensive and rigorous recruiting, intensive and continuous training, persistent innovation, *and* the servant leadership to bring increasing strengths in these many disciplines together and correct the inevitable troubles to ensure continuing excellence.

Meanwhile, we can celebrate the great firms and encourage all contenders because those that excel provide their clients with superb service, provide their professions with high standards, and provide individual professionals with profoundly meaningful careers.

We all know the advertising tagline "Wheaties, the breakfast of champions." But do all champions eat Wheaties? Are all those who eat Wheaties champions? No and No. There is no direct causal connection between eating Wheaties at breakfast and becoming a champion. Similarly, proving causation in professional fields—exactly why a few firms rise to and sustain professional excellence—is impossible.

However, the characteristics of the truly great professional firms are stunning in their consistent repetition. Every great firm is clearly strong on every one of the vital strengths—each in its own way—and superb on several. That's why they excel.

Individual and organizational excellence is always deliberate. Champion athletes share a compelling determination to do their very best in every competition. For a certain few of the most talented and driven people, being part of a great firm is so important, fulfilling, and rewarding that they could not accept less any more than a great musician could always be flat or a great dancer out of step. They want to excel more than they can explain or others can understand. They need to excel. That's who they are. For the superbly capable professional, something special comes with being part of the very best: the satisfaction of knowing you belong there as a member of a championship team and that you are meeting the high internal standards that keep you striving to excel—and the quiet confidence that nobody does it better.

Thanks

Over 300 partners of the great firms have given generously of their time, experiences, and insights in the course of my years of research. Their wisdom, candor, and interest have been both professionally inspiring and personally delightful. Sam Butler, Evan Chesler, Ron Daniel, Jon Lovelace, Jim Rothenberg, Leonard Spacek, Stephen Swensen, and John Whitehead have been particularly important guides toward understanding what it takes.

Linda Lorimer, my wonderful wife and best friend, gave me steady encouragement, astute critique, and interested questioning that opened the way to new and better explanations.

Bill Rukeyser, my good friend and superb editor, combined patient good humor, persistent diligence, toughness on standards of relevance and clarity, and his deep understanding of both storytelling and reporting to the great benefit of all readers. He made it fun.

Andrew Wylie's "Don't do it that way; do it this way" led to a far better structure and complete revision. Heidi Fiske provided decisive help with pleasing grace.

Jennifer Peterson, Kimberly Breed, and Catharine Schilkowski patiently converted rough drafts through multiple revisions into "final" text.

During the summer of 2004, six Yale College seniors—Daniel Bernstein, Anatoly Brekhman, Tiffany Clay, Andrew Korn, Elliott Mogul, and Nelson Moussazadeh—helpfully devoted their summer to research on the history of the great firms.

Finally, thanks and good luck to all who strive to advance their own professional firms to excellence. As John F. Kennedy explained, when asked why America should land a man on the moon: "Because it's hard."

Notes

Chapter 1: Mission

6   *The firm that eventually became Jones Day* ᐧTolles, Hogsett, Ginn & Morley, the predecessor of Jones, Day, Reavis & Pogue.

6   *He made a list of the key factors* Marvin Bower, The Will to Lead Harvard Business School Publishing, 1997), p. 11.

7   *Recognizing that advising was not doing* Ever the professor-entrepreneur, McKinsey gave an 8:00 A.M. lecture course to the managers of Marshall Field and asked a colleague, W. H. Newman, to work the lectures into a book published as *Business Policies and Management* by Newman after McKinsey's death.

7   *[McKinsey] decided to take this challenge* After committing to join Marshall Field, McKinsey got a dozen letters from firms wanting to acquire his small firm. One offer came from C. Oliver Wellington of Scovell, Wellington & Co., then a large, prestigious accounting and consulting firm headquartered in Boston. Meeting over a single weekend, Wellington agreed to acquire James O. McKinsey & Co. In the merged organization—named McKinsey, Wellington & Co.—Horace G. "Guy" Crockett, a CPA who had led the management engineering practice at Scovell, Wellington, would head the combined consulting group—with the irrepressible Bower effectively his co-head.

8   *threats on Mac McKinsey's life*   In Chicago's business establishment, the name McKinsey had a black mark as a result of his many hard decisions at Marshall Field & Co. He had nearly been forced out of the company.

8   *saved Marshall Field but ruined*   With McKinsey's death and the economic downturn of 1938, which stopped a large study for U.S. Steel that had represented 55 percent of its billings, the firm incurred a brief loss. In the aftermath, the consultants, in disagreement over various policy matters and in rebellion against Oliver Wellington's autocratic management, agreed to buy back their operations and split them into two new but operationally linked companies: McKinsey & Co., led by Crockett with offices in New York and Boston, and McKinsey, Kearney & Co., led in Chicago by McKinsey's first partner, A. Thomas Kearney. Bower, who had initiated the separation in confidential letters he typed himself and sent to home addresses, would manage the New York office of McKinsey & Co.

Financing was an urgent problem. Nearly $70,000 was needed to buy the small new McKinsey & Co. Bower was just 35 and could put up only $3,200. Crockett and another partner each put up $28,000. Still short, Bower turned to a Harvard Business School Club friend, Ewing W. "Zip" Reilley, who was wealthy and well connected, and interested in leaving Lehman Brothers. He agreed to lend $10,000 and join the firm as an associate, but not as a partner—at least until the firm was safely prospering. (He did not want to risk his family fortune as a partner with unlimited personal liability.) While two of his three co-investors were in their sixties, they believed in Bower and his vision even though most people had never heard of management consulting and usually confused consultants with "efficiency experts." On September 2, 1939 (the day after World War II began), the agreements were signed. The announcement defined the practice as "management engineering."

With a staff of only 22, Bower urged that McKinsey & Co. should commit to becoming the leading management consulting firm in the United States. Even though it had few competitors, the tiny firm certainly had a long way to go. Billings for 1940—with 44 clients—were only $284,000. With low salaries, this produced a "profit" of $57,000, even after paying 21 percent to the McKinsey estate. The next year, billings increased to $323,000 and profits to $73,000. Although per-diem billing was the norm, Bower started charging his clients "value-based" project fees, which he had seen used at Jones Day.

8 *Mac also thought managing should be* Bower always said he could not have done it without his hero and predecessor. James Oscar McKinsey had appeared doomed to live an inconsequential life in the early twentieth century. Raised in a three-room farmhouse in the Ozarks, he knew poverty. Fortunately for him and for the preeminent firm that now bears his name, McKinsey was brilliant, articulate, and determined to get ahead. Refusing to follow his father into dirt farming, he ran away from home at 14 to get a high-school education. (The school principal soon recognized his exceptional talents and hired him to teach algebra—to the teachers.) He earned a modest Bachelor of Pedagogy degree at modest State Teachers College in modest Warrensburg, Missouri, in 1912. A year later, McKinsey passed the exam for a Bachelor of Laws degree at the University of Arkansas and then moved to St. Louis, the nearest big city, to teach bookkeeping. He got a scholarship to the University of Chicago where he earned a Bachelor of Philosophy degree in 1916 and promptly started work on a Master's. Equally fortunately, his studies were interrupted by military service. As a lieutenant in Army Ordnance during the Great War, he traveled all over the country and saw firsthand that business managers badly needed accurate, timely information and good advice on the techniques of management.

After the war, McKinsey decided he would need three factors to succeed as a professional: respectability, professional exposure, and recognized competence in an area of interest to managers. He persistently pursued all three. To get professional exposure, McKinsey ate half of his breakfasts, all of his lunches, and a third of his dinners with either clients or prospects. At six-foot-two with piercing blue eyes, he was known as a superb listener. As his field of expertise, he chose accounting as a guide to management decisions. Returning to the University of Chicago, McKinsey completed his master's degree and became a CPA. Even before graduation in 1920, he was hired as an instructor by the dean, who also hired him as a senior professional in his accounting firm.

In 1919, McKinsey wrote the first of his 10 books, *Bookkeeping and Accounting*. It presented accounting as an analytical tool needed to manage all the different parts of a business organization and introduced the innovative budgeting process we now call *management by objectives*. His books earned McKinsey recognition for competence, even mastery, in his chosen field. And as one of the nation's first professors of business policy, he achieved respectability as an outstanding member (from 1917 to 1935) of an unusually strong faculty at the University of Chicago's School of Commerce.

In 1925, McKinsey split off from the accounting firm where his peers considered him "brilliant, energetic, and quite tireless." Continuing to teach an early morning class at the university, he devoted most of his time and energy to building his own firm, James O. McKinsey & Co. He built his professional reputation through speeches and service to such organizations as the American Management Association, which he helped form and then served as president. Starting with Armour & Co., McKinsey developed a reputation as an effective consultant. By 1935, McKinsey's firm had offices in New York and Chicago with five partners and 15 associates.

As a conscientious student, Bower was delighted that Mac McKinsey taught powerful lessons by example: devotion to work and the firm; the importance of earning a reputation though writing and speaking; reaching out to clients and prospects for luncheons and dinners; attracting and training young men; candidly telling associates about their mistakes and how they could improve; and a total lack of interest in repetitive routine work of a standardized "product" nature when time could, and therefore should, be spent on understanding new problems and developing creative solutions. As Bower later said, "Mac was not a theorist, but he believed strongly in principles because he believed that only principles can be transferred from one situation to another. He was a very practical person."

An enduring contribution to his firm's consulting was Mac McKinsey's 30-page General Survey Outline to help—and oblige—his associates to work through any complex problem by approaching it in the most effective manner. The Outline took consultants through a systematic examination of the outlook for a client's industry—its structure, the major competitors, the forces of change; the client's industry position and each competitor's principal strengths and weaknesses; and specific actions for improvement to be recommended to the client.

9   *Bower insisted on the term*   Booz Allen & Hamilton followed McKinsey & Co. and converted to the term *management consultants* in 1950. Arthur D. Little and Boston Consulting Group converted in the 1960s and Bain & Co. in the 1970s.

9   *Since major prospective corporate clients operated nationally*   Central to McKinsey's becoming a "one-firm firm" was the willingness of the New York office to transfer both the most experienced and the most promising consultants to new offices as they were opened and the willingness of individuals to move to new offices and of others to fill the voids they created by leaving.

10 *"By applying the professional approach*   Marvin Bower, *Perspective on McKinsey* (McKinsey & Co., 1979), pp. 157–158.

11 *At Capital Group Companies*   Capital began in 1929 as a small investment sideline for a taciturn 34-year-old finance whiz who had just moved to distant California when few Easterners had ever been there or even thought of going to the Far West. Jonathan Bell Lovelace had accumulated a small fortune as an investor and partner in a stockbrokerage firm in Detroit that specialized in serving the newly rich leaders of the booming automobile industry. (Adept at mental arithmetic, Lovelace had served during World War I in the artillery unit that was the first to figure out how to shoot down a German plane.) As an objective investment analyst, he recognized that the "New Era" stock market had risen to excessive prices, so he sold all his stocks and got out of the securities business. In California, he continued to invest and started a small firm, Lovelace, Dennis & Renfrew, serving as an expert financial adviser to such local corporations as Walt Disney, Lockheed, and Capitol Records.

Two years later, Lovelace's new firm agreed to succeed his old Detroit stockbrokerage firm as investment adviser to two small closed-end mutual funds. The directors were facing up to the funds' serious troubles and wanted both Lovelace's research capabilities and his integrity. In 1933, Lovelace took over a third closed-end fund, Investment Co. of America, which was later converted to the open-end fund structure that now dominates the industry. Managed at breakeven for 20 long years, Lovelace's firm was still a small firm in the very small mutual fund business in 1950, with only 28 employees managing just $36 million.

13 *[Capital] wouldn't offer such a fund*   Even in Capital's institutional Emerging Markets Growth Fund, the new shares made available to investors each year are carefully limited.

15 *"Mayo Clinic is an idea*   Some aspects of the culture are explicit: care for patients unable to pay and unreimbursed care under Medicare cost Mayo Clinic some $200 million each year. Another $350 million supports Mayo's medical research and education.

15 *the list was expanded* Originally written in 1979, the list was modified in 1998 to include shareholders and in 2001 to reflect the commitment to diversity.

18 *Barr's strategy* Loyalty to the team and to Tom Barr were central for what was often called Barr & Co. Some examples may, at first, seem foolish, but they signal the intense dedication that characterized the group. Here's one: Barr had a habit of leaning back from the conference table in a particular way: By carefully moving his legs, he would balance his straight chair on its back two legs, sometimes holding the balance for even 10 minutes at a time. But once, he lost his balance entirely. Barr and his chair fell over backwards and slammed to the floor. Silence. Then silence was broken by a junior teammate saying, "Okay, guys, here we go!" and falling backward to the floor in his chair, too—followed by one after another after another amid peals of laughter including Barr's.

The "band of brothers" intensity of the commitment to competitive excellence at Cravath creates a distinctive mass in all it does. This mass is why when two Cravath lawyers—one partner and one associate—representing giant IBM in a lawsuit against a small plaintiff, arrived in court to find the plaintiff represented by 12 lawyers, the associate immediately identified the reality: "Boss, we've got 'em outnumbered!"

18 *In early October 1972, the* New York Times *reported* Robert J. Cole, "Accord Unlikely in Suit on IBM," *New York Times*, October 6, 1972.

19 *Barr then requested postponement of the trial* William D. Smith, "Judge Denies IBM Bid for Delay," *New York Times*, October 12, 1992.

22 *"The sheer manpower* The executive mainly responsible for monitoring IBM's costs was general counsel Nicholas Katzenbach. "We provided Cravath an unlimited budget for both time and expenses," he said, adding wryly, "and Cravath went beyond that every year."

23 *"We lost only one of the twenty-one cases* Actually, the record is more complicated. In the case of *IBM v. Allen-Myland* the appeals court reversed the lower court's finding in favor of IBM and remanded the antitrust claims for retrial, using the market definition proposed by a distinguished economist. Before the refile, IBM won a counterclaim of patent infringement. IBM agreed to drop the patent claim if Allen-Myland dropped the antitrust claim. So that case was not won; it was settled.

Chapter 2: Culture

27   *"Every man has some inspiration*   Helen Clapesattle, *The Doctors Mayo* (New York: Simon & Schuster, 1969), p. 338.

27   *Those who stay for five years*   Staff turnover is very low, and two-thirds of that low turnover results from a spousal transfer or some other change beyond the individual's control.

28   *attacks by Indians*   In 1862, the Minnesota Sioux revolted when the Indian agent refused to distribute their annual allotments of food until their cash allotments had also arrived. Several settlers were killed and the militia was called out. Two thousand Sioux were captured, and 307 were condemned to death. President Lincoln pardoned all but 39, who were hanged on December 26, 1862.

28   *with his wife's active help*   Mrs. Mayo, according to her family, once resourcefully dressed in Dr. Mayo's clothing to convince a Sioux uprising that there was a man in the house.

29   *Religious prejudice against Catholics*   The American Protective Association, successor to the Know Nothings and a predecessor of the Ku Klux Klan, was organized in Clinton, Iowa, in 1887 and was strong in Minnesota.

29   *pay the hospital first*   Hospital rates were $6 a week for a ward bed and $9 for a private room. Mother Alfred was replaced by Archbishop Ireland in 1890 following complaints by several Sisters that their mission was teaching, not health care. She was succeeded by Sister Joseph in 1892.

29   *The Mayo brothers had an unintended monopoly*   Of course, the Mayo boys wanted to go to medical school, but in the late nineteenth century only a few schools were any good. Most were just diploma mills that took only 10 or 12 months and relied entirely on lectures. Most students would graduate without ever feeling a sick man's pulse or listening to a heart or lung. But this was changing. In 1880, the University of Michigan matched Harvard's pioneering commitment to a three-year program of medical education based on clinical teaching and strong science. Will Mayo went there to study and, at 22, decided his life's goal: Remain in Rochester, Minnesota, and become the greatest surgeon in the world. In 1885, Charlie Mayo left for the Chicago Medical College at Northwestern, aiming to get a somewhat different perspective and education.

Will and Charlie Mayo would soon take over their father's already large practice as both surgeons and physicians with an increasing emphasis on surgery. They also adopted their father's dictum that, no matter how busy they were, they should devote one full hour each day to reading and study to keep up with proliferating medical discoveries. (Determined to be a specialist in eye surgery, Dr. Will practiced on the eyes of sheep and pigs at the local slaughterhouse.) The Mayo brothers made a lifelong habit of taking postgraduate courses, visiting leading practitioners to study the latest developments, and participating actively in medical meetings. After Will gave a paper on his experience with appendectomies at only 27, he was considered so impressive that he was elected head of the surgical section of the state medical society. To keep up with others' advances, the Mayos each took a month's "vacation" each year to visit and observe other surgeons—Will going in the fall and Charlie in the spring. Some of the surgeons they visited were not only brilliant but arrogant and had no commitment to advancing their associates through education. For the Mayo brothers, this behavior reminded them of the wisdom of their father's admonition: "No man is big enough to be independent of others."

Louis Pasteur's proof that bacteria caused fermentation and putrefaction had been translated in 1867 by the English surgeon Sir Joseph Lister into a strict antiseptic procedure in surgery with extraordinarily favorable results. While stalwartly resisted by most established practitioners, the new ways of thinking would eventually transform surgery. While chloroform and operations on the kitchen table had long been professional norms, Dr. Will convinced his reluctant father to switch over to "Listerism" when he returned in 1885 from a second graduate course, at Chicago Medical College.

With new knowledge and Lister's pioneering practices, surgery was changing. Before Listerism, the great majority of surgical deaths were due to infection, but with Listerism, surgery flourished, particularly in antiseptic internal operations. Mortality in appendectomies dropped from 30 percent to less than 1 percent. The annual number of surgeries in Rochester's 250-bed hospital multiplied 10 times from about 400 to over 4,000 while the percentage of amputations dropped from 25 percent to 1 percent. Use of ether began at Mayo Clinic in 1885, but not until 1895 at Johns Hopkins and 10 years after that in Boston. From 1890 to 1910, the new wonders of surgery created an unprecedented opportunity for fame and fortune for leading practitioners. As Will observed modestly, "As I look back over those early years, I am impressed with the fact that much of our success, if not most of it, was due to the time at which we entered medicine."

31 *The Properties Association leased its buildings* Administration was vested in a board of governors, and supervision of all professional activities became the responsibility of an executive committee of five appointed by the governors from a list of 15 nominated by the professional staff. At Dr. Will's initiative, the various tasks of administration would be overseen by standing committees with rotating membership appointed from the professional staff.

31 *The interests of the patient* It was no surprise that less than a week after his law firm had been hired by five cigarette companies in 1997, Senator Howard Baker resigned as chairman of the Mayo Foundation board of trustees "rather than allow any perception of conflict to adversely affect the institution."

34 *Ed Benjamin became Cravath's first Jewish partner in 1964* Only one year later, Benjamin was killed in an Eastern Airlines plane crash in the East River.

36 *"The work habits I developed* Walter Isaacson and Evan Thomas, *The Wise Men* (New York: Simon & Schuster, 1986).

37 *Nor did Capital* A mutual fund director of the then recently acquired Anchor Group resigned from Capital, at least in part over this decision not to press charges.

38 *There may also be a belief* Perspective on McKinsey, p. 164.

Chapter 3: Recruiting

52 *the people who survive the drawn-out process* Leonard L. Berry and Kent D. Seltman, *Management Lessons from Mayo Clinic* (New York: McGraw-Hill, 2008), p. 135.

53 *highly selective . . . programs* Mayo Clinic consistently gets outstanding physicians by selecting the best and most committed in its various training programs. Sixty percent of physician recruits have had at least some Mayo training. They know Mayo and the clinic knows them. And 80 percent of new hires fit in so well that they will stay for their full careers. "Mayo Medical School is the most competitive medical school, with a 100:1 ratio of applicants to admission," reports Dean Lindor. In admissions, Mayo Medical looks for alignment of values. Has an applicant shown a commitment to service, particularly as a leader in a service organization? Being a leader is important because depth of commitment is more important than quantity of commitment. With 80 percent of medical school applicants nation-wide coming from the top 20 percent of the socioeconomic spectrum, Mayo Medical makes a special effort to achieve diversity and looks particularly for applicants who are the first in their families to graduate from college and needed to work to help pay for college.

54 *McKinsey's MBAs*   At first, Bower's idea of recruiting freshly minted MBAs met with great resistance. No other consulting firm did anything like hiring inexperienced young people to work as consultants on major issues. Most new MBAs were in their mid-twenties and, except for military service, had had no experience beyond routine summer jobs. They wouldn't know the subtleties of behavior—and would show that every day. They were a full generation younger than the senior executives McKinsey aimed to work with, so having "a bunch of kids" representing McKinsey would be courting disaster. Bower, as usual, persisted. He had seen it work at Jones Day and he was, as always, determined. He believed brainpower was sure to prove itself better than experience if new consultants worked on teams with senior consultants and would, as expert learners, not only catch on quickly with good training and mentoring, but be more open to new ideas and new ways and be easier to train and develop. As so often with new ideas, the compromise—after long discussions and many doubts—would begin with a small experiment: hiring one or two. With its rigorous emphasis on analysis, the firm was soon developing the competence to manage the process of developing an appropriate solution for practically any business problem.

55 *the best one or two nationals*   In Germany, McKinsey typically receives 1,000 job applications a year. They are screened by senior staff for such factors as schools attended, grades earned, and the range and richness of activities in which applicants have engaged. After this screening, about 300, or 30 percent, are interviewed in marathon days: two interviews in the morning and, for those who seem most promising, two more interviews in the afternoon. About half—or 150—will get offers and, of these, 90 percent will typically accept. McKinsey deliberately holds recruiting workshops in nice places, partly to sell the candidates on McKinsey and partly to observe the candidates closely. Graduates will often be offered a three-year agreement that includes two years of work at McKinsey followed by one year to do their dissertation or go to a business school like INSEAD.

56   *the most talented business graduates across Europe agreed*   Author's interview with Michael Muth, July 2006.

57   *Any one of those schools may be a pipeline*   A trick question in recruiting for many years: Name the top two colleges represented in the firm. Most candidates just assumed Harvard and Yale. The answer was actually Yale and the Indian Institutes of Technology because of the many engineers recruited from India.

59   *the starting salary at Cravath*   Back in the sixties, when competition was less intensive and Cravath sought far fewer associates, the firm had made itself the acknowledged price setter on compensation. In 1968, the going rate of pay to associates was $10,000 a year, up by $1,000 from 1967. Cravath stunned its competitors by setting the pay for first-year associates at $15,000. "We didn't want anyone deciding that they would not come to our firm because they could not live here adequately," said a partner. While Cravath's change in compensation for "first-years" outraged several less powerful and less profitable firms, law graduates were naturally delighted. At the University of Virginia, a student note was posted: "Definition of the 'going rate'—$15,000 or we're all going to Cravath!"

Chapter 4: Developing People

65   *People are mentored*   A McKinsey mentor is called a personal group leader.

66   *not be confined overlong*   Robert T. Swaine, *The Cravath Firm and Its Predecessors, 1819-1948* (two volumes, privately printed; New York: Ad Press, 1946-48), Volume I, p. 4.

68   *The case for law schools*   After considerable argument, automatic admission to the bar and to practice for law school graduates was ended.

68   *equal rank to any of the great law firms of the City."*   Edwards Patterson, "A Successful Life: Address in Memory of C.A. Seward," Phi Beta Kappa Society of Hobart College, Geneva, New York, June 22, 1898.

68   *Paul Cravath*   Cravath was born in Berlin Heights, Ohio, the son of the local Congregational pastor. When his father went to New York to work on spreading Sunday schools, young Cravath went to Brooklyn Polytechnic and then for two years to Geneva, Switzerland, and then to Oberlin. After graduating at 21, he went to St. Paul, Minnesota, to clerk for Frank B. Kellogg, who decades later became Calvin Coolidge's Secretary of State. Cravath caught typhoid fever, recovered,

and worked in sales for a Standard Oil subsidiary to earn enough to go to Columbia Law School, where he graduated in 1886 at the top of his class. He was admitted to the bar in 1886 and joined Carter, Hornblower & Byrne.

68   *an uncanny sense for the right solution*   Swaine, p. 572.

68   *a new kind of law firm*   The practice of law changed greatly during the early years of the twentieth century as the federal government moved to regulate railroads and break up monopolies. Young lawyers were increasingly trained at newly established law schools. Institutional clients displaced individual clients, and increasing numbers of lawyers worked within those institutions—governments, corporations, and nonprofit organizations—which grew both larger and more international. Regulators became stronger and their regulations more numerous and specific. The national economy was shifting from local proprietorships to large national corporations, and private ownership was changing to public ownership. The problems lawyers worked on became increasingly complex blends of business considerations and legal issues. The financial scale ballooned, and the tempo accelerated as bankers strove to keep pace with dynamic stock and bond markets. Law practice switched from analysis of the past to anticipation of the future. This new kind of law practice involved prospects of much larger gain or loss for clients and so was substantially more lucrative for lawyers.

As complexity of legal problems increased, so did specialization. Firms that were concentrated in a single city at the beginning of the twentieth century would, by the end of the century, have offices in a dozen American cities and another dozen overseas. The larger size of law firms called for changes in management and governance. Fifty years ago, only a dozen firms had 100 or more lawyers; today over 1,000 firms do, and the 25 largest firms average nearly 1,000 lawyers apiece, with revenues over $500 million. The loss of personal friendship as an important bonding glue in a partnership and the increasing power and discipline of impersonal business economics have produced intense pressure in most firms for more billable hours. A century ago, law firms were remarkably different.

68   *he knew how to build a great firm*   With Paul Cravath in charge, billings tripled in a few years; the increasing volume, handled largely by associates, changed the economics of the firm favorably and substantially. During his era, his firm went from three partners to 22 and from 16 associates to 72 with a support staff of well over 100 as it became one of New York's and America's largest and most respected law firms. Cravath also started what would become a formidable strength of the firm—its professional support staff—by hiring a Columbia University librarian to systematize a filing system. Before long, the firm was transformed from the loose relationships of partners and staff to the closely integrated teamwork of the Cravath firm.

69 *each partner train his own* The differences between partners in their approach to training 40 or 50 years ago were still clear. At the end of his first year at Cravath, Sam Butler was assigned by 65-year-old senior partner Donald Swatland to draft a joint venture agreement for Allied Chemical. Swatland suggested a few ideas and Butler got to work. When Butler gave him the draft, Swatland asked Butler to come in that Saturday morning to work on it with him. As Butler recalls, "We went through that entire document—line by line for five straight hours—examining the selection of individual words on up to exploring a few major concepts. Together we clearly improved the document, but what we were really engaged in was even more important: training."

In contrast, at about the same time, a Yale Law School summer associate was assigned to study a complex issue and write up a memorandum for senior partner Roswell Gilpatric, who was away all summer. The work was submitted after an extraordinary effort as the "summer" returned to law school. He received the following feedback:

Dear Bedrick:

Read your memo. Presumably you left "not" out of your conclusion.

Yours sincerely,

R. Gilpatric.

70 *. . . even if it took all night long."* Amy Singer, "A Passion for Organization," *The American Lawyer*, December 1959.

70 *"His first great object* Prior to 1926, most new partners had been at the firm for five or six years, but by 1940 the norm had become eight years. During World War II, the apprenticeship period lengthened briefly to 10 years, but that proved too long. As Swaine explained: "Ten years is too long for a man to remain a Cravath associate under normal conditions unless he has been told that the chances of his being made a partner are still good. A man who is not growing professionally creates a barrier to the progress of the younger men within the organization and to himself [and he] tends to sink into a mental rut and to

lose ambition . . . and loss of ambition induces carelessness. It is much better for the man, for the office, and for the clients that he leave while he still has the self-confidence and determination to advance. The frustrated man will not be happy, and the unhappy man will not do a good job."

74   *the Bar Association's continuing education requirement* Twelve hours a year of CLE (continuing legal education) credits are required by the Bar Association, with two hours specifically on ethics. Each CLE hour a lawyer teaches provides three hours of credit. An outside instructor gives an intensive course in forensic accounting.

77   *Gordon Crawford* When recruited to Capital, he claims to have been a bartender at the Boar's Head Inn in Charlottesville, where he was earning his MBA at the University of Virginia's Darden School following a BA in classics at Wesleyan. Crawford was initially recruited to cover insurance companies. After a year at Capital, he switched to cover media.

78   *by removing impediments* Two unusual examples: Bill Newton worked out of his office-home in Jackson Hole, Wyoming, and Shanahan worked out of his home in Palm Desert after 30 years in the Los Angeles offices.

80   *virtually no politics or bureaucracy* Even at Capital, politics can be part of reality so it's important to have an arbiter with a long-term perspective. Jon Lovelace performed this role for many years; today there are several other decision arbiters, including Jim Rothenberg and Mike Shanahan. In the Capital tradition, each would deflect the importance of his role and point out that at Capital virtually no one ever gets exactly what he or she originally wanted.

81   *restructures again and again into smaller teams* Similarly, the working limit on the size of a shareholder services center is 500 associates so the senior manager will know all the people who work there. If volume calls for more capacity, a new unit will be started.

81   *greater diversity* Today women and men are treated as equals in responsibilities, respect, and compensation. It was not always so. Acknowledging the differences so evident in the United States 50 years ago, Marj Fisher, the first woman professional Capital hired, believes today's reality had early roots: "JBL [Jonathan Bell Lovelace] had two very capable daughters, and his experience with them may have contributed to his strong belief that women should be given ample opportunities to demonstrate their capabilities. When I joined

Capital in 1951, there were only 19 employees, and I was our first professional woman. When one of our analysts came back from a meeting of the Los Angeles Analysts Society and announced that the first woman had just been made a member, the clear implication was that I should apply, too." Fisher did apply and became the second woman in the society and the first to serve as president.

83 *Fosters mutual respect* "We respect our employees and we respect their choices," said the Mayo Clinic's chief human resources officer, Jill Ragsdale. Mayo was offering domestic partner benefits in the early nineties and now sponsors networking opportunities including a gay, lesbian, bisexual, and transgender website.

91 *protects the institution* In 1994, at age 60, Charles Shaw's personal question was whether he should retire. He had no interest in that, so he worked out an arrangement: 60 percent of pay for two years, 30 percent for another two years, and then 15 percent for two final years. Three other consultants were offered the same deal, but the arrangement was dropped two years later because several other senior consultants wanted the same deal while the firm didn't really want them.

91 *decline in energy* European consultants generally leave early, but Americans, particularly those in New York City, tend to stay on. This may be linked to their being in a second or third marriage and having kids to put through school and college. (New York's divorce rate is higher than the firm-wide average, but other offices are closing the gap.) Some complain candidly, "If I didn't stay, I'd have nothing to do. I can't just sit around the apartment all day." So some strike a deal to work two or so extra years at the firm. The firm was going to offer Herb Henzler an exception on retirement when he was serving on the executive committee, but Henzler insisted the question be put on the partners' agenda. At their next meeting in Rome, the younger partners were in favor of staying consistent with the policy. So Henzler said, "Fine, I'll go."

91 *last three years' average compensation* After officially retiring in 2001, Michael Muth continued working on training consultants at the Munich office at a per-diem rate of $5,000.

92 *seventieth percentile of peers* Peer organizations include Leahy Clinic, Cleveland Clinic, and Memorial Sloan Kettering. Nursing pay is set at the market—essentially Minneapolis-St. Paul.

92 *Chairs rotate* Rotating leaders gives them variety in their experiences and gives each working unit exposure to leaders with different styles.

In leadership selection, such as for departmental chairs, every person in the department will be asked for an opinion. This gives the selection committee the maximum knowledge of how each candidate is perceived. This same process is followed in choosing administrators, but since administrators rotate from one department to another, positions are posted and individuals apply.

Chapter 5: Client Relationships

101 *undisputed leadership in investment banking*   This was Whitehead's second strategic masterstroke. His first—restructuring investment banking into two coordinated parts: relationship management and transaction specialists—took Goldman Sachs up into Wall Street's prestigious "bulge bracket."

102 *I was explaining how I lost an opportunity*   Jon R. Katzenbach, *Why Pride Matters More Than Money* (New York: Crown Business), p. 5.

105 *preset hourly rates*   The billing rates are identical for associates in each annual cohort and are set for three levels of partners. If an associate takes more time than necessary on a task because she or he is learning how to do that type of work, the associate's supervising partner can toss out the extra hours, but must clear it with the partner in charge of that department so the firm knows.

106 *Chesler wrote an article*   *Forbes*, January 12, 2009.

109 *the odds in favor of effective implementation*   Years ago, Bower scoffed at the futility of producing elaborate reports that did not lead directly to profitable action, frequently declaring: "A report is *not* an action-getting document!" His conviction had a story behind it. On the train to New York City, Bower had met a successful banker who told of his frustration in having several handsome reports, all with sound recommendations, that were not being used at all. "If your firm can get its clients to adopt its recommendations, I predict a brilliant future for you."

109 *"radiating references."*   Alumni originate 10 percent or less of a typical McKinsey year's work. And alumni are not always ideal clients. Many alumni, thinking they know who is particularly capable, will try to tell the firm which consultants to assign to their team. It takes most alumni about 10 years to mellow enough to let McKinsey manage its engagements.

Chapter 6: Innovation

113   *all four managers' best efforts*   An important "cushion" was invented to manage the process when one of the counselors working on a fund wants to sell all or a part of a fund's holding. First, the stock is offered to the other portfolio counselors working on the fund. If they wish to take the position over, an internal exchange is made and the seller's investment performance will be measured as though an actual sale had been made into the stock market. If other portfolio counselors do not want to take it over, the stock is sold into the market.

113   *several people opposed the idea*   With all the necessary records kept by hand, the multiple counselor system began operation on April 1, 1958. Naturally, skeptics reminded the proponents that this was April Fool's Day.

114   *no other investment organization has chosen to replicate*   Primecap, organized by Capital alumni, uses a version of the multiple counselor system. Vanguard employs multiple managers for some actively managed funds, but while their performance is of course measured and used in decisions to reward or retain them, their activities are not coordinated as at Capital.

114   *Replicating . . . is difficult*   As though to prove that the multiple counselor system is hard to implement effectively, even Capital failed with its introduction in one instance. The portfolio managers at Capital Guardian Trust—several of them new to Capital at the time—tried their own version. Different portfolio managers were simply paired, but there was too much differentiation in investment styles and too little communication among portfolio managers, so when two institutional clients with the same mandate compared portfolios, they were often very different. In the competition for new business, the investment consultants who advise institutional funds on the selection of new investment managers found the differences simply unacceptable and often vetoed hiring the firm. Finally, Mike Shanahan went over to Capital Guardian Trust and got the portfolio managers to adopt the disciplines of the multiple counselor system.

115   *He certainly did not believe in predicting*   Bower had no intention of having McKinsey be an exciting, creative intellectual leader. He aimed to be a deliberately cautious "fast follower"—arguably a sensible position for a consulting firm serving large industrial clients who were conservative in their own values and would want consultants who could be trusted never to overpromise. McKinsey's unstated strategy was to excel in managing client relationships, be a few steps ahead of clients on new ways of thinking, and be consistently reliable, particularly in getting clients to take action.

116   *tough, smart, creative experts*   BCG also attacked McKinsey in recruiting talent, advertising in student newspapers that it had hired one-quarter of Harvard Business School's "high distinction" graduates and offering large "exploding" bonuses.

117   *expertise in areas of greatest interest to clients*   Tom Wilson, formerly employed at Procter & Gamble, challenged McKinsey consultants to a test of their competence in consumer goods: If they were such marketing experts, could they interpret Nielsen reports on the sales of consumer products? All consultants who took that test except Wilson failed. That led McKinsey to hire marketing experts.

119   *McKinsey would need to change*   Twice each year, consultants from many offices worldwide in each of the major industry practice groups met together for two full days in a search for ways to help each other by sharing new developments. Over the years, this fostered bonding and teamwork and became an important growth engine for McKinsey. Bringing consultants together to exchange experiences and information inspired each consultant to keep learning more. As Don Waite recalled, "Bringing all our banking consultants together for two or three days of sharing information, ideas, techniques, *and* war stories—10 consultants at first, but many more later on—pooled all our knowledge and experience and clarified who knew what and so who could help in any particular way. This also increased our personal and professional bonding and steadily raised the norm or standard of those in our group. We *all* got better. And we enjoyed our work together more, too."

119   *it's not necessarily a handicap*   Not only was the traditional generalist model being displaced, but also the powers of the geographically defined office heads were eventually balanced by industry expertise. These same changes enabled McKinsey to preempt national markets by borrowing consultants from one office to work in another office rather than waiting for critical mass in demand to build up in each office. With this portability and aggressive local recruiting of consultants, McKinsey also staked out many countries preemptively before BCG, Bain, or Booz Allen could get established.

119   *industry expertise would almost always trump*   Korea and Japan are exceptions: Both require national "insiders." China is more open.

124   *the best day's work*   The Doctors Mayo, p. 221.

125   *The files were cross-indexed*   Today over four million patient records are kept on file. Anyone wanting to study cases of any one kind simply gets a list of the cases and requests those files.

126   *commitment to continuous improvement*   Launched in 2008, the Center for Innovation employs 70 people. Dr. Douglas Wood teaches innovation capabilities and started the Quality Academy to seek innovation that can transform health care. "We strive to understand the latent or unstated needs of the public. This is important because physicians will typically start their thinking with themselves. Organizing has greatly accelerated progress with innovations at Mayo Clinic and permeates the organization."

127   *a committee recommended*   Members were Tom Barr, Sam Butler, Wayne Chapman, George Gillespie, Jack Hupper, Henry Riordan, and Richard Simmons.

127   *For their second year, partners receive*   Capital percentages are equal to partnership percentages, rising and then falling with the bell curve of a career. In the old days, there was no help from the firm on making capital contributions, but now the firm helps arrange bank loans to young partners. (The firm does not borrow for operating capital.) Today the firm also makes sure that ample credit is available to young partners so they can buy attractive homes.

128   *mandatory retirement at 65*   Partners have two choices in retirement compensation: either an annual income at one-quarter of the three-year average of the five highest paid partners or, if a survivor's benefit is chosen by age 60, at an actuarially reduced rate. (The total payout to retired partners is capped at 10 percent of the partnership's net income, reduced from 15 percent in the 1980s. The firm exceeded the cap in 2011.) Retired partners are provided with stationery, business cards, office space, and secretarial assistance, but no extra pay for working for clients of the firm. They can have a few outside clients, but most who decide to continue working do so entirely pro bono. Some litigators serve as arbitrators. A partner can choose to retire at age 60 with an actuarially discounted payout and, with the permission of the firm, a partner can retire as early as 55.

Chapter 7: Macro Innovation

135   *taking too much out for themselves* Bower was fully aware of the personal opportunity but refused to take advantage of it. "Marvin was absolute about never going public," recalled Vance. "The firm should be serving only one master: clients, not public shareholders." As Bower explained in his oral history, "If it does happen, it will be to satisfy the greed of the partners instead of following our deeply embedded policy of passing along the firm to succeeding generations of partners stronger than those partners received it from their predecessors. That move would violate our founding mission of establishing a firm that would continue in perpetuity."

135   *seriously burdensome obligations* Bain partners credit Mitt Romney with the leadership required to lead Bain out of its severe financial problems. One indication of the stress caused by Bill Bain's extraordinary deal was that two partners committed suicide.

135   *began on a vacation trip* Bower sometimes claimed he began thinking of international expansion in 1940 after hearing Wendell Willkie's presidential campaign speeches on "our one world."

143   *a joint venture was soon agreed* Goldman Sachs would own 20 percent, Kleinwort Benson 40 percent, and McCowan's group 40 percent. The new firm's initial name was Kleinwort Benson McCowan.

143   *looking for a new manager* Paul Nagel, chairman of the board of the fund, called Institutional Liquid Assets, served with Whitehead as a director of Household Finance. The fund's co-advisers—Salomon Brothers and First Chicago—had made a wrong bet on the yield curve and "broke the buck." While the managers were ready to cover the losses, the trustees were determined to make a quick change.

144   *A series of possible acquisitions* In 1987, Steve Friedman tried to acquire Roll & Ross, an institutional firm owned by two brilliant academics: Stephen Ross and Richard Roll. But they didn't want to be a part of a large organization and turned him down. In 1994, Miller, Anderson & Sherrerd, a prestigious institutional investment manager, was interested in selling, and Goldman Sachs had the inside track. Negotiations were going ahead rapidly until Friedman refused to pay $350 million for the business. A year later, after Jon Corzine declined to reconsider, that firm was sold to Morgan Stanley for . . . $350 million. It became the core of a substantial business. Corzine initiated acquisition discussions with a series of investment managers, including

Robeco, Wellington, Grantham Mayo, Van Otterloo, and T. Rowe Price. None succeeded.

147 *the idea of a one-company holding company* One-bank holding companies had by then become common.

148 *Capital's acquisitions had positive attributes* Capital's largest acquisition began with a failure, while its largest startup failure began with a dazzling success. The Commonwealth group of mutual funds had come up for sale in 1963, but the controlling shareholder, a proud San Franciscan, declared he would never sell to a Los Angeles firm. So Capital was ruled out as an acquirer. Commonwealth was sold to Fireman's Fund, which was itself acquired two years later by American Express and its funds rebranded as the American Express Funds. Ten years later, in the worst of the 1973 to '74 bear market, those funds had dreadful investment performance, so American Express was nearly desperate to get out of the mutual fund business. Heavy redemptions were serious, but not the worst problem: That was the harm being done to the AmEx image. Poor performance also produced serious fears of class-action lawsuits and all the bad publicity they would bring. AmEx was relieved to get out of the mutual fund business by selling the management company to Capital. For just $8 million in 1975, Capital picked up sizable mutual fund assets, a group of capable investment managers, and the prestigious Stanford University endowment fund.

Capital also bought the Anchor Group of mutual funds for $1 plus 1.2 times book value—almost all in cash—minus an "adjustment" depending on future redemptions. These adjustments were eventually large enough to eliminate almost all of the original premium over book value. Only one Anchor fund, Fundamental Investors, was continued as a separate mutual fund. The assets of others were merged into Capital's existing funds, adding substantial assets with minimal incremental cost—enhancing Capital's profitability when it was needed most.

Not everything Capital tried in corporate development worked. One move could have been a major winner. Alliance Capital was nearly acquired from Donaldson, Lufkin & Jenrette for $5.5 million, but Alliance's chief investment officer managed to block the sale. Later Alliance would go public and have a market value more than 100 times greater.

Investors Overseas Services (IOS) was also briefly considered. Capital's Ken Mathysen-Gerst was a neighbor of IOS's Bernie Cornfeld in Geneva, Switzerland, so Cornfeld easily made the initial contact. However, takeover talks were quickly aborted when serious study of the IOS books revealed that the firm owed large contingent payments to mutual fund salespeople. Also, Cornfeld's flashy, unsavory personal reputation meant there was little chance of making a successful arrangement with a conservative outfit like Capital. The adverse publicity of IOS and its contractual sales programs later hurt sales across the whole mutual fund industry for several years.

Ironically, IOS management and Capital both failed to recognize the real strength of the IOS business. IOS management, fixated on cash-basis business economics and large front-end sales charges, worried that investors would terminate their investments early. If so, the sales compensation already paid out to the IOS salesmen would never be recovered through investment management fees. They were wrong. IOS redemptions proved to be unusually low by industry standards for a simple reason: The IOS funds were among the few safe-haven alternatives then available anywhere to "flight capital" investors from the Arab world or Latin America as well as some communist countries. These flight capital buyers put their IOS fund certificates in safe-deposit boxes in safe countries and left them there indefinitely. Because there were so few redemptions, managing IOS funds was a surprisingly strong continuing business.

149   *Ask Mayo's Expert*   The complexity of medical knowledge, multiplied by the complexity of the structure of health care, is overloading the nation's health system and the physicians in it. Mayo believes its knowledge management system can be used anywhere. It is programmed to guide a physician by identifying decision rules, alerting the physician to possible errors, such as an alert not to prescribe a particular medicine for an unusual malady, or, in a rare syndrome, what to look for, what actions to take, and which Mayo specialists to bring in on the case—even one who joined Mayo Clinic just one day before. This system frees the patient's "quarterback" from having to depend on his own informal network of acquaintances to make up the right team. The system is designed to work toward continuous improvement through extensive cooperation.

In the early eighties, Mayo added public distribution of health-care information, beginning with Mayo Clinic Health Letter in 1983, followed by Mayo Clinic Family Health Book in 1990. Nearly one million subscribers now pay for the letter and over one million copies of the book have been purchased. MayoClinic.com receives over 15 million Internet visits a month.

Cooperative group practice has been called the most important practical development in modern medicine. Group practice had been conducted in public and university hospitals, but Mayo Clinic was the first *private* group practice.

150   *"in the center of the ring . . . facing the bull."* Ernest Hemingway, *Men Without Women* (New York: Penguin Press), 1955.

Chapter 8: Leadership

153   *a law firm . . . must have strong executive direction,"*   Swaine, Volume II, p. 12.

153   *a brilliant businessman and promoter* "Paul D. Cravath Dies Suddenly," *New York Times,* July 2, 1940.

154   *Cravath realized he was wrong* Swaine, Vol. I.

154   *Good work doesn't call for comment* Swaine, p. 127.

154   *four senior partners* Carl Painter, Tex Moore, Bruce Bromley, and Donald Swatland.

156   *To facilitate the selection of a successor* In the managing director election process, all directors had one vote. All directors were presumed to be candidates, with the rule that there would be no self-promotion and no campaigning. (Looking back, some feel Gluck and Rajat Gupta both made or implied promises to others to win more votes.) Today directors vote initially for seven candidates in order of preference. The balloting process is repeated until one candidate has over 50 percent. Several weeks separate the rounds of voting to allow time for inquiry and discussion of the candidates. Younger candidates have an inherent advantage because, in the organizational pyramid, there are always more young directors.

158   *"Now we'll be okay!"* With six years as head of the New York office and 12 as managing director, Daniel was at the center of firm leadership for 18 years.

159   *for 25 years* after *he had retired* Bower actually "retired" three times— at 60, at 80, and at 87.

159   *managing director for 12 years* At 58, he was, by the firm's bylaws, too old to serve out another three-year term. Some felt his third term was served without passion or conviction and that four three-year terms was just too long, as he seemed to be staying on because he had no alternative role to turn to.

161   *promoting consultants* Becoming a principal takes about six years
and becoming a director typically takes six more. Principals and
directors are evaluated on the same three factors: client development, client service, and value to others within the firm. Election
to director is made by the firm, not by the individual office. Of 700
principals, about 120 are reviewed each year as candidates for director and, of these, 80 to 100 will advance. Over time, about half of
the principals become directors. Other principals leave before they
are evaluated and about half of those who are elected to director
will leave, typically to join a client in a high-ranking position. The
firm now has over 400 directors.

McKinsey prunes 5 to 10 percent off the bottom each year—
and some of the best people get bid away. "We weed out those who
are too financially interested," explained Peter Walker. "Success in a
career at McKinsey depends on not overtly showing a 'need to succeed.'" (Senior McKinsey consultants don't talk about compensation
but do enjoy being well paid.) As a result, considerable homogeneity
is ensured, a potential problem. Jürgen Kluge worried: "McKinsey is
a culture of the top one-third. We must fight the culture of upper-
middle acceptance and reach higher and higher."

Given the firm's current scale—over 8,000 consultants and
nearly 7,000 additional employees in support roles worldwide—
McKinsey's leaders believe that, with the integrity of the process
well established, the firm can expand its internal evaluation process without change to virtually any scale desired as the firm grows
by simply devoting more people to the established process. On the
other hand, the firm does not expect to enjoy scale economies.
"The idea of seeking scale economies in this work is irrational," said
Kluge. "There are no economies nor diseconomies to scale. Also,
we don't know whether we are slightly overinvesting or underin-
vesting, but we do know we are *investing*, not spending, on rigorous
evaluations."

165   *the decision was made . . . to build, not buy* When Phil Murphy, the
newly appointed head for Germany, stated his goal was to be number
one in Germany, his German colleagues scoffed. But Murphy wouldn't
listen. He made a list of the 30 best prospects by volume of securities
business done and insisted on figuring out who at each giant prospect
really made decisions on which investment banks to use. Murphy's first
two names were Daimler-Benz and Siemens.

"Not a chance—*ever*," laughed Murphy's German associates. Deutsche Bank owned 30 percent of Daimler-Benz and *always* did all its financing. And Siemens was started in 1885 by . . . Deutsche Bank. Even today, its chairman is always provided by Deutsche Bank. For the finance director, there would be serious career risk in using any new firm for any investment banking service, particularly a foreign firm like Goldman Sachs.

Murphy wouldn't listen. He was determined.

In those Saturday and Sunday sessions and back at the office, there was no talk by anyone about Goldman Sachs' traditional first priority: profitability. For now, the focus was on becoming first in the "league tables" based entirely on volume of business done because that would establish Goldman Sachs as number one in Germany. After that, it could and would focus on profits. Corporate prospects were separated into three groups—"super league," major, and important—according to how much they paid or would pay in investment banking fees. Then everyone went to work to be sure that every capability of Goldman Sachs was brought forward so vigorously and persistently that any opportunity to do business would be exploited. Siemens was one of the first major German corporations to pay fees for investment banking services, and soon became a large fee-payer. Among many other transactions, Goldman Sachs worked with Siemens on its acquisition of Westinghouse.

The next major target was another giant: Deutsche Telekom. In the run-up to the selection of lead underwriters for the enormous Deutsche Telekom privatization offering, international adviser Hans Friderichs quietly arranged a private meeting for Goldman Sachs with Chancellor Helmut Kohl. Later, at a special meeting of the Bundestag, Goldman Sachs bankers gave legislators a detailed briefing on every aspect of the complexities involved in the Deutsche Telekom privatization. This helped create the solid political base that enabled Goldman Sachs to win the mandate as the lead international underwriter for what was then the world's largest-ever IPO—with Goldman Sachs coequal to Deutsche Bank as lead underwriters, a dramatic demonstration of Goldman Sachs's ascendance in Germany. Chairman Hilmar Kopper of Deutsche Bank paid the firm a high compliment by saying, "Nobody irritates me like Goldman Sachs. You get mandates we have not expected you to be even considered for!"

This triumph for Goldman Sachs had come after six years of persistent hard work and an important lucky break: Deutsche Telekom's capable future chairman, Ron Sommer, had previously been an

employee of Klaus Luft, who was also a Goldman Sachs adviser in
Germany. Luft insisted on Goldman Sachs being chosen. "If that transaction had been Luft's only major contribution—and it could *not* have
been done without him—it was plenty," said Steve Friedman.

In one of many moves toward an increasingly aggressive pursuit
of profit and dismissing what he called the PR factor, Hank Paulson
decided that the firm should abandon its celebrated "no hostiles"
policy. This was such a dramatic change in policy that two conditions
were set. First, any hostile deal would be done outside the United
States and involve no U.S. companies. Second, the fee would have
to be large enough to make absorbing the likely negative reactions
worthwhile. The chosen deal was Krupp's 1997 hostile acquisition
of Thyssen—a multibillion-dollar deal in terms of market capitaliza-
tion that would produce over $10 million in fees to Goldman Sachs.
Moreover, this takeover would give Goldman Sachs an opportunity
to outflank the dominant national competitor in Germany: Deutsche
Bank.

With detailed advice from Goldman Sachs, Krupp's execution
of the surprise attack was timed perfectly. In Germany, Easter weekend is a four-day tradition that includes both Good Friday and Easter
Monday as holidays. Most senior executives make this long weekend
a special event for their families by leaving instructions not to bother
them with calls. Many travel considerable distances to one or another
of Germany's numerous resorts, usually departing early Thursday afternoon. Their assistants also "disappear" with their own families. So, by
announcing the tender offer late that Thursday afternoon, *Blitzkrieg!*
Krupp caught Thyssen unprepared and unable to respond. For four
straight days, Thyssen executives, all widely dispersed to "unknown"
locations—with no assistants on duty at headquarters—were unable to
contact one another. With no communication, no defense was possible
to organize until well after all the newspapers, magazines, broadcasters,
and financial news services had reported the story just the way Krupp
and Goldman Sachs wanted it defined.

Reactions in Europe to Goldman Sachs advising on the raid were
muted and cynical: "Every bank does such things." Increasingly, clients
saw Goldman Sachs change from a dual client-serving *and* profit focus
to a single profit-making focus—often surprising those who had been
led to believe they were clients. Recognizing its own increasingly formidable strengths, the firm increasingly did what it could because it

could and it made money. But as Whitehead and Weinberg had long understood, to earn and keep the trust of large, sophisticated clients—and repeatedly be their first firm of choice—requires always acting and being seen to be acting in a reliably trustworthy way. No firm can be the trusted leader if it "does what everybody does."

One aspect of leadership has never changed. More is always expected of the true leader. John Weinberg and John Whitehead had both understood that embracing this qualitative challenge was crucial to Goldman Sachs being accepted as the industry leader and as each major corporation's lead investment banker. Leadership integrity—organizational character—was why Her Majesty's representative, Lord Cuckney, had decided, after many probing meetings with Gene Fife, the partner responsible for Goldman Sachs's business in Europe, that partner Eric Scheinberg's unsavory dealings with Robert Maxwell were the acts of a single person and *not* systemic; Cuckney allowed the firm to settle the matter by paying a record-setting $254 million "voluntary contribution" to the pension funds of Maxwell companies.

168 *a merger with a major commercial bank* Corzine initiated merger discussions with Chase Manhattan Bank, Mellon Bank, and J.P. Morgan.

168 *"This is an evolutionary transition* "Chief Resigns from Shared Post at Goldman," *New York Times*, January 12, 1999, p. C1.

169 *Goldman Sachs would soon be stronger on its own* In 2002, an agreement with Sumitomo-Mitsubishi Bank provided the firm with quick access to low-cost credit up to $1 billion.

Chapter 9: . . . and Luck

175 *a disappointed employee* Janet Hickey, who went on to a senior position at GE's in-house investment unit.

Chapter 10: Trouble

182 *Gupta had known for nearly two years* Based on a July 29, 2008, wiretap of a call between Gupta and Rajaratnam.

182 *Anil Kumar* Kumar, arrested in 2009, had bargained for a lighter sentence by cooperating with prosecutors in their case against Gupta. Kumar and Gupta had been classmates at Wharton and had worked closely together to establish the Indian School of Business. They also violated a McKinsey policy when they jointly set up a separate consulting business in 2011.

183   *six counts of insider trading*   The SEC originally brought its case before
an administrative law judge in March 2011. Another 26 cases had been
brought in federal court. Gupta sued, claiming his constitutional rights
were being trampled and demanding a jury trial. Later the SEC withdrew the administrative case. In October the U.S. prosecutor filed a
six-count indictment and Gupta was released on $10-million bail.
Meanwhile, Gupta went off the boards of American Airlines, Procter &
Gamble, Goldman Sachs, the Bill and Melinda Gates Foundation, and
the Rockefeller Foundation.

183   *trading profit of $840,000*   David Glovia and Patricia Hurtado,
"Galleon Partner's Eyes 'Popping' After Trade, Trader Says," Bloomberg,
May 23, 2012.

183   *While a director of Procter & Gamble*   Prosecutors accused another
Goldman Sachs employee, David Loeb, of providing inside information to Rajaratnam on Apple, Intel, and Hewlett-Packard.

183   *[Gupta] was also negotiating*   "Gupta Trial: Day 9 Dispatch," Law Blog,
June 1, 2012.

183   *letters of admiration from over 400 prominent people*   Several McKinsey
directors, having been asked by Gupta's friends to write letters to the
judge, were cautioned by senior members of the firm that McKinsey's
own investigation by lawyers indicated that not all the adverse facts
came out at trial.

184   *at $115 a share*   Margaret Collins and Andrew Frye, "Buffett Says
Berkshire to Retain Goldman Sachs Warrants in Wager on Bank,"
Bloomberg, May 1, 2011.

184   *"a major, major event*   Peter Lattman, "Buffett's Goldman Deal," *New
York Times*, May 23, 2012.

184   *"The decision has been made*   Gupta continued to be in denial, sending an e-mail to Ajit Rangnekar, dean of the Indian Business School,
that was forwarded to its faculty and alumni, saying: "The SEC's allegations are totally baseless. I am informed by my lawyers that the case
is based on speculation and unreliable third-hand hearsay. Just to be
clear: There are no tapes or any other direct evidence of me tipping
Mr. Rajaratnam. I did not trade any of the securities involved, nor did
I share in any of Mr. Rajaratnam's profits. In fact during the period in
question, the business relationship between Mr. Rajaratnam and I was
strained." But as *Bloomberg Businessweek* reported: "There are a number

of obvious inaccuracies in Gupta's e-mail: The government did indeed have a tape; Gupta's investments in Galleon's funds suggest that he did profit from Rajaratnam's trading, illegal or otherwise; and, although he says his relationship with Rajaratnam was 'strained' during 2008, the easy, friendly tone of their wiretapped conversation belies that, as does testimony from a Galleon trader that Gupta was seen in Rajaratnam's office biweekly during the month of September 2008."

187   *The traditional disciplined process with which the firm managed its mutual funds*   On the mutual fund side of Capital, performance challenges came later—after exceptionally good returns from the sharp market drop in 2000–2002 through 2007. Good investors know to stick to their knitting and are prepared to be publicly overglorified in their best years only to be pilloried in their worst years. These are twin realities in the mutual fund world, which is why going with what the experienced investment professional really believes in—not current market trends—is the key to long-term investment success. Back in 1999, Capital's analysts and fund managers had been accused of being "dinosaurs" out of touch with the dot-com market. But when the millennium market collapsed, Capital's investment results looked great—200 basis points ahead of market averages—because Capital had avoided the NASDAQ "stars" and did not own them as they plunged in price.

Looking at Capital's superior results, investment consultants brought in a slew of new 401(k)-plan assets on behalf of their institutional clients. Numerous broker-dealers, many with a salesperson's short-term focus, switched over from other, troubled mutual fund groups to Capital's American Funds. Money from new accounts poured in. When the American Funds got over 50 percent of *all* mutual fund inflows, "we knew those big inflows were not sustainable and we knew our stellar results were not sustainable—particularly in international markets," said Rothenberg. "We knew we just were not that good and we said so to our mutual fund directors." Still, the new money from new accounts represented by new brokers was cheerfully accepted.

But Capital did *not* recognize how quickly those same broker-dealers—new to Capital—would cut and run at the first sign of underperformance, taking their customers with them. Turnover among investors in Capital's mutual funds nearly doubled from traditionally less than 15 percent to almost 30 percent as brokers, attracted by Capital's earlier superior performance, abruptly switched their customers to other fund groups during 2008–2010.

188 *A painful series of lost accounts . . . got attention* Capital's professionals
have other personal motivations. Not only does their annual compensation depend on producing superior results, but most of their own
and their families' investment assets are in funds managed by the firm.

190 *Capital's management is now grappling with questions* Other problems were
not at all systemic, but were externally visible and somehow became part
of a "Capital has problems" story. In information technology, two separate groups had served the institutional and mutual fund units, with the
implicit goal of *perfection* in each case. A new executive, experienced in
IT management, was hired to figure out the real problem and propose
the right solution. After nearly three years of study, she made her recommendations. A single IT organization was established with the more realistic objective of "great" rather than "perfect" service. The IT staff, which
had mushroomed to 2,700, was reduced by 600 employees and numerous
part-time IT consultants. Simultaneous staff reductions in the American
Funds Services organization—almost all by attrition—were caused by an
external change in demand: stockbrokers combining individual accounts
into "Street name" omnibus accounts. As a result, AFS now services
28 million shareholders though only 20 million separate accounts.

195 *one of the most important and least recognized changes* As Jamie Dimon
would learn when a trader called The London Whale lost $6.2 billion
for JPMorgan Chase on a series of trades in 2012.

195 *even minutes to do a trade* In the eighties, transactions were always done
by teams with up to 10 signing the memo describing the success.

197 *"a giant vampire squid"* Matt Taibi, "The Great American Bubble
Machine," *Rolling Stone*, April 5, 2010.

197 *angry Americans . . . looking for someone to blame* In artillery, when the
timings of several thousand guns' firing are coordinated so all their
shells arrive on target at the same time—certain to be terrifying—the
exercise is called "synchronous serenade."

199 *Wall Street had been bailed out* Actually, it was Main Street that got
bailed out. The Great Recession could easily have been far worse and
far longer lasting without the massive intervention by the Federal
Reserve and TARP, but perceptions became reality because most people believed them.

199 *no firm suffered so much* Experienced observers of Wall Street could
easily point "he was worse" fingers at Merrill Lynch under Stanley

O'Neal or Lehman Brothers under Dick Fuld or Bear Stearns under Jimmy Cayne or even Morgan Stanley under Phil Purcell. Everyone has heard shopworn excuses like "everybody does it" or "we have to keep up with the competition."

200 *The board of directors was widely considered weak* Given the extraordinary capability of many former partners, it has been surprising to see how few have been asked to serve as directors.

202 *a hedge fund* Managed by Paulson & Co.

203 *bribe . . . was apparently never paid* "Meet Goldman's Rock Star in Libya," *Wall Street Journal*, May 31, 2011.

204 *not . . . admission of fraud* Carla Main, "Goldman Huddles," Bloomberg, June 10, 2011.

204 *"This isn't meant to say* Andrew Ross Sorkin, "The Fine Print of Goldman's Subprime Bet," *New York Times*, June 6, 2011.

204 *The Senate report stated* The report of the Senate subcommittee had serious factual errors, however unintentional. Net revenues from residential mortgage-related products were only about 1 percent of the firm's net revenues, or less than $500 million.

205 *"The problem isn't that Goldman went short* Jesse Eisinger, "Misdirection in Goldman Sachs's Housing Short," *New York Times Dealbook*, June 15, 2011 (edited by Andrew Ross Sorkin).

206 *but no clients* The firm would argue that it did survey clients' views and that a subcommittee of the Business Standards Committee regularly discusses client-related topics, but outsiders emphasize that the survey was based on a relatively small number of clients and did not compare the firm to other firms, and that having insiders speak for clients is not the same as having clients speak for themselves.

209 *recast its public relations strategy and leadership* Now led by Richard Siewert, a former Clinton press secretary and senior adviser to Treasury Secretary Geithner.

209 *an admiring report in the* New York Times N.R. Kleinfeld, "It's a Goldman World in Battery Park City," *New York Times*, June 29, 2012.

210 *Justice . . . decided to close its examination* Senator Carl Levin, who had been particularly accusatory in April 2011 during hearings before the Senate's Permanent Subcommittee on Investigations, was unrepentant. He declared, "Whether the decision by the Department of Justice is the product of weak laws or weak enforcement, Goldman Sachs actions were deceptive and immoral." Legal experts had expressed doubt about the case for some time. (*Source:* Peter Lattman, "U.S. Goldman Disclosure a Rare Break in Secrecy," *New York Times,* August 11, 2012, p. B1.)

210   *the firm had weathered the storm*   A *New York Times* op-ed piece, "Why I Am Leaving Goldman Sachs" (March 14, 2012), won its author, Greg Smith, a lot of attention and got him a reported $1.5 million advance for a book that came out in October and left readers yawning. Smith had been with the firm in a lower-middle position for 11 years and was apparently disappointed not to have earned a promotion to managing partner and substantially more than the $500,000 he was paid.

Chapter 11: Arthur Andersen

213   *more than 360,000 CPAs*   American Institute of Certified Public Accountants.

214   *Andersen resolved to recruit only college graduates*   A Vision of Grandeur, Arthur Andersen & Co., 1988, p. 11.

215   *. . . a great promoter and a very egotistical individual*   Leonard Spacek, *The Growth of Arthur Andersen & Company 1928–1973, An Oral History* (New York: Garland, 1989),   pp. 9.

215   *When we got into a difficult argument*   Ibid, p. 11.

216   *If it weren't for our clients*   A Vision of Grandeur, p. 15.

217   *. . . "We did all this work in the off-peak months*   Oral History, p. 204.

218   *We had classes virtually all day*   Author's interview with Ed Jenkin, June 22, 2004.

218   *There was no opposition to it*   Oral History, pp. 46–48.

218   *Arthur Andersen Would Rather Be Right*   New York Times, March 7, 1944, p. 7.

219   *He could inspire confidence and commitment*   Born in 1907 in Cedar Rapids, Iowa, Spacek got a job at 17 with Iowa Electric Light & Power Co., hoping to become an electrical engineer. But since there were no engineering openings, he tried accounting, liked it—particularly his work with auditors from Arthur Andersen—and took corre-

spondence courses. He joined the firm in 1928, becoming a manager in 1934 and a partner in 1940.

219   *I can tell you*   Oral History, p. 50.

220   *We made those investments*   Ibid.

220   *He believed that you couldn't have the influence you had to have*   Author's interview with George Catlett, Evanston, Illinois, June 30, 2004.

221   *"I've been asked for years*   Oral History, p. 47.

221   *"You do the right things*   Author's interview with Robert Medwick, June 2004.

221   *"Spacek's philosophy was that every partner*   Author's interview with Robert May, July 6, 2004, Chicago.

221   *"Is our profession so impressed*   Speech at Milwaukee Controllers Institute of America, February 12, 1957.

223   *"Everyone else thought this was ridiculous."*   Thomas Watson of IBM had estimated total global demand at only five or six computers, and retired General Douglas MacArthur, then at Sperry Rand, assured Spacek that Sperry was so far ahead, nobody could possibly catch up.

223   *"Don't go overboard*   "The Fall of Andersen," *Los Angeles Times*, September 2, 2002.

232   *"The culture changed*   Ibid.

232   *Profit participation would be based on the economic performance*   Economist, August 17, 1991, p. 66.

233   *"It seemed innocuous*   Author's interview with Robert Kelley, June 31, 2004.

234   *As DeLorean's auditor*   Chicago Tribune, September 2, 2002.

235   *the average partner's earnings*   Ibid.

235   *"Clients that were either not growing*   Barbara Ley Toffler and Jennifer Reingold, *Final Accounting: Ambition, Greed and the Fall of Arthur Andersen* (New York: Broadway Books, 2004), p. 142.

237   *This meant, of course, that the entities*   Final Accounting, p. 212.

239   *just a "business problem"*   Ibid., p. 215.

240   *Volcker said no*   Chicago Tribune, September 8, 2002.

243   *"Mr. Andersen had great courage*   Final Accounting, p. 253.

Afterword

246   *We all know the advertising tagline*   The Wheaties questions were first posed in this context by Richard N. Foster, Yale PhD in chemical engineering with a long and distinguished career with McKinsey & Co. where for several years he led research and wrote two strong fact-based business books.

About the Author

C HARLES D. ELLIS serves as a consultant on investing to large institutional investors, government organizations, and wealthy families, and as managing partner of a *pro bono* partnership of nearly 100 Harvard Business School classmates and friends, The Partners of '63, which commits time and treasure in support of entrepreneurial, change-oriented ventures in education, particularly those focused on children born into tough circumstances.

Charley's professional career centered on three decades with Greenwich Associates, the international strategy consulting firm he founded in 1972. Recognized worldwide for the proprietary research which informs its consulting, the firm grew in the 30 years he was managing partner to serve the leading firms in over 130 professional financial markets around the world.

Services to the investment profession include: Chair and two terms as governor of the profession's CFA Institute and an associate editor of both the *Journal of Portfolio Management* and the *Financial Analysts Journal*. He is one of 11 people honored for lifetime contributions to the investment profession.

Academic activities include two appointments (in 1970 and 1974) to the faculty of the Harvard Business School and one (in 1986) to the Yale School of Management, both to teach the advanced course on investment management, and 20 years on the faculty of the Investment Workshop at Princeton.

Charley chairs the Whitehead Institute for Biomedical Research, where he also chairs the investment committee, and is a trustee of the Robert Wood Johnson Foundation, where he chairs the finance committee. He has previously served as a successor trustee of Yale University, where he chaired the investment committee, as trustee of Phillips Exeter Academy and Eagle Hill School, as an Overseer of the Stern School of Business at New York University, as a member of the Visiting Committee and the Board of Directors of the Associates of the Harvard Business School, and as a director of the Vanguard group of mutual funds and several business ventures.

The author of 16 books, including *The Partnership: The Making of Goldman Sachs* (Penguin), *Winning the Loser's Game (McGraw-Hill),* and *Joe Wilson and the Creation of Xerox, Capital,* and, with Burton Malkiel, *The Elements of Investing* (all John Wiley & Sons), Charley has written over 100 articles for business and professional journals. His article "The Loser's Game" won the investment profession's Graham & Dodd award in 1977. *Joe Wilson* was selected as one of the best business books of 2006.

A graduate of Exeter and Yale College, Charley earned an MBA (with distinction) at Harvard Business School and a Ph.D. at New York University. He is married to Linda Koch Lorimer, vice president of Yale University. Their four children are Harold, Chad, Kelly and Peter.

Index